A HISTORY OF THE ISRAELI ARMY (1870~1974)
BY ZEEV SCHIFF

translated and edited
by Raphael Rothstein

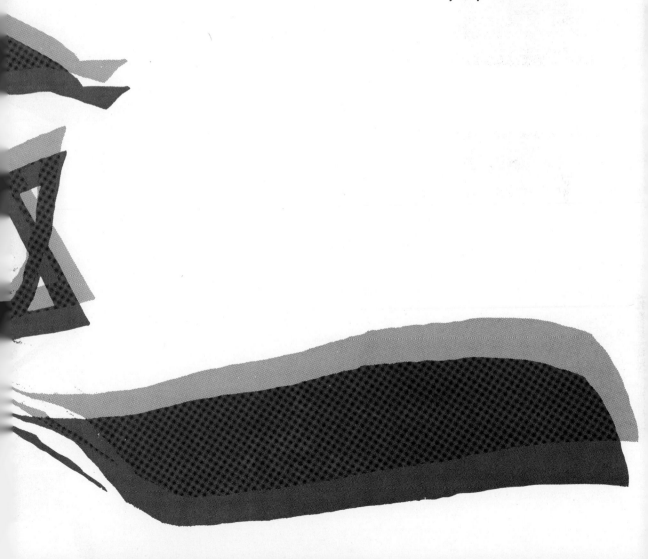

Library of Congress Catalog Card Number:
74-76602
ISBN: 0-87932-077-X

Straight Arrow Books
625 Third Street
San Francisco, CA 94107

Distributed by Simon and Schuster
Simon and Schuster order number: 21889

0 9 8 7 6 5 4 3 2 1

Book design by Jon Goodchild
Printed in the United States of America

Acknowledgments

Zeev Schiff (right) on the west bank of the Suez Canal during the Yom Kippur War, with Chief of Staff Lt. Gen. David Elazar (left) and Maj. Gen. Ariel Sharon.

I wish to thank the many former IDF officers and enlisted men who helped me assemble material and were kind enough to grant interviews for this book. I also owe a special debt of thanks to the owners of private archives who made these rich sources of information available to me.

I would particularly like to thank those former chiefs of staff of the IDF, Intelligence officers and even censorship officers who adopted a positive approach toward this work. Special acknowledgment is given to Mordechai Makleff, Haim Laskov, Yitzhak Rabin, Haim Bar-Lev and David Elazar. In addition, Generals Mordechai Hod, Ezer Weizman, Israel Tal, Avraham Tamir, Ariel Sharon, Shlomo Lahat, Yitzhak Hofi and Shmuel Gonen; former Intelligence chiefs, Isser Harel, Yehoshofat Harkabi and Haim Herzog; former Army attachés in Washington, Yosef Geva, Yehuda Prihar and Ram Ron; the first two commanders of CHEN, Shoshana Werner and Shoshana Gershoniwitz; as well as officers of NAHAL and GADNA, Moshe Netzer, Yitzhak Pundak, Elhanan Yeshi and Baruch Levy must be mentioned for their assistance.

And, finally, special thanks are due to Louis Williams, who aided me with his counsel and translator's skill in preparing material for the English-speaking reader. I sincerely appreciate his devoted attention.

Zeev Schiff
Tel Aviv
May 1974

The editor, Barbara Kelman-Burgower, and publisher gratefully acknowledge the invaluable assistance of Cheryl Bishop, Brent Beck, Joshua Chaikin, Susan Cohen, Bill Cruz, Bond Francisco, Vickie Golden, Linda Gunnarson, Victoria Jackson, David Laidig, Larry Miller, Rosemary Nightingale, Arne Norberg, Maxine Nunes, Dian-Aziza Ooka, Richard Reynolds, Mick Stevens and Michele Strutin.

FOREWORD

In interviews near the end of his life, David Ben-Gurion would often cite the Israeli Army as perhaps the most notable achievement arising from the return of the Jewish people to Israel. Ben-Gurion was one of the first Israeli leaders to realize the importance of a Jewish defense force. He perceived that, beyond the bloody wars with the Arabs, the forging of a strong and well-motivated army was part of the struggle to unify a nation of Jews coming from the exile of many lands. Yet at times he stood alone in his zealous determination to defend and fortify Israel with a Jewish Army.

As an instrument of both defense and social integration, the Israel Defense Forces, as the Army is officially known, has been highly successful. It is understandable that, despite the many wondrous accomplishments during Israel's brief history, David Ben-Gurion should have singled out *TZAHAL* (the Hebrew acronym for the IDF) as among the most encouraging and gratifying results of the Zionist movement and the rebirth of Israel.

This book attempts to describe the development of this unique army by examining its battles, doctrines and leaders as well as its special place in Israeli life. The emergence of the IDF is one of the great stories of modern Jewish history, not only because it made Israel a reality, but also because it compelled Jews throughout the world to alter their view of themselves.

Until recently, Jews revered scholarship above all other callings. The notion of a warrior was an alien, repugnant one. Few Jews willingly sought military careers in the armies of Europe. However, just as Israel has wedded Jews once more to the land, so too has the biblical tradition of the Hebraic warrior been revived. With the renewed Jewish settlement of Palestine in the late nineteenth century, there emerged a deeper appreciation and understanding of a tradition exemplified by Bar Kochba's revolt against the Romans and the Maccabees' uprising. The settlers who joined the first defense organizations in Palestine understood only too well that armed defense in the face of hostile marauders was a pursuit as honorable as the study of the Talmud. The great theorists of the Zionist movement had already put forth the idea of redemption through working the land. Inevitably, defense followed as a path to redemption.

The Nazi Holocaust and the destruction of Jewish life in much of Europe gave new impetus to the conviction that the defense of Jews could be left to none other than the Jewish people. It is futile but instructive to think how many lives might have been saved in Poland, for example, if there had been a Jewish tradition of self-defense and militance. The lesson of the Holocaust was not lost on the struggling, postwar Jewish settlement in Palestine. In the aftermath of Auschwitz, survival became as important as faith. This conviction enabled Israel to undertake the transformation of the Jewish character which was necessary if the new State was to survive.

Zeev Schiff, the highly respected military commentator for the Israeli daily, *Ha'aretz,* and author of several books on the Arab-Israeli conflict, writes the history of the IDF with the view that it is at once the army of a modern, developing nation and one of the most respected and affectionately esteemed institutions in contemporary Jewish life.

The uniqueness of the IDF has struck many foreign observers: the women's army, the relaxed discipline, the tradition of officers who lead in battle, the easygoing *esprit* and the remarkable successes on the battlefield against enormous odds. Schiff describes these notable features and also provides the background for understanding that the IDF is a true people's army which faithfully reflects Israeli attitudes. It is an army in which the senior commanders

Below: Raphael Rothstein. [Charmian Reading]
Opposite: [Starphot]

are known by childhood nicknames, an army that teaches immigrant soldiers Hebrew and even how to use a knife and fork. A complex relationship exists between civilians and their army in both political and cultural terms— hardly a corner of Israeli life is untouched by the IDF. Schiff examines all this, looking closely at causes and results.

He writes with pride of the IDF as the means of ensuring that Jews can determine their destiny in their own land. And he writes critically— his analysis of Israel's failures in the Yom Kippur War is no less important than his description of her stunning victory in the Six-Day War.

It has been an honor and a pleasure to be involved in the preparation of this work. I hope it will contribute to a more accurate understanding of one of the most interesting elements of modern Israel at a time when Israel's destiny is even more closely tied with that of the rest of the world. Both Zeev Schiff and myself are grateful to Alan Rinzler of Straight Arrow Books. His imagination and vision are responsible for commissioning this book. We also owe a special debt of thanks to Barbara Kelman-Burgower, whose considerable editorial skills and good-natured devotion made it possible for us to complete the manuscript, and to Jon Goodchild, whose excellent design added a graphic dimension which complements and enhances this saga.

Raphael Rothstein
New York City
April 1974

CONTENTS

A Brief History of Israel, 2000 BC—1974 AD

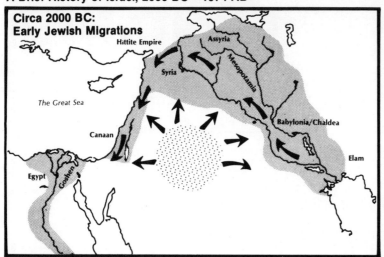

**Circa 2000 BC:
Early Jewish Migrations**

Hittite Empire
Assyria
Syria
Mesopotamia
The Great Sea
Canaan
Babylonia/Chaldea
Egypt
Goshen
Elam

**Circa 1400 BC:
The Twelve Tribes of Israel**

1. Asher
2. Naphtali
3. Zebulon
4. Issacher
5. Manasseh
6. Gad
7. Ephraim
8. Dan
9. Benjamin
10. Reuben
11. Judah
12. Simeon

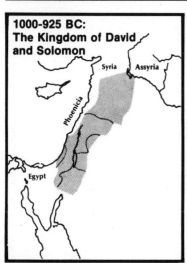

**1000-925 BC:
The Kingdom of David
and Solomon**

Syria
Assyria
Phoenicia
Egypt

**800 BC:
Assyrian Invasion**

Syria
Assyria
Phoenicia
Israel
Ammon
Philistia
Moab
Judah
Edom

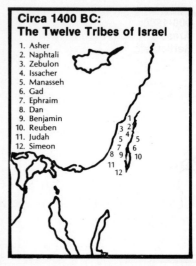

**586 BC:
Invaded by the Babylonians.**

**(Then by the Persians,
C. 550 BC; Alexander
the Great, 323 BC; &
the Egyptians, 270 BC)**

**142 BC:
Hasmodean Jewish
Kingdom**

Jerusalem

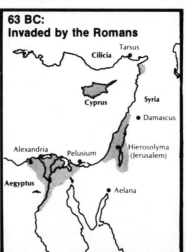

**63 BC:
Invaded by the Romans**

Cilicia
Tarsus
Cyprus
Syria
Damascus
Alexandria
Pelusium
Hierosolyma
(Jerusalem)
Aegyptus
Aelana

**Circa 650 AD:
The Islamic Invasions**

Antioch
Bagdad
Damascus
Ramleh
Damietta
Fustat
Independent
Jewish tribes
Khaibar

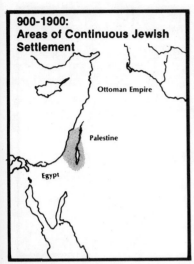

900-1900:
Areas of Continuous Jewish Settlement

Ottoman Empire

Palestine

Egypt

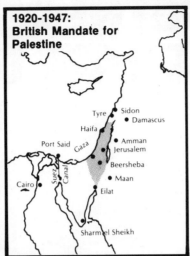

1920-1947:
British Mandate for Palestine

Tyre
Sidon
Damascus
Haifa
Port Said
Gaza
Amman
Jerusalem
Beersheba
Cairo
Suez Canal
Maan
Eilat
Sharm el Sheikh

1914-1918:
Principal Battle Zone for Jewish Troops

Jerusalem

1947:
UN Partition Plan

Gaza
Jerusalem
Cairo
Sinai
Elath
Sharm el Sheikh

Jewish sovereignty
Arab sovereignty
★ International Control

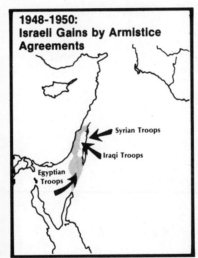

1948-1950:
Israeli Gains by Armistice Agreements

Syrian Troops
Iraqi Troops
Egyptian Troops

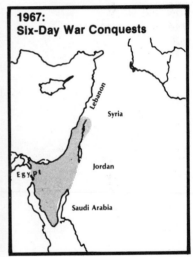

1967:
Six-Day War Conquests

Lebanon
Syria
Jordan
Egypt
Saudi Arabia

1973:
Yom Kippur War Gains

Damascus
Kuneitra
Suez Canal
Negev
Sinai
Sharm el Sheikh

1974:
UN Cease-Fire Lines

Lebanon
Syria
UN Buffer Zone
Suez Canal
Jordan
UN Buffer Zone
Saudi Arabia
Egypt

1. FATHERS OF THE ISRAEL DEFENSE FORCES

Opposite: Members of Hashomer (The Watchman),
1909. [Israeli Army]

Below: A group of Bedouin fighters, 1911. [Frederic
Lewis]

The roots of the modern Israeli Army go back to
the 1880s when the problem of self-defense for
the Jewish settlers in Palestine began. From the
moment Jews decided to return to Israel and to
cultivate their own lands the question of pro-
tecting life and property became real. The first
Jewish settlement, Mikveh Israel, was founded
in 1870, when there were some 25,000 Jews in
Palestine. It was followed by Petach Tikvah,
Rehovot, Gedera, Hadera and others. These
semi-collective settlements or *moshavot* were
built for all-round defense as though the houses
were covered wagons making a stand against
Indian attack. Yigal Allon, one-time Commander of the Palmach, the commando corps
founded in the 1940s, and himself the son of
one of these *moshavot,* wrote that the men
spoke and thought in nationalist terms and saw
their modest villages as forward positions that
would some day have a role in determining the
borders of a Jewish state.

Security was then nonexistent in Palestine
and Bedouin tribes robbed and plundered settlements and travelers. There was no Jewish
settlement that had not been attacked by its
Arab neighbors or by Bedouins.

Late Nineteenth Century:
The Shomrim

This first period of Jewish self-defense in
Palestine was noteworthy for a group called the
Shomrim (Watchmen). Its outstanding members, such as Yehoshua Shtemper, one of the
founders of Petach Tikvah, and Yehuda Raab,
who had come to Palestine from a small Hun-
garian village, are considered to be the first
Jewish watchmen among the settlers.

In the early stages, the Jewish self-defense
force consisted of farmers, idealistic workers
and socialists. A new consciousness arose
among Jews because of the pogroms in Czarist
Russia. These anti-Jewish massacres began in

A group of Jewish students from Russia studying
farm work at Rishon le-Zion, 1905. David Ben-
Gurion, who was to be Israel's first Prime Minister,
can be seen in the first row center. [Culver Pictures]

the 1880s and persuaded the Jewish masses
that they had to aspire to national freedom and
independence. This feeling was accompanied
by spontaneous and largely disorganized self-
defense groups.

In 1903, an historic event took place in the
town of Homel on the borders of the Ukraine
and White Russia. Jewish youngsters, members
of the Zionist Socialist Party, organized themselves into self-defense units and for three days
repelled the mobs and the Russian police who
were among the organizers of a pogrom. Some
of the men of the Homel socialist group immigrated to Palestine in 1904 and helped or-

ganize the first real Jewish defense organization there.

1907: Bar-Giora

In September 1907, ten men met in Jaffa and
established a secret association of watchmen
called Bar-Giora, named for the Jewish warrior
who distinguished himself in the rebellion
against the Romans in 70 A.D. The organization placed on its flag that same biblical slogan
that had marked decades of blood-soaked
history in Palestine: "Judea fell in blood and
fire—in blood and fire shall Judea arise!"

The Arabs, who opposed renewed Jewish

Members of Hashomer, 1909. [Israeli Army]

settlement, cursed the Jews and called them *Walad el Mita,* the Sons of Death. But the members of Bar-Giora wanted to change the Arabs' attitude toward Jews. They were encouraged in this hope by the example of the Circassian villages in Palestine. Although the Circassians were a minority group, the Arabs stood in awe of them and respected them as fierce fighters. The members of Bar-Giora underwent training in the use of weapons and then accepted their first assignment, the protection of the *moshava* of Sejera in Galilee.

1909: Hashomer

By 1909 the members of the Bar-Giora had decided that a secret association of watchmen was not enough. If they wanted to become a national force, they would have to create a larger and partially open organization. In April 1909 they held a general meeting and decided to establish a new defense organization to be named *Hashomer* (The Watchman). Although still a primitive defense organization, Hashomer represented an important stage in the development of a Jewish force in Palestine. It accepted responsibility for the protection of additional Jewish agricultural settlements and

replaced the hired Arab watchmen who had often joined hands with Arab thieves and divided the loot with them.

Bar-Giora and Hashomer were founded and nurtured by the men of the Second *Aliya* (immigration). This wave of immigration, which began in 1904 and continued up until the First World War, brought to Palestine men from the ghettos of Eastern Europe who had been influenced by the experience of the Russian Revolution. Youngsters who wanted to liberate themselves from the stagnation of a life of commerce and to fulfill themselves as pioneers were drawn by the Zionist vision. From an ideological viewpoint, they espoused a mixture of nationalist and socialist opinions.

When they established Hashomer, they spoke of the bond uniting Jewish agricultural colonization and military training. This thread, which began with Hashomer, was to run through the formation of Haganah in the 1930s,

the Palmach in the 1940s, and the NAHAL soldier-farmer units of the Israel Defense Forces. Members of Hashomer participated in the founding of the first *kibbutz* or agricultural commune in Palestine—Degania—as well as other settlements. They tried to start a "labor legion" within which each youngster would devote two years to defense and labor on the land, but the idea never got off the ground.

Although Hashomer concentrated primarily on watch duties, here and there they did undertake small punitive actions against Arabs who harmed Jews. They also tried unsuccessfully to manufacture arms and bombs. Many of their members were killed in clashes with Arab brigands. Their bravery fired the imagination of many Jews and a fund was even set up in Russia to acquire arms, equipment and horses for the watchmen and to compensate their families in the event of death or disablement.

Hashomer waned during World War I. They

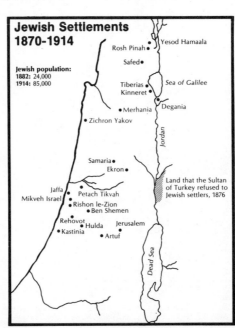

Jewish Settlements 1870-1914

Jewish population:
1882: 24,000
1914: 85,000

Yesod Hamaala
Rosh Pinah•
Safed•
Tiberias• *Sea of Galilee*
Kinneret•
•Degania
•Merhania
•Zichron Yakov
Jordan
Samaria•
Ekron•
Jaffa• •Petach Tikvah
Mikveh Israel• •Rishon le-Zion
•Ben Shemen
Rehovot• Jerusalem
•Hulda
•Kastinia •Artuf
Land that the Sultan of Turkey refused to Jewish settlers, 1876
Dead Sea

Zeev Jabotinsky, who urged formation of a Jewish Army.

Bottom: Rehovot, one of the earliest Jewish settlements in Palestine, 1905.

had proposed to the Turkish Ottoman authorities the establishment of a Jewish militia in Palestine but the idea was rejected and Hashomer was outlawed.

World War I: The Zion Battalion

The next stage in the development of a Jewish force emerged in Egypt in the camps of Jews who had been exiled from Palestine by the Turks. It was here that two Russian Jews promoted the idea of establishing Jewish battalions to fight as part of the British Army for the liberation of Palestine from the Turks, who had joined the Axis. Zeev Jabotinsky, an Odessa newspaperman, writer and gifted orator whom many Zionists still see as their spiritual leader, joined forces with Joseph Trumpeldor, a Jewish officer in the Czar's Army who returned from Japanese captivity after losing his left arm in the Russo-Japanese War. At first the British refused to hear of the proposal and agreed only

Opposite: The swirl of Great Power interference and designs in Palestine—With oil and the Suez Canal at stake, Britain increases its collusion with Arab leaders at Paris Peace Conference, 1919 (above) where Prince Faisal, center, stands with former Allenby aide T.E. Lawrence to his right. [Culver Pictures] French troops (below) operating with British Army in Palestine. [Frederic Lewis]

Below left: British agents in Palestine, 1918—Maj. John Bagot Glubb, uncrowned king of Transjordan, gives orders to one of his officers. [Culver Pictures]

Below right: Leaders of the *yishuv* before World War I—(from left to right) David Ben-Gurion, Yitzhak Ben-Tzvi, second President of Israel, and Joseph Sprinzak, first Speaker of the Knesset.

to establish a battalion of mule drivers. Jabotinsky, who had envisioned a Jewish Legion, was disappointed but Trumpeldor became one of the battalion's officers. Six hundred and fifty men of the "Zion" Battalion were transferred to the Gallipoli front where they served bringing arms and supplies to the besieged British. When the campaign drew to a close the British, impressed with their courage, sought to transfer them to suppress the rebellion in Ireland. The men refused and the battalion was disbanded. Jabotinsky, meanwhile, continued to press for a Jewish army.

cruits were David Ben-Gurion and Yitzhak Ben-Tzvi, who was later to become the second President of Israel. Both had been expelled from Palestine by the Turks.

In 1918, the Jewish battalions reached the front in Palestine, and an additional battalion was organized with Palestinian Jews. They fought against the Turks as part of General Allenby's forces. This was the largest Jewish military formation in modern times. Veterans of these Jewish battalions brought their military experience to the Jewish settlement in Palestine, the *yishuv*.

1917: The Judean Battalion

In 1917, after publication of the Balfour Declaration in which the British recognized the Jewish right to establish a national home in Palestine, the idea of Jewish units was raised again. Jabotinsky and Trumpeldor were invited to the Defense Ministry in London to discuss the subject. After considerable discussion Jabotinsky prevailed and three units of the Royal Fusiliers were combined to form the First Judean Battalion.

Many volunteers from England, the United States and Canada joined and the unit became known as the Jewish Legion. Among the re-

Joseph Trumpeldor: Prototype of the Modern Hebrew Warrior

While Jabotinsky enlisted as a private in the Judean Battalion, Joseph Trumpeldor went to Russia to negotiate the establishment of a Jewish army with the authorities there. He dreamt of Jewish fighters breaking into Palestine by way of the Caucasus and Persia. By 1917, Trumpeldor was considered the outstanding military leader in the *yishuv*.

In 1902, when he was twenty-two, he had enlisted as a young Caucasian in the Russian Army. A year later, he was sent to the Port Arthur front and distinguished himself in

Emblem of the
Jewish Legion

battle. Though he lost his arm, he asked to be returned to the front and was granted permission. He returned from the war with many decorations and was the only Jew to receive an officer's commission in the Czar's Army. While in Japanese captivity, he organized Jewish prisoners who wished to immigrate to Palestine into a group called *Bnei Zion* (Sons of Zion). In 1912, Trumpeldor himself reached Palestine and joined the first kibbutz in Degania. As a Russian citizen, he was deported by the Turks during the First World War.

Like Jabotinsky, he traveled widely urging the idea of a Jewish army. He was a unique

mixture of a war-loving knight and a zealous settler on the land. When the first Jewish soldier of the mule drivers' battalion was killed in Gallipoli, his men contended that it was a day of celebration for Trumpeldor because Jewish blood had been spilled in battle without a pogrom.

Trumpeldor was a tall, handsome Nordic type. He was keen on anything Hebrew—Hebrew labor, a Hebrew army and a war that would be fought for the goals of Zionism. Yet he did not speak Hebrew well and to the day of his death his conversation was interspersed with many Russian words and curses.

When his idea of forming a Jewish army in Russia failed, he persuaded many Jewish youngsters to emigrate. Among them was Yitzhak Sadeh who would himself become one of the fathers of the IDF.

When Trumpeldor returned to Palestine at the end of 1919, relations with the Arabs were tense. In the north of Palestine, the Arabs were rebelling against the French who had received the mandate for Syria and Lebanon after the First World War. Trumpeldor went to the northern border settlement of Tel Hai, where he took command over the small workers' and shepherds' settlements. In March 1920, Trumpeldor was killed in an Arab attack on Tel Hai. Tel Hai became a symbol of resistance and self-defense, and Trumpeldor an example for generations of Israeli youngsters. His dying statement, according to legend, "No matter, it is good to die for our country!" became a motto for later Jewish underground organizations. Some historians suggest that in view of Trumpeldor's shaky Hebrew and his penchant for salty language, he probably died with a Russian curse on his lips.

Tel Hai fell and another three Jewish settlements in the north were abandoned. There were riots in Jerusalem and many Jews were killed. Jabotinsky, who stood at the head of Jewish self-defense in Jerusalem, was arrested and deported by the British, who had been given the mandate for Palestine. He never returned to Palestine, though his influence was felt for many years. He died in 1941 in New York while on a speaking tour.

1920: Haganah

By 1920 Arab attacks had spread to Jaffa, where many new immigrants were killed. Among them was the Jewish writer, Y.H. Brenner, whose writings had vigorously argued for a Jewish defense force. The Jews were shocked and bewildered by the outbreaks of

Eliahu Golomb, commander of Haganah during World War II. [Photo Rex]

Bottom: The Third *Aliya*. Immigrants arrive at Jaffa from Russia and Eastern Europe. An Arab ferryman takes them from boat to shore.

violence. They realized that their political situation in Palestine had changed for the worse and that the British authorities were not interested in keeping the promises of the Balfour Declaration. The shock was all the greater because of the failure of Jewish defense. The organization of watchmen was obviously not enough; there was a need for a more extensive, comprehensive and popular defense organization. Jewish settlement watchmen on horseback were not the answer when the security problem also existed in cities like Jerusalem and Jaffa.

The Hashomer organization was voluntarily disbanded in May 1920. A month later the Haganah was established at a conference of one of the major workers' parties. The Haganah was later transferred to the jurisdiction of Histadrut—General Federation of Labor. Because the British forbade Jews in the territory under their mandate to bear arms, Haganah was, from the beginning, a clandestine organi-

zation. The Haganah was the creation of the Jewish Labor Movement in Palestine and even when more rightwing elements participated in the National Command of Haganah, the workers' representatives set the tone.

If Hashomer had been the creation of the Second *Aliya*, the Haganah received its impetus from the members of the Third *Aliya*. This immigration had begun at the end of the First World War and continued up to 1924. Many of the men of this *aliya* were Russian and Polish refugees who had been displaced and also deeply influenced by the Bolshevik Revolution. They mostly believed in colonization on a cooperative basis. Thirty-four thousand immigrants were added to the 90,000 Jews in the *yishuv* during this period. Most of them were young and unmarried and ready for the challenges Palestine presented.

In the 1920s, the first attempt was made to set up permanent armed defense units within

A gang of Jewish pioneers crushing stone to be used to pave the network of roads built between new settlements in Palestine, 1922. [Frederick Lewis]

the Haganah. The idea was to convert the labor and defense battalion, numbering a few hundred men, into the center of a permanent military structure. This unit was called the Trumpeldor Battalion and its men did agricultural work, paved roads and quarried throughout Palestine. This effort represented a recognition on the part of the Jewish leadership of the increasingly dangerous tension between Arabs and Jews heightened by the Arabs' rejection of the Balfour Declaration or of any program aimed at affording the Jews a national presence in a land that was historically theirs and had been under various foreign rulers for centuries. Arab hostility burst forth in three major outbreaks of terrorism: 1921, 1929 and 1936-39.

1921: Arab Riots

In 1921, the Arab Riots, as the attacks on Jewish settlements and centers of population came to be known, were aimed at both discouraging the Zionist enterprise and pressuring the British to alter their favorable attitude toward the idea of a Jewish national homeland. Although Arab hostility was confined at first to a small section of the Arab community, it was fanned by the Arab nationalist movement that sought to oust the foreign mandatory powers and to unify Palestine and Syria into an independent Arab kingdom.

The anti-Zionist disorders took on the complexion of a political and religious struggle. The slogans *Itbahu al yahud!* (Slaughter the Jews) and *Falastin bladna wa al yahud clabna* (Palestine is our land and the Jews our dogs) were heard for the first time. The extremism of the Arabs stunned many members of the *yishuv* and relegated to myth the notion that the Arabs were willing to live peacefully with their Jewish neighbors.

Acts of terrorism spread from Jerusalem to Jaffa, the Arab seaport north of Tel Aviv. Longtime Jewish residents and Jewish newcomers to Palestine alike were murdered. From Jaffa the first wave of terror struck in Petach Tikvah, Hadera, Rehovot and other Jewish settlements and erupted in Jerusalem again. The Jewish community in Palestine emerged from this first experience of violent Arab opposition determined to take measures to protect itself against recurrences of similar terror and to develop economic institutions that would make it less dependent on the Arabs. Thus the Arabs' hostility had provided the impetus to expand and develop the Haganah.

In its efforts to seek countries that would agree to train its men, the Haganah sent representatives abroad. In 1925 contact with the Soviet Union was established through the agency of the Russian Ambassador in Berlin and, in 1926, a delegation of three Haganah members went to Russia. Its sole achievement was an agreement by the Russians to accept one Jewish youth from Palestine for flight training. But to the Haganah's chagrin, the candidate completed the course but decided to stay in the Soviet Union.

Haganah leaders then decided to seek the assistance of Jews abroad to acquire men, money and arms. They began smuggling arms into Palestine in defiance of a British ban and formulated ambitious plans for equipping themselves. But the relative tranquility of the late 1920s lulled the leaders of the *yishuv* into a complacency about security problems, and the Haganah elicited little support for its procurement program.

1929: The Second Wave of Arab Terror

However, in 1929 the *yishuv* was shocked by violent Arab attacks on Jews that spread throughout Palestine, beginning in Jerusalem with a religious dispute. The spark that ignited the outbreak was the refusal of Arab authorities in Jerusalem to allow Jews to pray during the High Holy Days at the most sacred site in Judaism—the Western Wall, a remaining fragment of Solomon's Great Temple, which adjoins a compound of mosques sacred to Islam. In defiance of the Moslem religious authorities' prohibition, a group of Jews worshipped at the Western Wall on August 23, 1929 and were attacked by an Arab gang shouting, "Allah and Mohammed command the killing of the Jews."

A few days later an Arab mob murdered fifty-nine Jews in Hebron. The massacre was described in an eyewitness account in the London *Times* of Friday, August 30, 1929:

The first house attacked was a large Jewish house on the main road, and the occupants locked themselves in. For some unknown reason the gates were opened to allow two young boys to leave, and they were immediately killed. This inflamed the crowd, who entered the house and beat or stabbed the inmates to death. The local police force, which consisted of only a British officer, two Arab officers and 30 Arabs, made every effort to control the situation, but the crowd was out of hand, and attacked other Jewish homes, beating and stabbing the inhabitants—men, women and children. The police fired, but the situation was not definitely in hand until the arrival of 12 British police and 12 Royal Air Force personnel from Jerusalem.

Palestine early 1900s

Masada
Lake Hula
Acre
Sea of Galilee
Mt Carmel
Jezreel Valley
Ein Harod
Bet-Shaan
Hadera
Jordan
Tulkarem
Nablus
Mediterranean Sea
Tel Aviv
Amman
Palestine
Gedera
Jerusalem
Dead Sea
Hebron
Gaza

In addition to Hebron, the historic Jewish community of Safed in northern Palestine was hit hard by Arab terrorists. Following the violence of 1929, the Jewish communities in the Arab cities of Nablus, Gaza, Tulkarem, Jenin and Bet-Shaan were abolished, the Jews having learned that their greatest security was in banding together in all-Jewish settlements and neighborhoods.

The Jews suffered greatly in 1929 but the Arabs failed to bring about their total annihilation because of the presence of the British who sometimes intervened to establish peace and order. The British could not always reach beleaguered areas and the Jews resolved to strengthen their own defense arrangements. The Haganah was impelled to plan defense on a national scale. The settlements were organized in groups linked to each other for all-round defense and procurement of weapons abroad gained momentum. In Vienna, the

A band of Arab marauders advances on a Jewish settlement, 1936.

Haganah was assisted by the secret defense organization of the Austrian socialists, the Schutzbund. Antwerp, Belgium was also a base for weapons purchase. In 1935, the Haganah's Intelligence Service was expanded and improved and its efforts directed against the Arabs and British officialdom. A clandestine arms industry was begun in Palestine and abroad and bombs, hand grenades, cartridges and even tear gas were manufactured in small secret plants.

1930: Conflict and Development within Haganah

The lessons derived from failures changed the Haganah for the better, but the commanders were still idealists rather than practi-cal military men. Ideological debates preoccupied them. One of the focal points of repeated conflict in the 1930s was the principle of community control over the military force. A number of the senior commanders of Haganah were removed from their positions when they resisted orders from *yishuv* leaders.

Along with the need to fight against extreme pacificism, which is always rampant in Jewish society, there was a need to fight tendencies toward militarism that were developing among Haganah commanders. To protect public control over the Haganah, a national command was set up comprised of representatives of all political groups in the *yishuv*—not just the Histadrut but the civilian rightwing population as well. Nevertheless, the representatives of the

The Arab Revolt of 1936-39: Arab fighters in the Shomrim Hills (above) and a British policeman chasing rioters in Tel Aviv (below) [Frederic Lewis].

Right Wing continued to argue that the Left controlled the Haganah.

In 1934, the constitution of the Haganah was amended. It no longer spoke of a popular militia, but of an organization that was clearly meant to be an essential stage in the development of a national defense force. It stipulated that men and women, from the age of seventeen, could be accepted into the Haganah. A period of six months was set aside for basic training followed by a year and a half of active service. After this period—and only after it—a member was transferred to the reserve units. This was the embryonic structure of the IDF.

1936-39: The Arab Revolt

In April 1936, a severe test of the Jewish community began. Known today as the Arab Revolt, the third wave of Arab terrorism was aimed against British authority as well as the *yishuv*. A key figure in the three-year uprising was the pro-Nazi Grand Mufti of Jerusalem, Amin el Husseini. He exploited hatred of the Jews and Moslem religious fanaticism to inflame Arab emotions. Arab terrorist organizations inspired by the Mufti carried on a sustained guerrilla campaign in the name of religion. One of these groups, Fighters of the Holy War, called on the local Arabs to become *fedayeen*, i.e., to sacrifice themselves for the sake of Allah. Those who fell were promised a place in heaven.

The Arab Revolt of 1936 began in the urban centers and then spread to the villages. The city Arabs, however, quickly abandoned the struggle to their lesser-educated rural brothers who attacked non-Arab vehicles traveling Palestine's roads and formed into guerrilla bands whose favorite targets included the pipeline carrying British-owned petroleum from the Kirkuk fields in Iraq to Haifa's port. The guerrillas were commanded in a rather loose and

haphazard manner by a former Ottoman army officer named Fawzi Kaoukji who had been dispatched by Syrian nationalist extremists to press the Arab reaction in Palestine against both the Jews and the British.

The British Army's initial response against the Arab guerrilla bands in 1936 was ambiguous. Although heavy casualties were inflicted on the Jewish community, the British forces often showed themselves unwilling to suppress the wave of violence. The British Foreign Office feared that drastic action would turn the entire Arab Middle East against Britain at a crucial time, and Whitehall was mindful of the

It was not until the late thirties that the British Mandatory Authority was clearly committed to putting down the Arab Revolt. The Second Battalion Scots Guard stands for inspection before departing for service in Palestine. [Frederic Lewis]

Bottom: *"Falastin bladna wa al yahud clabna!"* Arabs gather to hear a speech during the riots in Palestine. [Frederic Lewis]

inroads Nazism had made among rightist Arab political groups in Egypt. Only later, when the Arab Revolt was well underway, did the British Army receive authorization to effectively put down the rebellion.

The Haganah realized the danger to both life and property the new situation represented as well as the implicit political threat. It was clear that under the circumstances the neutrality of the British and their occasional indirect support of the Arabs would undermine the Jewish presence in certain parts of the region and might lead to a reversal of Britain's commitment to the Balfour Declaration.

At first the leaders of the Jewish settlement were in favor of defensive actions in the face of Arab hostility because it was assumed that the British would eventually intervene in the Jews' favor. Seventy percent of the Jewish community at that time lived in the three major cities of Tel Aviv, Haifa and Jerusalem. The remainder were in fortified agricultural settlements and villages. The nature of Jewish defense was static. The settlers tended to garrison themselves and large areas of property and fields were abandoned to marauding Arabs.

The military initiative was in Arab hands, but despite this tactical advantage they made a number of serious errors in the 1936-39 period. Not a few of their commanders exaggerated the power of their own forces and minimized the potential of the Jews. The clashes of 1936 were essentially between two nationalities and the Arabs were mistaken in directing their hostility against the British too. The latter were preoccupied with the deteriorating international situation. It was natural, therefore, that the British authorities would be in need of the Jewish community's cooperation, even if it meant military collaboration with the still officially illegal Haganah.

Faced with the prospect of civil chaos and alarmed by attacks on the Iraqi Petroleum Company's pipeline, the British embarked on an offensive to suppress the Arab guerrilla fighters. Severe punishment was imposed on terrorist gangs and the local Arab population. Hardly a search of Arab communities was made without several civilians being killed and hundreds of homes, vineyards and orchards destroyed by the angry British troops and Palestine police both as revenge and deterrent measures.

To prevent infiltration by Arabs from neighboring countries the British set up fence-and-watchtower police stations in frontier areas. A further British measure was the occupation of

Armed Supernumerary Police guard Jewish workers rebuilding a settlement destroyed by an Arab attack during the Arab Revolt. [Frederic Lewis]

Bottom: British police dispersing crowd during riot in Jaffa, 1936.

twenty-five Arab villages in the Galilee to the north and on the west bank of the Jordan River in the middle of 1938. This was done to prevent supplies from reaching guerrilla and terrorist groups.

The Haganah was surprised by the magnitude of the clashes and was not prepared for them. The Arab war potential had been underestimated. The Arabs had more fighters, more weapons and were bold.

Recovery came slowly. While the Arabs almost succeeded in wresting control over large areas of land, the Jews responded by strengthening the Haganah. Losses were heavy. At the beginning of the disturbances, the Jewish population numbered 385,000 and increased to 460,000 by the end, but of these, 520 were killed and some 2,500 wounded.

1937: Plan Avner and the Supernumerary Police

The *sabra* sons of the second generation began to reach the command levels of the Haganah. This generation was free of the psychological burden of its elders who remembered the pogroms in Eastern European ghettos. Youngsters like Yigal Allon and Moshe Dayan were outstanding in this group and soon

Yohanan Rattner, first Chief of Staff of the Haganah.

Below left: Haganah women practicing with English rifles at the Hanita settlement, 1938. [Haganah Archives]

Bottom: A fence-and-watchtower settlement on the Lebanese border, 1936.

the Haganah into divisions. It foresaw the establishment of an army of 50,000 men with an additional garrison force of 17,000. Meanwhile, working under the circumstances of that time, the ranks of the Haganah were clandestinely augmented by volunteers as well as professional men—doctors, engineers and scientists. In July 1938, a Chief of Staff was appointed for the Haganah: Yohanan Rattner, a Haifa Technion professor. Until then, the Haganah had been an underground army with management but not a command. Military problems moved from the jurisdiction of political leaders into the hands of professionals. Jewish settlement was planned in accordance with strategic and political needs. The intent was regional concentration to prevent settlements from being cut off in the event of partition. Fence-and-watchtower settlements sprang up and access roads were paved. In the previous disturbances many settlements had been abandoned, but in the

brought about changes in planning and organization. In 1937, the Haganah, for the first time, prepared a plan to achieve control over the whole country in the event the British Army left Palestine. This scheme was known as Plan Avner and included provisions for reorganizing

Hayedid, the Friend: Orde Charles Wingate. [Haganah Archives]

Below: A Jewish watch patrol guards the settlement of Rosh Pinah. [Frederic Lewis]

1936-39 round of war fifty-two new ones were built. Many kibbutzim were transformed into paramilitary bases where agriculture was only one activity. Because of this the majority of top Haganah commanders, and later those in the IDF, came primarily from kibbutzim.

A new mood emerged in the Haganah during the Arab Revolt. A number of commanders criticized the weakening of their defensive strength that could be expected if they sat waiting in prepared defensive positions. They called on the Haganah to "move out beyond the fence," to set ambushes and mount preventive attacks. Outstanding among these activist commanders was Yitzhak Sadeh, a tough Russian Jew who had established a Jerusalem-based mobile patrol unit called "Nomad." Similar mobile Haganah guard units were organized throughout the country and were subsequently integrated into a new Jewish defense organization called the Supernumerary Police.

The British were reluctant to sanction a Jewish force but the problem of putting a quietus on Arab terror made the British acquiesce to Jewish demands for a legitimate peacekeeping force. The creation of the Supernumerary Police enabled thousands of Jews to be trained in the use of weapons under its auspices and it greatly strengthened the Haganah since so many members of the police were secret members of the Haganah. The Supernumeraries, or settlement police as they were also known, became the basis of a forthcoming Jewish army. The Jewish Agency bore the burden of paying the Supernumeraries, but the small arms came from the British.

The Supernumerary force reached its peak at the beginning of 1939 when it was reorganized and reconstructed into ten territorial battalions. In total, the Supernumerary Police encompassed some 22,000 members of the Jewish community or about five percent, with about 8,000 rifles at their disposal. The Haga-

nah had at the peak of the disturbances only 6,000 rifles, 24 machine guns and 600 medium and submachine guns. By the time the Arab attacks subsided the Jewish community had come of age in the military sense and was well on its way to being psychologically and physically prepared for the possibility of overall confrontation with the Arabs of Palestine. It was thus that the Arab refusal to accommodate Jewish national rights served to increase the *yishuv's* determination to develop the force it needed to guarantee Jewish survival and to defend Jewish nationhood.

Orde Wingate: A Modern Gideon

Perhaps the most significant development for the *yishuv* at this time was the advent of a slightly built, eccentric British officer named Orde Charles Wingate. He arrived in Palestine as a captain in 1936 and left his mark as the single most important influence on the military thinking of the Haganah. Born in India to a Scottish family with a long tradition of military service and religious dissent, Wingate was imbued at home with Puritanism and a deep love of the Bible. He served in Palestine as an Intelligence officer. With the blazing eyes of a visionary he viewed the scores of Jewish settlements and kibbutzim as proof of biblical proph-

Orde Wingate's Night Squad, 1939. [Haganah Archives]

ecies concerning the redemption of Zion.

His behavior was strange, his clothes were slovenly and his manners crude. He could be bad-tempered and he ate lots of onions as though to keep people away. But within a short period of time he became an enthusiastic Zionist. He wrote to his cousin, Sir Reginald Wingate who was British High Commissioner in Egypt: "When I was at school I was looked down on and made to feel that I was a failure and not wanted in the world. When I came to Palestine I found a whole people who had been treated like that through scores of generations, and yet at the end of it they were undefeated, were a great power in the world, building their country anew. I felt I belonged to such people."

And in another letter: "I have seen the young Jews in the kibbutzim. I tell you that the Jews will provide a soldiery better than ours. We have only to train it."[2]

Orde Wingate saw the Jewish people and their struggle to return to the land of Israel as a just and righteous cause and he dedicated himself to making the Haganah an effective fighting instrument. He was a man of brilliance, reserve and discipline. He often quoted the Bible and saw himself as a modern Gideon, operating in the same terrain where the biblical Gideon fought the Midianites. He instilled in the men of the Haganah a sense of mission and professionalism. His word was law and he insisted on meticulous discipline. Although he prepared every operation thoroughly, he was gifted in improvisation and trained his men to respond resourcefully to changing battle conditions. As a military adviser, he set a personal example in courage and endurance and regarded the Haganah men in his command as partners in thinking and action. The members of the Haganah thought of him as one of themselves and he was known affectionately as *Hayedid* (the Friend).

Wingate persuaded the British Army command in Palestine to allow him to train special

Supernumerary Police patroling border settlements
during the Arab Revolt.

"We, the Jews, will teach the Arabs to fear night more than they fear day."—Orde Charles Wingate [Nancy Reese]

Haganah night squads to fight bands of Arab terrorists. He received grudging permission for this because the British, worried over Arab sabotage of the major petroleum pipeline in northern Palestine, were willing to close their eyes to the Haganah's participation in the night squads.

"The Arabs think the night belongs to them. The British Army huddles in its camps at night. We, the Jews, will teach the Arabs to fear night more than they fear day,"[3] Wingate told his men. And so it was. The initiative was slowly taken out of the hands of the Arab gangs. Wingate preached face-to-face combat and encouraged mobile ambush units which moved throughout the country. He handpicked his men and the Haganah cooperated fully.

The nighttime raids and ambushes were carried out over wide areas of the Galilee on both sides of the pipeline. Dressed in blue shirts and Australian bush hats, the night fighters under Wingate's command helped drive Fawzi Kaoukji's guerrillas from the Galilee, away from the petroleum pipeline.

Orde Wingate gave Yigal Allon, Moshe Dayan and other future Israeli army commanders their first formal instruction in warfare, particularly counter-guerrilla tactics. Dayan greatly admired Wingate and throughout his career has been influenced by the Englishman's emphasis on striking at the center of enemy activity rather than assuming a static defense. Wingate's example inspired the Haganah to begin attacking instead of limiting itself to defensive guarding tactics. Wingate's maxim that the best defense is attack later became one of the primary combat doctrines of the Israel Defense Forces.

At kibbutz Ein Harod, Night Squad training headquarters, Wingate would say to trainees in Hebrew: "We are creating here the basis for the army of Zion."[4] His friendship for the Jews made him suspect in the eyes of the British

Command and it was decided to transfer him from Palestine and disband the Night Squads. In his final farewell speech, he said to his men: "I promise you that I will come back, and if I cannot do it the regular way, I shall return as a refugee. The force has been disbanded but this does not mean that the dream of Jewish strength has been forsaken. It has only been delayed for a while, a short while I hope. I hope the vision of a free people of Israel in its homeland will be fulfilled soon."[5]

In his personal file, his commanders wrote on the eve of his departure (May 1939): "Orde Charles Wingate, DSO, is a good soldier, but so far as Palestine is concerned, he is a security risk. He cannot be trusted. He puts the interests of the Jews before those of his own country. He should not be allowed in Palestine again."

Wingate never returned. After fighting the Italians in Ethiopia, he was transferred to

Menahem Begin, ETZEL Commander, disguised as a rabbi, 1947—and the ETZEL emblem.

Below: A patrol of the British Mandatory Authority stops and searches an Arab in Palestine. [Frederic Lewis]

Burma where he fought in the jungle and lost his life in a plane crash in 1944.

1937: ETZEL

A rival to the Haganah was another underground group: *Irgun Tzvai Leumi* (National Military Organization), known in Israel as ETZEL and abroad as the *Irgun*. It was founded in April 1937 in reaction to the Haganah doctrine of *havlagah* (restraint) in the face of Arab terrorism. ETZEL adopted many of Zeev Jabotinsky's ideas on the historic boundaries of the land of Israel and the importance of vigorous military action in defense of the Jewish community. The *yishuv's* socialist leadership at the time endorsed restraint as a policy and even though the Haganah's commanders contended that only retaliation would silence Arab terror, the Haganah had to follow the *yishuv's* civilian direction until later in the Arab Revolt when *havlagah* proved to be an untenable policy.

After publication of the White Paper by the British Government in 1939, with its severe restrictions on Jewish immigration to Palestine, ETZEL moved against the British mandate authorities as well as the Arabs. The badge of the organization was a hand grasping a rifle over a map of the land of Israel, including Transjordan. Below the badge were inscribed the words: *Rak Kach!* (Only Thus!)

1939: The British Issue the White Paper

As the Arabs found their activities to be increasingly costly in the face of British and Jewish counterattacks, their initiative gradually diminished until a relative peace was achieved in the spring of 1939. The Jewish settlement had survived and the Arab objective of driving the Jews out of Palestine had failed. But the Arabs scored definite political victories, particularly the White Paper of 1939.

The British had realized that the mandate was unworkable and that it could not be applied without large-scale and constant use of

force against the Arabs. On the other hand, the migration of German and Central European Jews to Palestine following Hitler's rise to power—by 1937 the Jewish population in Palestine was 400,000 as compared to 175,000 in 1932—made it equally difficult to reverse the moral-legal obligation to help establish a Jewish national home as implied in the Balfour Declaration.

Failing to achieve a settlement of the Palestine question by agreement in a special conference of Arabs and Jews, the British sought to retain Arab goodwill, which they believed was crucial to the war effort in the Middle East.

They settled on the issuance of the White Paper, which was, in effect, a reversal of the Balfour Declaration since it severely restricted Jewish immigration and property acquisition.

World War II: LEHI (The Stern Gang)

When World War II broke out the Haganah joined in the Allied war effort and ETZEL stopped its activities against the British and was even prepared to cooperate with them. An ETZEL commander, David Raziel, was killed in Iraq where he was sent to assist in putting down the pro-Nazi Kilani rebellion. In opposition to ETZEL's decision to cooperate with the British during the war, another group headed

Avraham Yair Stern, founder of LEHI, the
Stern Gang.

by Avraham Yair Stern broke away and established another military organization called *Lohamei Herut Yisrael* (Fighters for Israel's Freedom), known in Israel as LEHI and abroad as the Stern Gang. Stern and his men did not accept Ben-Gurion's thesis that Hitler should be fought as though the British White Paper did not exist. They contended that there was no cease-fire with the British. Their method consisted primarily of terrorism against the British. Stern was caught and killed by the British, but his comrades pressed on and in their most publicized action assassinated the anti-Jewish British Minister for Middle Eastern Affairs, Lord Moyne, in Cairo. A number of LEHI veterans later occupied senior positions in the IDF.

ETZEL also renewed its activities against the British at the beginning of 1944. Reports of the extermination of Jews in Europe filtered through to Palestine but the British refused to permit the refugees of the Nazi Holocaust to enter Palestine. ETZEL's harassment steadily increased and there is no doubt that it had considerable influence on the British government's decision to terminate its mandate over Palestine.

At its peak, ETZEL numbered some 5,000 men, and was led by Menahem Begin who often disguised himself as an orthodox rabbi to escape British arrest. It operated in small units and its military achievements were considerable. It blew up the British High Command and Administrative Center in the King David Hotel in Jerusalem in the summer of 1946; that same year it engineered a prison break at Acre where many members of Haganah and ETZEL were being held as political prisoners by the British; and it staged numerous attacks on British airfields in Palestine throughout the late forties. ETZEL even acted against the British outside the country and blew up the British Embassy in Rome. Many ETZEL members were killed in

battle and others were executed by the British. ETZEL and LEHI's activities, though for the most part without the sanction of the *yishuv's* institutions, served as an example of courage to many Palestinian Jewish youth. These organizations formed two important cornerstones in the infrastructure of the IDF.

World War II: Jews in the British Army

During World War II, 28,000 men and 4,000 women of the Jewish community in Palestine volunteered for various units of the British Army. Four hundred and fifty of them attained officer's rank. The percentage of volunteers was high—the Jewish community at the time numbered only 600,000. The volunteers acquired important military experience in infantry, commando, artillery and engineering units and in the Air Force. At the outbreak of the War of Independence, they constituted the backbone of the IDF and many senior IDF commanders were drawn from British Army veterans. Toward the end of the War, the Jewish Brigade was established and it participated in the battles for Italy.

As Rommel's forces approached Egypt and it became clear that the British intended to retreat from Palestine and set up their line of defense further to the north, the National Command of Haganah decided in 1941 to establish nine companies of commando troops—*Plugot Mahatz*—known as the Palmach. It would be a national reserve prepared for immediate action. The commandos were intended for the defense of the *yishuv* against the Arabs in the event of a German invasion and to wage guerrilla war, with the agreement and cooperation of the British, against the Germans.

Yitzhak Sadeh: First Commander of Palmach

Yitzhak Sadeh, founder of the Jerusalem Haganah "Nomad" unit, was appointed the

Far left: Palmach emblem.

Left: Yitzhak Sadeh, first Commander of the Palmach. [Israeli Army]

Below: Yitzhak Sadeh (center) with Moshe Dayan (left) and Yigal Allon, as members of Palmach, 1938. [Haganah Archives]

first Commander of Palmach. He himself chose his company commanders, among them Allon and Dayan. They began to handpick the recruits. There was nobody in the *yishuv* better suited for the job of organizing the Palmach than Sadeh, a fighter and a writer who by his courage and spirit became a legend and a symbol of the fighting spirit of the Jewish underground.

Sadeh was born in 1890 in Lüblin, Poland and was the son of a respected Jewish family. The grandson of the town rabbi, he attended a Russian gymnasium. In World War I, he served as a sergeant in the Czar's Army, a rank which was generally the highest that a Jew could attain. He received the George Cross for distinction in battle and after the Revolution was appointed commander of a company in Petrograd. It was here that he first met Joseph Trumpeldor, who appealed to him to emigrate to Palestine.

Before coming to Palestine, he went to the Crimea where he studied and earned money by wrestling. He was a burly, zestful man known for his Rabelaisian ways.

Sadeh was involved in every central defense happening in Palestine—the Labor Battalion, the defense of the Old City of Jerusalem in the disturbances of 1921 and the defense of Safed in the Arab Riots of 1929.

In 1937 Sadeh had attempted to form a permanent Haganah field brigade. He had about a thousand men in this brigade known as FOSH (Field Forces), but it was disbanded after a year and a half because the Haganah feared it would become a military elite.

Between these different tasks, he was employed in various occupations. He worked as a newspaperman and a farmer and for many years he worked in a quarry while writing articles, books and plays. He attracted the young by both his bohemian spirit and his abilities as a commander. "The Old Man," as his Palmach and IDF trainees called him, could take on the strongest among the young men. He set the free-wheeling, folksy tone of the Palmach and played a key role in moving the Haganah from self-defense to active defense. He was in ideological agreement with Wingate, although their personal styles varied greatly.

When the Haganah began its revolt against British authority Sadeh was appointed its Chief of Staff and was responsible for planning most Haganah and Palmach actions against the British. Later, when the IDF was founded, he was moved out of senior positions because of his leftist tendencies. In the War of Independence he was a brigade commander and the founder of the IDF's first armored units. He found himself under the command of his former pupils who had in the course of time overtaken him in rank. He died three years after his release from the IDF at the age of sixty-two.

In 1941, with funds put at the disposal of the

Jewish Army regulars. [Frederic Lewis]

Haganah by the British—one of the fruits of the new period of cooperation—600 men were recruited into the Palmach and began training in the forests around Kibbutz Mishmar Ha'Emek in the Jezreel Valley. A German-speaking platoon was set up with the intention of carrying out actions behind German lines and an Arab-speaking platoon was organized. Its task was to infiltrate and work in Arab territories. The Palmach participated in several dangerous missions. Its members were among twenty-three men who vanished in a boat on their way to a commando action near Tripoli in Vichy-occupied Lebanon. When the British forces invaded the Vichy forces in Syria and Lebanon, Palmach scouts led the invading units. One of these scouts, Moshe Dayan, lost his eye in the battle. Palmach men were also among the Palestinian parachutists dropped behind enemy lines in Europe on clandestine missions. When it seemed that the Germans would invade

Palestine, Yitzhak Sadeh, together with the Haganah Chief of Staff, prepared Plan Carmel. It called for concentrating most of the Jewish community on Mount Carmel which would be fortified. The Germans would be fought to the end much as the defenders of Masada fought the Romans in 70 A.D.

When Rommel was defeated by the British and the danger of Nazi attack ebbed away, the British decided to stop their cooperation with the Palmach. Nevertheless, the Haganah resolved to continue the Palmach, but the question was how. The solution was found in 1943 in a proposal by a leader of the kibbutz movement who suggested that Palmach units be attached to kibbutzim where half their time would be devoted to training, the remainder to farming. This work would cover eighty percent of the Palmach's expenses. It was thus that the Palmach took on the character of a workers' army rooted in the land and imbued with egalitarian ideals. The Palmach was enriched with the graduates of youth movements who came to kibbutzim with Palmach units.

In 1944, the Palmach numbered 1,000 men and 300 women, organized in battalions, and another 400 reservists on call. During the struggle against the British after the war, the Palmach played a key role. Its men escorted the illegal immigrant ships that ran the British blockade.

Yigal Allon succeeded Sadeh as Commander in May 1945 and Palmachniks were sent to the displaced persons camps in Europe and Cyprus to teach the youngsters the use of weapons. The Palmach also organized Jewish communities in the Arab countries and prepared them for self-defense and emigration.

The unique quality of the Palmach lay in its *esprit de corps.* It was an elite volunteer unit with the highest level of training of any Haganah units. It was especially noteworthy for its ideology. Commanders emphasized educa-

Emblem of the Jews in service with the British Forces, World War I.

Below: Jewish women soldiers in the British Army during World War II, marching in a Tel Aviv parade. [Haganah Archives]

tional and informational activities that inculcated socialist ideals. Education of the soldier was considered the basis for discipline. Their slogan was taken from one of the sentences of the Palmach anthem: *"Rishonim Tamid Anahnu!"* ("We are always first!"). The Palmach Bible was a small book called *Panpilov's Men* by the Russian author, A. Beck. It describes the experiences of a Russian unit in World War II and how its commander led his men.

At a Palmach campfire gathering in 1943, Yitzhak Sadeh addressed his troops. The following excerpt from his oft-quoted speech re-

veals something of the spirit and nature of the Palmach and why to this day it is thought of in Israel as having been akin to a knighthood:

The fellowship of men fighting for a common cause is surely the perfection of camaraderie. Without it nothing can be achieved. The realization of any goal requires a joint effort, a common insight into its purpose and a high degree of individual preparedness. Fighting as an independent Jewish force we already achieve part of our goal. The rest is the building and restoration of this whole land, and of a better, juster society in it.

The Haganah on the Eve of Independence

The Haganah on the whole developed in strength and scope. The Haganah Command received its orders from the Executive of the Jewish Agency, which was the pre-Statehood governmental authority. Within the Agency, Ben-Gurion controlled defense matters. His assistants were the chiefs of the Haganah, Yisrael Galili and Yaakov Dori. The latter would become the first Chief of Staff of the IDF. In the spring of 1947, 46,000 men were in the Haganah and its activities extended beyond the borders of Palestine to Europe where it arranged for smuggling tens of thousands of Jewish refugees to Palestine in defiance of the British ban. The British, wishing to wash their hands of the increasingly explosive situation, decided to relinquish their mandate.

On November 29, 1947, the United Nations voted to partition Palestine into Jewish and Arab states. The Arab nations immediately invaded in an attempt to crush the Jews and to prevent the State of Israel from coming into being. A new war began in Palestine and the underground Jewish forces—the Haganah and its commando force, the Palmach, as well as ETZEL—went into battle. Before the war would end, these fighting Jews would be merged into one army—*Tzva Haganah Leyisrael,* the Israel Defense Forces.

Footnotes

1   Collected letters of Orde Wingate. Haganah Archives, Tel Aviv.
2   Ibid.
3   Igal Allon, *Keshet Lohamin* [Fighter's bow] (Jerusalem: Weidenfeld and Nicholson, 1972), p.99.
4   Speech at Kibbutz Ein Harod, 1939. Haganah Archives, Tel Aviv.
5   Ibid.

2. THE WAR OF INDEPENDENCE

Opposite: [Frederic Lewis]

TZAHAL, the Israel Defense Forces, came into being in the midst of Israel's hardest and cruelest war, the War of Independence. On the eve of the war, in November 1947, Israel's very existence was in peril; an Arab victory could have forever destroyed the dream of Zionism as it wiped out the politically independent Jewish nation.

Israel did win her War of Independence, but the result was armistice, not peace. The loss of Jewish life in the war was heavy. Out of a *yishuv* settlement of some 600,000, more than 6,000 men were killed—one out of every 100 was killed and many more were wounded. Nor was the threat of Arab hostilities removed. To this day Israel has no permanent, recognized borders as far as her Arab neighbors are concerned. In a sense, all the other wars that have followed 1948 have been a continuance of the War of Independence.

November 29, 1947: The End of the British Mandate

On November 29, 1947, the UN General Assembly voted to end the British Mandate over Palestine by May 1, 1948 and to partition Palestine into a Jewish state, an Arab state and an International Zone comprised of Jerusalem and its environs, extending as far as Bethlehem.

It would have been difficult for a non-Jew to understand the feverish dances and the joyous singing that swept the *yishuv* that night. Perhaps only one whose people had been denied freedom for thousands of years and then had struggled to regain it could appreciate the happiness that enveloped the Jewish nation on November 29, 1947.

But the celebrations were short-lived. Arab threats had not been empty. Those who opposed the UN decision sought to alter it by force of arms. Scattered incidents that resembled the guerrilla and terrorist tactics of the anti-Jewish actions of 1929 and 1936-39

quickly assumed the dimensions of full-scale hostilities.

The War of Independence began as a confrontation between two populations: the Jewish *yishuv* and the Arab community which, at that time, numbered about 1.2 million. But Amin el Husseini, the Mufti of Jerusalem and religious leader of the Moslems in Arab Palestine, sought to involve the armies of his allies. Before the war ended, Jewish forces battled with the regular armies of five Arab states which invaded Palestine to thwart the creation of an independent Jewish nation.

The Jewish force began as an underground organization but emerged from the battle as an organized national army of twelve brigades. Facing well-equipped enemy forces, the Jewish fighters began with scanty equipment but in the course of the war aircraft, ships, tanks, guns and ammunition poured into Israel.

1947 Partition Plan

Arab State
Jewish State (Israel)
Jerusalem (International)

A Jewish patrol on guard near Haifa. [Frederic Lewis]

The Arabs of Palestine and the neighboring countries set out to prove that the UN resolution was unenforceable. On November 30, a Jewish bus was attacked en route to Jerusalem, and five Jews were killed. This was the starter's gun for a war which was to last intermittently for a year and seven months. It reached its formal conclusion when the last armistice agreement with Syria was signed on July 17, 1949. This was preceded by similar agreements with Egypt on February 24, 1949; with Lebanon on March 23, 1949; and with Jordan on April 4, 1949. The Iraqi Army withdrew from Palestine without any formal cessation of warfare.

Makeup of the Jewish Fighting Force

When hostilities broke out the enlisted Jewish force numbered 2,100 men of the Palmach. Another 1,000 reservists could be called on. The Supernumerary Police numbered 1,800 men on regular full-time duty. But the Haganah could also quickly muster 9,500 men in the eighteen to twenty-five age group. Two other Jewish military organizations, ETZEL and LEHI, numbered 4,000 men.

At that time military cooperation existed between ETZEL and LEHI and the Haganah. These forces were not to be merged into the unified IDF until after May 1948. As the war escalated, the Haganah began to recruit from the higher age groups; an estimated 32,000 men were recruited in stages throughout the war. Another 9,500 youth, from fifteen to eighteen, were organized in GADNA youth battalions.

At the beginning of the war, the Jewish community possessed what few weapons had been collected, one by one, over the years. The arsenal inventories listed 10,000 rifles, 3,500 submachine guns, 160 medium machine guns, 885 light machine guns, 670 light mortars and 84 three-inch mortars. There was no heavy armament, but the Haganah had nine light aircraft and forty pilots, including some who had served as fighters for the RAF and U.S. Army Air Force in World War II.

Makeup of the Arab Forces

The Arabs possessed more weapons and more fighters, but their organization was weak. Arab political leadership had been splintered since the failure in the uprisings of 1936-39. An exception was the extremist Mufti, who controlled two Palestinian Arab military organizations, the Najada and the Futuwa. Altogether, some 6,000 local Arabs had acquired military training in the British Army and almost every male Arab villager was experienced with weapons. Some 3,000 Arabs were enlisted in the British Palestinian Police but were at the immediate disposal of the Arab military. Even before the November 30 invasion a number of units of the British-trained Jordanian Arab Legion were in the country and assisted the local Arabs, even capturing some Jewish settlements for them. Both sides accepted volunteers from abroad, but at first the Arabs were more successful in this respect. Some 6,000 volunteers, the majority Syrians, were organized in fighting units and sent to Palestine as the Arab Liberation Army. This force was led by an Arab officer, Fawzi Kaoukji, who had commanded

terrorist bands during the Arab revolt and had spent World War II in Nazi Germany. Another military leader who had spent time in Nazi Germany was Hassan Salameh, whose units fought in Central Palestine. The most talented Arab military leader in Palestine was Abdul Kader Husseini, who commanded units in the Jerusalem area. Volunteers also poured in from Egypt, drawn from the fascist Moslem Brotherhood. Other volunteers came from among Yugoslavian Moslems, deserters from the British Army and ex-Nazis.

Weighing the Advantages

The Jews had the advantage of superior organization, resolution to fight to the bitter end and united political and military leadership. The Arabs possessed other advantages. In addition to better armament, they enjoyed important geographic strength. Much of the area allotted the Jewish State by the UN partition plan was either in fact in Arab hands, or was isolated, such as the bulk of the Negev Desert and part of Eastern Galilee. Jewish areas, such as the Etzion Bloc near Jerusalem and Western Galilee, were surrounded by Arab districts. The Arabs also controlled the major transportation arteries. Jerusalem, with its Jewish majority, was surrounded by Arab communities. Tel Aviv and Haifa were adjacent to large Arab towns and settlements. And more important, the Arab community enjoyed land frontiers with neighboring Arab countries, while the sole border through which the Jewish community could bring vital supplies was the sea. The ports were in British hands until their departure from Palestine. In May 1948 the British, who displayed open hostility to the Jewish side, endeavored to hand strategic points over to the Arabs. This hostility had its source in the years of the *yishuv's* struggle against the British regime. Hundreds of British police and soldiers had been killed by ETZEL and LEHI.

The Egyptian and Iraqi armies and the Arab Legion were equipped with British weapons, and the latter was commanded by English officers. Even after the evacuation of the British Army, which numbered some 80,000 men, English hostility to the young Jewish state continued. At the height of the War of Independence, London threatened Israel with implementation of her mutual defense pact with Egypt.

December 1947-March 1948: The First Stage

In the first four months of the war initiative was mainly in Arab hands. The fighting broke out in mixed Arab-Jewish towns, such as Jerusalem, Haifa, Tiberias and Safed, and between neighboring towns like Tel Aviv and Jaffa. Sniping and sabotage were the order of the day. The Arabs' usual method of warfare was to send camouflaged vehicles loaded with explosives into Jewish districts. Thus, for example, they blew up a car in Ben Yehuda Street, a main street of Jerusalem, killing fifty people. A short while later, with the help of a driver from the American Consulate, they exploded a consulate car in the courtyard of the Jewish Administration building in Jerusalem. Twelve were killed.

As fighting went on in the towns, a battle began for the country's roads. The Arabs' objective was to isolate and destroy individual Jewish settlements, and to impose blockades on the towns. The Jewish Command, trying to hold off the Arabs while building up its forces for the later battles, took a defensive stance.

The question soon arose whether it would be wise to shorten supply lines and evacuate isolated settlements. This matter became even more acute when Kaoukji's Arab Liberation Army, Abdul Kader's units and the Moslem Brotherhood opened attacks on isolated Jewish settlements. A number of Jewish military experts said it would be better to evacuate

Abdul Kader Husseini confers with Kamel Effendi Arekat, commander of Arab Futuwa forces, 1948. [UPI]

Below: Abdul Kader Husseini (white straps over shoulders) successfully confers with local Arab leaders in Hebron to muster support for his Liberation Army, 1948. [UPI]

A sandwich armored vehicle patroling road
between settlements.

those settlements that were in danger of fall-
ing, but the decisive consideration was political
and not military. It was decided to risk the settlements on the assumption that the area and
borders of the Jewish state would ultimately be
determined by the area that the Jews succeeded in holding. There was also no possibility
of strategic withdrawal without adversely af-
fecting the *yishuv's* morale. There were about
300 Jewish settlements throughout the country. At first commanders refused to permit even
the evacuation of women and children. The
assumption was that where there were children
and wives to be defended, defense would be

more spirited. As pressure grew, children and
some women were evacuated from the Etzion
Bloc, but the children remained in the Negev
settlements until the Egyptian Army's invasion.

The Jewish military effort at this stage was
directed toward maintaining communications
with isolated settlements by means of armored
truck and bus convoys. The armor was prepared by using two layers of steel with wood
in between thereby earning the name "sand-
wiches" for the armored vehicles. Supplies
and ammunition were transferred to Jerusalem and other settlements by means of these
convoys, but the Arabs improved their methods

of warfare and the blockade of Jerusalem
tightened daily. Most of the offensive actions in
the early stage were carried out by Arabs. It
went badly for the Jews. The convoys were
hard hit, especially on the road to Jerusalem.
In Jerusalem itself, the regular convoy to
Mount Scopus and the Hadassah Hospital was
destroyed and scores of doctors and research
personnel were killed.

On March 27, 1948 a big convoy was trapped
on its way back to Jerusalem from the Etzion
Bloc. The following day, forty-two men were
killed in Galilee on a convoy to isolated Kibbutz Yehiam. A force of thirty-five, mostly students and Palmach men, went on foot to reinforce the Etzion Bloc but they encountered
Arab villagers en route and were wiped out.
On March 31, 1948 the road to Jerusalem was
cut. One of the convoys was forced to return
after sustaining heavy casualties. Abdul
Kader's forces were not great, but he could
summon thousands of villagers every time a
Jewish convoy approached. They would shoot
and hurl rocks at the vehicles, slowing them
and increasing their vulnerability.

In March 1948, the daily Jewish losses
reached their peak: an average of ten men
every day. The total death toll in this stage was
1,200 Jews, of whom half were civilians.

The success of the Arab offensive and Jewish
military failures influenced diplomatic developments. U.S. support for the partition plan
waned. On March 19, Herschel Johnson, the
U.S. representative in the United Nations, suggested reviving the international trusteeship
plan for Palestine. In effect, this was a proposal
to withdraw the UN resolution to establish two
states in Palestine. Washington was persuaded
to drop its international trusteeship proposal
only after the Jews were able to turn the tide
in battle.

Failure in the field and the British transfer
into Arab hands of such strategic points as the
huge army camps in Sarafand and Tel Litwin-

Elderly men and immigrants building the Burma
Road to Jerusalem as part of Operation Nahshon.

ski as well as Lydda Airport, forced the Jews
to recognize the need to mount a counter-
offensive. It was clear that it was impossible to
be strong everywhere at once and the only
chance was to concentrate forces at a strategic
point. The site for the first great counter-
offensive was Jerusalem, a city under siege.
The fact that this city was a religious symbol to
Jews was an important factor in the decision.
Ben-Gurion said, "The Arabs were right. The
capitulation, conquest or destruction of Jewish
Jerusalem would strike a heavy, perhaps
mortal, blow to the *yishuv* and would break
Jewish willingness and ability to withstand
Arab aggression."[1]

April 1948: Stage Two Begins
the Counter-Offensive

On April 3, 1948, Jewish forces began Operation Nahshon. Named for a biblical hero, this
military action marked the beginning of the

second stage of the War of Independence.
Nahshon was the first operation in which Jewish forces actually moved on the offensive to
seize territory. Until this time units had ven-
tured out only to return to their starting points,
or had broken through on roads that would
again be closed. According to operational
plans, a breakthrough would be made on the
road to Jerusalem and control of the areas on
both sides of the main road would be secured
prior to the transfer of a large convoy to the besieged city.

Haganah was used for this operation which
relied on surprise and boldness. The boldness
lay in a willingness to expose other fronts,
which would be depleted in manpower and
weapons in order to focus strength at one point.
It was the first time a Jewish force had operated in large formations. At the beginning of
the War of Independence the largest operative unit was the company. In Operation Nah-

shon three battalions or about nine companies participated in a single action. Because of the large number of men, rank badges were distributed for the first time in order to differentiate between officers and enlisted men. To equip this force it was necessary to take arms from fighting units on other fronts and to strip some settlements of almost all their defenses.

On the eve of the operation, March 31, a transport plane flown by a hired American pilot landed with the first delivery of arms purchased from Czechoslovakia: 200 German rifles and 40 machine guns. These were immediately transferred to Nahshon Command. A second and even larger shipment from Czechoslovakia arrived the following day by sea in the *SS Nora*. Over 4,000 rifles and 200 machine guns were hidden beneath a load of onions.

The Nahshon Operation succeeded in securing the road to Jerusalem, but only temporarily. The Haganah's new strategy was countered by the Arabs who activated large units. Kaoukji's forces attacked Kibbutz Mishmar Ha'Emek in the Jezreel Valley, while a battalion of Druze, an Arabic-speaking religious minority who had come mostly from Syria, attacked another kibbutz. The Arabs used artillery for the first time on Mishmar Ha'Emek. Nonetheless Kaoukji's forces found themselves in danger of encirclement. They retreated but the Haganah had insufficient men to exploit its success.

The battle with the Druze at Kibbutz Ramat Yochanan was decisive for the future of Western Galilee, for it decided not only the fate of the kibbutz but also the control of the sole road that connected Galilee with the rest of the country. After repeated assaults by the Druze were repulsed, they finally gave up their attack. The Druze made no more attacks on Jews during this war, and many of their settlements in Galilee announced their willingness to assist the Jewish forces. They later became staunch

allies of the Jews and served in IDF border patrol units. As a people who had suffered religious persecution at the hands of orthodox Moslems, the Druze found the Jews to be natural allies. Israel was the first Mideastern nation to recognize the Druze as a distinct ethnic and religious group and to grant it full civil rights.

In April, a battle which was to become a milestone in the Israeli-Arab dispute took place on the approaches to Jerusalem. This was the battle for Dir Yassin, a small village that controlled the road to Jerusalem. The attack was the job of ETZEL and LEHI. Haganah commanders in Jerusalem knew of this attack on April 9 and had approved it. Later, when the outcome was known, the Haganah repudiated the action. Of 400 inhabitants of the village, 250 men, women and children were killed. Though ETZEL commanders did not justify the killing of civilians, they later contended that the conquest of Dir Yassin was of strategic significance, since it was armed and the first Arab village to be conquered by a Jewish force.[2] The battle caused masses of Arabs to flee in fear of further atrocities. This made the battle for Haifa all the more easy for Jewish forces. The story of the massacre spread among the Arabs, gathering detail. It was a serious blow to the morale of the civilian Arab population. The wealthy had already been moving to neighboring countries and now the middle class and proletariat panicked and fled.

Many who fled did so despite Jewish appeals that they stay. They hoped to return within weeks supported by the Arab armies and take over Jewish property.

In May, the Jews won additional victories. One of the most difficult triumphs was in the north of the country when the siege of Safed was lifted. In this ancient town 1,200 Jews faced 12,000 Arabs. The Mufti was convinced that victory was already his, and had even

Dir Yassin, site of the infamous slaughter of 250
Arab inhabitants at the hands of ETZEL and LEHI
in 1948.

planned to establish a Palestinian government
in this town. But the faulty organization of the
Arabs was their undoing. The town's Arab inhabitants, hearing of Dir Yassin, had begun to
flee and the Jews assisted in the exodus from
surrounding villages by spreading rumors and
threats.

The conquest of Safed was carried out as part
of an overall operation named Yiftach, after the
Palmach commander's code name, in which
Jewish forces took control of part of Eastern
Galilee. Yiftach was also a Jewish warrior hero
whose triumph over the armies of Ammon is related in the Old Testament book of Judges.

During the battle, when Lebanese forces and
local Arabs descended on Moshav Ramat
Naphtali (which was also called Yemin Orde,
after Orde Wingate), Wingate's widow came to
visit Palestine. At her insistence, the Jewish
command put her aboard a reconnaissance
plane that flew over the settlement named for
her husband. She dropped a parcel to the
fighters containing a Bible and a letter. It read:
"To the defenders of Yemin Orde: Since the
spirit of Wingate is with you, even if he cannot
command you in person, I am sending you the
Bible that he carried with him on all his war
travels, and from which he drew the inspiration of his victories. Let this be a mark of the
pact between you and him, in victory or defeat, from now to eternity!" The Jews broke the
Arab siege of Yemin Orde and the settlement
was saved.

The local Arab leadership crumbled; Arab
military leaders could not overcome the disin-
tegration and stem the exodus. Two superior
military leaders were killed in battle—Hassan
Salameh and the talented commander, Abdul
Kader Husseini.

In this second stage of the war another 1,253
Jews, among them 500 civilians, were killed.
Following Operation Nahshon, the road to Jer-

usalem was again closed to Jewish convoys. Also in May four settlements of the Etzion Bloc near Jerusalem fell. Proposals made to the Haganah Command to evacuate the Bloc settlements had been rejected. But the shock caused by the fall of the Bloc resulted in a decision to evacuate a number of settlements around Jerusalem (Atarot, Neve Yaakov and Hartuv, and the potash works at the north of the Dead Sea).

The Arab irregular forces that descended on the Etzion Bloc settlements were joined by a battalion of the Arab Legion and the last charge was mounted in the morning of May 13. Legion armored cars penetrated the village, followed by thousands of armed men from the local Arab villages. One hundred and fifty inhabitants of Kfar Etzion were massacred. In the last stage of fighting, only eighty men and women remained. They surrendered and were brought to a field. Suddenly, machine gun fire was opened on them. A few tried to reach their weapons, and then all were eliminated save four. Two of these succeeded in reaching a nearby settlement. One hid and was saved by an old Arab, while the fourth, a girl, was caught by two irregulars who attempted to rape and kill her, but an Arab Legion officer shot them and took her into captivity. The following day, when the fate of the inhabitants of Kfar Etzion became known, the three other settlements of the Bloc surrendered. Two hundred and fifty defenders of the Etzion Bloc had fallen in battle.

The name of the Etzion Bloc has found its place in Israel's annals of courage. It is often claimed that by their bravery, the settlers saved new Jerusalem. The truth is that the Etzion Bloc was eliminated by irregular forces and a small Legion unit before the invasion of Arab regular armies began. In this respect, the role played by the Bloc was different from that played by settlements like Yad Mordechai and Negba, which were on the invasion axis of the Egyptian Army to the south and which effec-

tively delayed the Egyptian advance on Tel Aviv. The question arose more than once as to whether it would not have been better at a certain stage to evacuate the place and transfer the defenders to Jerusalem where they were sorely needed.

The fall of the Etzion Bloc marked the end of the second phase of the War of Independence. During this stage the Haganah had an opportunity to establish territorial continuity within and between Jewish areas, as well as extending Jewish control over areas previously held by Arab forces. Most of the Arab attacks during this period were repulsed and Jewish forces liberated vital areas, including the upper and lower Galilee which included several Arab towns and mixed Arab-Jewish towns like Safed and Tiberias. Jaffa was taken by ETZEL and Haganah forces. Haifa and sections of western Jerusalem were also captured along with several strategically significant villages. Nahshon was typical of the operations undertaken to clear the Jerusalem corridor.

The Haganah suffered heavy casualties during this period and Jewish convoys were hit hard. But the Jewish fighters were, as a result of their successes and experience during the second stage, prepared to meet the third phase of the war, which lasted from May 15, the day after Israel's statehood was declared, until June 10.

May 14, 1948: The State of Israel Is Born

On May 14, 1948 in a museum in Tel Aviv housed in a low, squat, white stone building, David Ben-Gurion proclaimed the birth of the State of Israel, the first Jewish republic in 2,000 years. He moved soon afterward to unify the Jewish fighting forces and create the IDF. The Haganah was the basis of the new state's official army. ETZEL and LEHI were ordered disbanded and gradually integrated into reorganized battalions. The Palmach Command staff

Golda Meir and Moshe Sharett sign Israel's
Declaration of Independence.

Bottom: David Ben-Gurion declares the State of
Israel, May 14, 1948. A portrait of Theodore Herzl,
father of the Zionist Movement, hangs on the wall.

was integrated into the IDF, but three Palmach
brigades were kept intact. All the troops took
an oath of allegiance to the State. An official
uniform was introduced and ranks were created for officers and NCO's. The Chief of Staff
of the Haganah, Yaakov Dori, became the new
Chief of Staff of the IDF with the rank of
major general.

The entire field army consisted of twelve
regular brigades and one armored brigade in
addition to the Palmach brigades. The Israeli
forces were still inferior to those of the Arabs,
but were now better equipped. The Army had
Czechoslovak and French arms and the Air
Force had acquired a number of Czech-made
Messerschmitts and English-made Spitfires—all
bought in Europe.

An attempt by ETZEL in June 1948 to land the
Altalena, a ship loaded with sorely needed
rifles, ammunition, armored vehicles, bombs
and other arms, was at first agreed to by the

new government and then opposed, presum-
ably because the government feared an armed
revolt by ETZEL. The IDF sunk the ship and the
arms. Several men were killed on shore. Although the incident might have been seen as
cause for civil war, Menahem Begin, who lost
one of his closest friends in the shelling of the

Altalena, vowed that his men would not use arms against fellow Jews. Civil war was avoided. The *Altalena* Affair has haunted Israeli politics for many years and was the cause of a bitter feud between Begin and Ben-Gurion.[3]

May 15-June 10, 1948: Stage Three

The third phase of the war brought the simultaneous offensive of all the neighboring Arab armies on all fronts. The offensive initiative had returned to the Arabs. Encounter with regular armies, supported by aircraft, armor and massed artillery, was a shock for the Jewish units. At the end of this stage, the Arab armies had indeed been blocked, but at the cost of 1,176 Jews of whom 300 were civilians. Israel was in fact saved by the first truce of the Independence War which was declared by the United Nations on June 11, after four weeks of bitter fighting.

The defeat of the local Arabs and the irregulars in the early stages of the war convinced the Arab states that they would have to commit their armies. The scales were tipped in favor of invasion by inter-Arab strife.

In April 1948, King Abdullah of Jordan, King Hussein's grandfather, announced that he intended to take control of the UN-proposed

Arab part of Palestine. A month earlier the British had given their agreement to Abdullah's plan. Their thinking was that it would be better to support the Bedouin ruler of Transjordan rather than choose the Palestinian alternative, which would have meant the rise of the Mufti Amin el Husseini, who had collaborated with the Nazis and was considered a war criminal.

Abdullah's decision gave rise to considerable anxiety among Egyptian and other Arab leaders. The Egyptians feared that the inter-Arab balance would be upset, and that King Abdullah would gain strength. There was also information that indicated that Abdullah in-

Field Marshal Montgomery, British Mideast watcher, meets with American General Dwight D. Eisenhower. [Authenticated News]

Yigal Allon and David Ben-Gurion during War of Independence.

tended to reach an understanding with the Jews of Palestine. Before the invasion, Abdullah did indeed meet a Jewish delegation headed by Golda Meir. It was these fears that induced the Egyptians to invade Palestine, even though the Egyptian Chief of Staff warned his government that the army was not prepared for war.

The Arab armies lacked an overall operational plan. They did not use their weapons efficiently and because of conflicting interests abstained from coming to each other's assistance in time of need. It was decided that Abdullah would head up the coordinating staff of

be destroyed within two weeks. In their evaluation, the Jewish force could not withstand the heavy weapons. The British acted on this evaluation and upon the establishing of the State of Israel increased diplomatic and economic pressure on the young state. She expelled Israel from the pound sterling currency bloc and then abrogated all existing arrangements for the supply of vital commodities to Israel.

Israel Faces Five Invading Armies

Five Arab armies invaded Israel: the Syrians, the Arab Legion, Lebanese, Iraqis and Egyp-

the Arab armies. But from the beginning he formulated a limited strategy against the Jews. It was assumed that a secret agreement would be reached between Ben-Gurion and Abdullah, under which both would employ limited strategy. The Jordanian Arab Legion, therefore, did not invade the areas allocated to the proposed Jewish state. The large-scale clashes between the IDF and the Legion were in the Jerusalem sector and this was explained by the fact that Jerusalem, according to the partition plan, was to be a part of an international zone.

British experts, among them Field Marshal Montgomery, estimated that the *yishuv* would

tians. Token units of other armies, such as the Sudanese Army, were added to the Egyptian Expeditionary Force. On May 15, Tel Aviv was bombed for the first time by Egyptian aircraft. The city was to be bombed another fifteen times before the first truce. Ben-Gurion, who had already become the leader of a fighting Israel, said that one morning when returning from a bombed area, he saw the faces of people peering out at him from the windows of their homes. He looked closely at them and knew that this nation could stand in war. "I saw in their eyes anxiety, but no sign of panic, and this convinced me that the nation would be able to

Tel Aviv central bus station after Egyptian aerial attack during War of Independence.

IDF Loyalty Pledge: I pledge my honor to believe in the State of Israel, promise to carry out unconditionally orders given by my commanders and those in authority, and to give all my efforts and my life, if necessary, to the defense and freedom of the Jewish homeland.

sustain the many sacrifices that it could expect."[4]

Ben-Gurion understood, even before the battle began, that this would not be a war of armies alone. The victor would be he who could recruit all his resources. He told IDF commanders: "We will not win by military might alone. Even if we could field a larger army, we could not stand. The most important thing is moral and intellectual strength."[5] A short time after his speech to the Army officers, bombs dropped near the Israeli General Staff headquarters which was located on a hill in Ramat Gan. After the evacuation of the dead and wounded, Ben-Gurion summoned the members of the General Staff and told them that he wanted them to adopt Hebrew names before they took the oath of loyalty to the new official Army. The eleven officers who were members of the General Staff, and those who were later appointed as front commanders, obeyed and chose Hebrew names for themselves.

The first Chief of Staff, Yaakov Dori, was ill so the main burden fell on the shoulders of a talented young officer who was head of the Operations Division. His name was Yigal (Sukenik) Yadin, a student of archaeology, who had been summoned in October 1947, at the age of thirty, to head the Operations Branch of the Haganah. He had held this position previously

at the age of twenty-six, but had returned to his studies. The *sabra* son of a noted archaeologist, Yigal had devoted most of his years since the age of fifteen, when he joined the Haganah, to security matters. Because of Dori's illness, he in fact became Number One in the IDF Command echelon.

During the third stage of the war, the Arabs had a clear advantage both in weapons and equipment and in manpower. Upon the invasion on May 15, the Jewish community mobilized an additional 30,535 men, including defenders of settlements. From the beginning of the war a superhuman effort had been made to acquire additional weapons, but the 21,000 rifles that had been secured was not sufficient to equip all the soldiers. The heavy casualty rate among officers resulted in a disturbing decline in the quality of the junior command. Their ranks were slowly replenished and luckily the new officers adapted themselves quickly to regular warfare tactics. Youngsters who had

מס' אישי	דרגה	שם משפחה	שם פרטי

סבועה לצבא־הגנה לישראל

הנני נשבע(ת) ומתחייב(ת) בחן צדקי לשמור
אמונים למדינת ישראל, לחוקתה ולשלטונותיה
המוסמכים, לקבל על עצמי ללא תנאי וללא
סייג עול משמעתו של צבא־הגנה לישראל.
לציית לכל הפקודות וההוראות הניתנות על־ידי
המפקדים המוסמכים ולהקדיש כל כוחותי ואף
להקריב את חיי להגנת המולדת ולחרות ישראל.

תאריך _____   חתימת הנשבע(ת) _____

_____ חתימת המשביע

(דרגה)   (שם אישי)   500 טפס (1/100) 7/64

Golda Meir [Frederic Lewis]

Below: Immigrants arrive in Israel, 1948. [Frederic Lewis]

Bottom: New immigrant dying at battle for Latrun. He came to fight for Israel's independence but never lived to see the country for which he fought.

been squad commanders in a partisan force at the beginning of the war were transformed in the later stages to company and battalion commanders in a regular army with its heavy support equipment.

A considerable part of the fighting force arrived from abroad during the war. Thousands of new immigrants were brought from refugee camps in Cyprus and Germany. They joined the ranks of the army straight from the ships. The second, more professional and superior force that came from abroad were the men of MAHAL *(Mitnadvey Hutz Leeretz),* overseas volunteers. They came from all over

the world. Most were Jews, but many were also of other religions. Among them were veterans of World War II who had been summoned to the assistance of the Jews. Some were legendary figures, such as George Bass Barling, an American pilot who had downed thirty-two German aircraft. He was killed in Rome, while taking off in a fighter aircraft to fly to Israel to fight. Another such American youngster was Ted Gibson, son of a Protestant minister, who had received his father's blessing to volunteer for the Israeli Army. Ted was a squadron commander in the Israeli Air Force. The men of MAHAL made a considerable professional and technical contribution to the young Army. Apart from pilots, there were gunners, tank crews, naval officers and doctors. Most of them spoke English. In the IDF of those days, orders were given in a babel of tongues; the most prevalent were Yiddish, English and Russian. One of the volunteer pilots whose plane was shot down landed near an IDF outpost. He spoke only English and, fearing that he would be shot by IDF soldiers, he blurted out two Jewish words he had heard in his parents' house: "Gefilte fish!"

There can be no doubt that what blocked the advance of the invading armies was the string of Israeli settlements, primarily kibbutzim, that stood in their path. The Arab forces wrongly thought they would be confronted solely by armed bands. They knew little of the Jewish fighting force and almost nothing of the morale and determination of Israel's citizens. They lost countless soldiers in small clashes and, more importantly, lost time. For the Jewish Army that needed every minute to organize, that time was golden.

The smallest Arab army to invade Palestinian territory was the Lebanese. This front was also the only place where IDF units had initiated operations in advance of the invading force. A Palmach-IDF unit penetrated into Lebanon by night and demolished the great bridge over the Litani River, an action which disrupted Lebanese troop movements. The Lebanese Army contented itself with retaking one kibbutz and grabbing some areas close to the Lebanese-Palestinian border. The IDF contained the Lebanese force and spoiled the Syrian plan to act jointly with the Lebanese in cutting off the Upper Galilee.

The clashes with the invading Syrian Army were more severe. The Syrian column, accompanied by armor, concentrated to the south of the Sea of Galilee with the intention of breaking through toward Tiberias and Nazareth. They first took the Arab township of Semach, inflicting heavy losses on IDF units. One day before their renewed offensive, a delegation from the settlements of the region reached the General Staff and begged for reinforcements and heavy weapons. A number of Ben-Gurion's comrades from the Second Aliya were included in this delegation. It was a tough conversation for Ben-Gurion. There were many pleas and even tears, but Ben-Gurion was compelled to reject the demand on the grounds that the reinforcements were all needed on the Jerusalem and Egyptian fronts. All that the delegation gained were two 65mm mountain artillery pieces of nineteenth-century vintage. These two guns, named Napoleonchiks, had reached the country two days earlier.

To block the Syrian armor, Yigal Yadin told the men of Kibbutz Degania, which would be the first to face the Syrian breakthrough, "There is no other way but to let the Syrians approach the fences, and then to fight face-to-face with their armor!"[6] And that was exactly what happened. The tanks broke through the fences of Degania and were set afire by Molotov cocktails thrown at close range by the defenders. The Napoleonchiks opened fire from the hills above and the Syrian attack was blocked. They retreated to Semach.

This battle persuaded the Jewish settlements on the front lines that a regular army with heavy equipment could be stopped. Degania was safe together with the whole of the Jordan Valley. Two other settlements, Masada and Sha'ar Hagolan, had been abandoned by night without prior approval from the High Command. They feared that additional advance by the Syrian Army would isolate them completely.

The Syrians made no further attempts to flex their muscles on this front. They transferred their efforts northward, and in the new area of operation succeeded in taking control, after bitter fighting, of the Moshava Mishmar Hayarden. They ended their advance at that point and made no further moves until the end of the war.

The Iraqi Army entered further to the south. One prong occupied the Naharayim Power Station, but was unable to advance further. The Napoleonchiks were summoned to bombard the Iraqi column, but were not very accurate. Another column forged ahead into the Arab regions of Judea and Samaria on the west bank of the Jordan River and threatened the center of the country. Minor battles flared up in this sector and one of the Jewish settlements changed hands. The IDF tried to draw the Iraqi Army's attention northward and opened an attack in brigade strength on the Arab town of Jenin. The opening proceeded well but because it lacked coordination, the IDF sustained one of its most severe defeats and retreated from Jenin and the surrounding hills. But the advance of the Iraqi Army had been stopped. The achievements of the Arab armies were limited to occupying positions on the periphery.

The Negev Brigade of the Palmach and the IDF Givati Brigade attempted to block the Egyptian Army that was advancing in the south of the country. The latter numbered five battalions with 2,750 men. At the time there were

Emblem: Veterans of Siege of Jerusalem, 1948.

Below: Food convoy moves toward the besieged city of Jerusalem during the War of Independence.

twenty-seven Jewish settlements in the Negev area. The Egyptian Army, which was the largest of the invading Arab armies, advanced in a two-pronged attack. The larger column moved up the coast toward Tel Aviv. The second turned eastward to Beersheba, and from there through Hebron to the south of Jerusalem. The major problem facing the IDF was to delay the column advancing toward Tel Aviv in order to gain time to organize defense lines.

This task was imposed on the Israeli settlements along the line of Egyptian advance. Though the inhabitants numbered only a few score men, some of these settlements were formidable obstacles to the Egyptians' advance. The Egyptian Command at first decided to concentrate on the settlements, thereby granting the Israelis considerable time. Fierce attacks were made on Yad Mordechai, a kibbutz where survivors of the Warsaw ghetto fighters lived. It had been named in honor of Mordechai Anilewitz, one of the leaders of the ghetto uprising. On May 24, the settlement was evacuated after most of its buildings had been destroyed and the majority of its defenders were killed. A second settlement, Kibbutz Nitzanim, fell to the Egyptians after substantially delaying them. The women and children of Nitzanim had been evacuated earlier. In their northward advance, the Egyptians finally reached Ashdod, but stopped at a bridge twenty miles south of Tel Aviv, and there they were attacked by four Israeli fighter aircraft. This was the first time that fighters, brought from Czechoslovakia and assembled in Palestine by Czechoslovak experts, had gone into battle. The Egyptians were shocked by the presence of aircraft in Israeli hands. The Negev remained cut off, but they advanced no further. The bridge where they were stopped by Israeli aircraft has been called ever since: *"Ad Halom!"* ("No Further!")

The most serious blows sustained by Israel's Army were on the Jerusalem front in the war with the Arab Legion. When the Legion joined the irregular forces that encircled the Jewish quarter of ancient Jerusalem the defenders were no longer able to prolong their resistance. On May 28, the Jewish sector of the Old City fell into Arab hands. Twenty-five hundred inhabitants were sorted out and all men taken into captivity. The IDF's success in taking control over a part of the Arab districts of Jerusalem outside the walls was not enough to compensate in even the smallest degree for the loss of the Jewish quarter in the Old City, with the Western Wall and its ancient synagogues.

Col. Mickey Marcus, the American who commanded the Jerusalem front during the War of Independence. [Israeli Army]

Bottom: Training senior citizens in the use of arms during the siege of Jerusalem.

It was a demoralizing blow.

The IDF sustained another defeat in the battles for the Jerusalem road. There the battles centered on the Latrun Police Fortress which controlled the road to Jerusalem before its entry into the Sha'ar Hagai ascent. The IDF attacked the police station five times, including one assault supported by a number of tanks, but each assault on the fortress was driven back. Some 200 men gave their lives in these battles. The most costly attack of all was that made by a brigade that had been organized only a few days previously and consisted of new immigrants who had just gotten off the boats. Though Yigal Yadin opposed this attack, Ben-Gurion would not withdraw his orders. All his resources were devoted to easing the pressure on Jerusalem. Many of the new immigrants were killed by Jordanian artillery fire without even having seen the country for which they died.

Most of Ben-Gurion's attention was given to Jerusalem. It was to this front that he sent Col. Mickey Marcus, an American-Jewish graduate of West Point who had come to Israel as a volunteer. Mickey Marcus was given command of the Jerusalem front over the objections of some of the Israeli commanders. He was killed one night when he left his tent to urinate and was challenged by a sentry in Hebrew. Marcus was asked for the password and when he replied in English the sentry shot him.

By the time of the truce, the Israeli forces had established a roundabout mountain route, called the Burma Road, through which they transported the first food to reach starving Jerusalem in weeks. Hundreds of men over call-up age were brought to the Burma Road to carry sacks of flour and crates of food on their backs.

Israel's small Air Force found an opportunity to flex its muscles for the first time. Just

English-made Spitfire fighter plane sold to Israel by Czechoslovakia during War of Independence.

Bottom: Joseph Stalin, the moving force behind Soviet military aid to Israel during the War of Independence, here poses with Winston Churchill. [Authenticated News]

before the truce, an Israeli transport plane dropped bombs over Amman, the capital of Jordan. This was the first Arab capital to be bombed, and it caused considerable shock among the Arabs who had not known the Jews had any planes. Later, Damascus was also bombed. The bombings of Tel Aviv continued until two Egyptian planes were downed in aerial combat. This success was achieved thanks to the fighter aircraft that Czechoslovakia had sold to Israel.

The Soviet Bloc Supplies Arms to Israel

Israel's arms deals with the Communist bloc are an interesting aspect of her War of Independence. The first Prime Minister and Defense Minister of Israel, David Ben-Gurion, told me in an interview before he died: "They saved the State. There is no doubt of this. Without these weapons, it's doubtful whether we could have won. The arms deal with the Czechs was the greatest assistance that we received."[7]

Ben-Gurion relates that the contacts with Czechoslovakia began during the days of the democratic regime in that country and continued after the Communists took over. This was not only business for the arms industry, but

was backed by the Communist Party and the government and, according to all signs, Czechoslovakia received Stalin's approval. The Secretary of the Israeli Communist Party, Shlomo Mikunis, says he was told by Communist officials in Bulgaria in 1949 that Stalin was the moving force in obtaining Eastern bloc assistance for Israel.

It seems that the Communist countries were interested in supporting any means to help remove the British from Palestine. At that time Ben-Gurion had declared that Israel would maintain a policy of neutrality but the Russians certainly thought they could acquire influence in the region through aid to the new State. The assistance encompassed a number of Communist-bloc countries. Bulgaria agreed to release Jewish youngsters for immigration to Israel and even offered to equip them with light arms. Rumania also agreed that 400 Jewish youths could go to Israel as volunteers. Poland announced that she would be willing to accept Palestinian Jews into her staff officers' school. Volunteers, though few in number, also arrived from the Soviet Union. Among others, an officer with the rank of major was dispatched to assist in training and a Jewish divisional commander from the Red Army was attached to Ben-Gurion's staff.

The greatest help came from Czechoslovakia. Her leaders were prepared to establish a brigade of Czech-Jewish volunteers. They came to Israel but were split up among all the units. The Czechoslovaks trained pilots and tank crews from among the Jews who asked to immigrate to Israel. The big arms transaction, in which Israel paid the full price, was a major affair. Prague demanded payments in dollars. The prices were high, though for Israel this was a most worthwhile transaction. At one point, when it became known to the Czechs that the IDF needed heavy mortars for the battle of Jerusalem, they bought twelve such pieces in

Switzerland and delivered them to Israeli representatives. Tens of thousands of rifles and thousands of machine guns were also transferred to the country.

The foundations for the Israeli Air Force can also be attributed to Czechoslovakia. In all, eighty-nine fighter planes were acquired there. The first were German Messerschmitts and they were followed by British Spitfires. The Czechs also began to train Israeli pilots within the Czech Air Force. An Israeli base, named Etzion, was established near the town of Zatec in Czechoslovakia. Most of the weapons acquired in America and in Europe were brought to this place and flown to Israel from there. Three Flying Fortresses acquired in the United States also landed at Etzion. They flew to Israel via Cairo where they dropped one and a half tons of bombs near one of King Farouk's palaces. Ninety-five missions were flown from Etzion to Israel until August 1948 when Prague gave in to American pressure to close the base and stop the aerial bridge.

The CIA was also worried over the fact that planes taking off in the United States were "vanishing" behind the Iron Curtain. Two Czech flying officers who had defected to West Germany reported an aerial link that began in the United States and extended from Czechoslovakia to Israel. Washington submitted a formal complaint to the Prague government and even noted the names of American citizens who were playing a role in the airlift. The United States threatened to bring the matter up in the United Nations. America also put pressure on the Bulgarian government not to permit Jewish youth to go to Israel to join the IDF.

June 11-July 9, 1948: The First Truce

A stalemate developed in late spring. The Arab armies were losing the offensive momentum and the Israelis were not yet ready for large-scale offensives. Both sides welcomed a breathing space and they agreed to a one-month cease-fire that began on June 11.

During this period the IDF made its plans for the future. Israeli forces were to take the initiative after the cease-fire and it was reckoned that the foremost priority was removing the danger to Tel Aviv and its immediate surroundings by liberating Lydda and Ramle. Next they planned to move to the hilly country east of the coastal plain to lift the siege of Jerusalem; then to outflank the Transjordanian-held Old City from the north. Another task was to secure the Haifa region by taking Nazareth and the remaining parts of the Lower Galilee.

Yigal Allon, Palmach Commander, led Jewish forces in Operation Dani in July 1948.

At the same time, the Egyptians in the south, the Iraqis in the east and the Syrians in the north had to be held back by the settlements until offensive action could be taken.

It was clear to the Israeli General Staff that battle would recommence and that this would be the decisive stage of the war. Four weeks of truce allowed rearmament and reorganization and injected blood into the arteries of the Israeli Army. It now stood on its feet. There was no doubt that the Arabs had made a military error by agreeing to the truce. In addition to the weapons that arrived from Czechoslovakia, Israel had acquired material from other countries, including fifty Krupp 75mm guns and six ships for the Israeli Navy.

The Army intensified its training and four fronts were established. Severe conflict erupted between the General Staff and Ben-Gurion over the appointments of commanders for these fronts. Ben-Gurion wanted to appoint Shlomo Shamir and Mordechai Makleff, graduates of the British Army, to these positions in place of leftist officers, whom he apparently considered to be less politically loyal. Yigal Yadin submitted his resignation.[8] Ben-Gurion, in turn, announced his resignation, and it was only thereafter that a temporary solution to the conflict was found. The way out was found when Yigal Allon, Commander of the Palmach, was appointed commander of the great Operation Dani in the Tel Aviv area that was designed to begin when the truce ended on July 9, 1948. The prestige associated with the appointment placated the dissident officers. It was also decided to move on the weakest enemy of all: Kaoukji's Arab Liberation Army in Galilee.

July 9-July 18, 1948: Stage Four

Fighting resumed on July 9 and the well-planned strategies were put into effect. The battles raged for ten days through July 18, at which point the United Nations again imposed a truce which lasted until October 10, 1948.

The IDF remained on the defensive on the Egyptian front at this stage. The Egyptian Army was repeatedly repelled by the residents of Kibbutz Negba, who effectively prevented their northward advance. Another settlement, Kfar Darom on the Gaza Strip, was evacuated on July 7 under Egyptian pressure. This was the last Israeli settlement to fall during the War of Independence.

During the ten days of battle, Israeli naval vessels bombarded the town of Tyre in Lebanon and land forces began operations against Kaoukji on the northern front. By penetrating from the rear, they succeeded in gaining control over the Arab town of Nazareth and in conquering a considerable part of Lower Galilee.

The biggest and most important operation of the ten-day battle was Operation Dani, which was intended to drive the Arab Legion from the area of Tel Aviv and relieve the pressure on Jerusalem. The Arab towns of Lydda and Ramle fell into IDF hands. Yigal Allon commanded a force of almost four brigades, including some armor (half-tracks and eight-tracks) and artillery. Yitzhak Sadeh, the founder of the Palmach and a past commander of Allon's, led the armored force. Moshe Dayan led a raiding battalion of commandos. This was the IDF's largest initiated operation and it led to the taking of Lydda Airport. Some 50,000 Arab inhabitants of Lydda, Ramle and neighboring towns fled the region, this time without the Israelis preventing them or suggesting that they remain.

The second truce came into effect on July 19 when the Israeli defensive was at the height of its momentum. During the last ten days of war Israel had learned that the Arab military coalition had, in effect, crumbled. When one of the Arab armies was hit, the others failed to come to its aid. This story was to repeat itself in the 1956 and 1967 wars.

October 10, 1948: The Final Stage Begins

When fighting resumed on October 10, Israel held the initiative on all fronts. It was no longer a war of few against many. The Arab forces had lost the numerical advantage and, at best, the opposing forces were equal in number. The Jewish community had mustered all its resources and at the peak of the battle fielded an army of 120,000 men. Weapons flowed into the country in considerable quantities. In the final stage of the war, the IDF had 60,000 rifles, 220 artillery pieces and 7,000 vehicles of various types.

The Israelis had the advantage of superior organization on their side. Throughout the war and during the cease-fire period, the IDF had undergone evolutionary change. It began to ·take on the marks of a regular army, with ranks and a well-developed command.

The Arab armies were large but they were peasant armies. The vast majority of fighting men were illiterate and the gap between soldier and officer was immense. Organization was faulty, ammunition stores ill-prepared and medical facilities inadequate.

The IDF carried out four big operations, three of which were in the south and one in the north of the country. In the north Kaoukji's Arab Liberation Army was driven out of the country in Operation Hiram, named for a biblical king of Tyre in the days of Solomon. The rout lasted only sixty hours. Four brigades operated in Upper Galilee, under the command of Moshe Carmel. The objective was to cut off Kaoukji's army without clashing with him directly. The move succeeded with relatively few losses, but Kaoukji and most of his army managed to escape to Lebanon. The IDF chased his

units as far as the frontier, and took twelve Lebanese border villages. Vanguard units even reached the banks of the Litani River but when the armistice agreement with Lebanon was signed, the IDF withdrew from Lebanese territory.

The IDF's major effort was directed southward to the Negev and was motivated by diplomatic and political considerations. The UN mediator, Swedish Count Bernadotte, had proposed a new plan for the partition of Palestine in which he suggested removing the Negev from Israeli hands. Israeli leaders suspected that the British were behind the plan which would permit them to establish military bases in the Negev. The area was, at that time, under siege by the Egyptian Army. The Egyptians had refused to allow convoys to reach the blockaded Israeli settlements in the Negev. The Israeli offensive was based on the short-term end of breaking the siege and blockade on the settlements and the long-term objective of securing the Negev against later attempts at a partition of the area.

On October 15, the battles of Operation Yoav began according to a plan that was one of the best in the War of Independence. For the first time during this war, the offensive began with an aerial bombardment by the Israeli Air Force on Egyptian planes that were stationed at El Arish Airfield. Three brigades opened the offensive, and were joined toward the end by a fourth and a battalion of armor. Planning was based on the assumption that the other Arab armies would not interfere or even open fire.

Before the breakthrough began, various diversionary actions were carried out. Forces from the besieged settlements attacked Egyptian supply lines from the rear. The only frontal assault took place around an Arab-held police fortress, which was stationed on the main road to the Negev. IDF forces attacked the fortress unsuccessfully a number of times before they took it and broke through to the Negev.

The Egyptian Army began a general retreat while the IDF was taking the Negev capital of Beersheba. Five thousand Egyptian soldiers remained behind in an area called the Faluja Pocket. One of the Egyptians was a young officer named Abdul Nasser who would later become the President of Egypt. The Egyptians sustained another defeat when, in the course of the operation, the *Emir Farouk*, flagship of the Egyptian Navy, was sunk by Israeli frogmen.

The commander of Operation Yoav was Yigal Allon, then thirty years old. He had previously led Operation Dani and was later to command two other big operations on the southern front. Yigal Yadin was the outstanding staff officer of the war but Allon was the most talented field commander. Yadin was a student, an intellectual-soldier; Allon a farmer-soldier. He was born in Kfar Tabor in Galilee, the birthplace of the Hashomer organization. He later studied in an agricultural school and joined Kibbutz Ginossar. He began his military career in the Palmach and was a student of the doctrines of Orde Wingate and Yitzhak Sadeh. He served as Palmach commander after Sadeh and his strategic theories were instrumental in shaping IDF

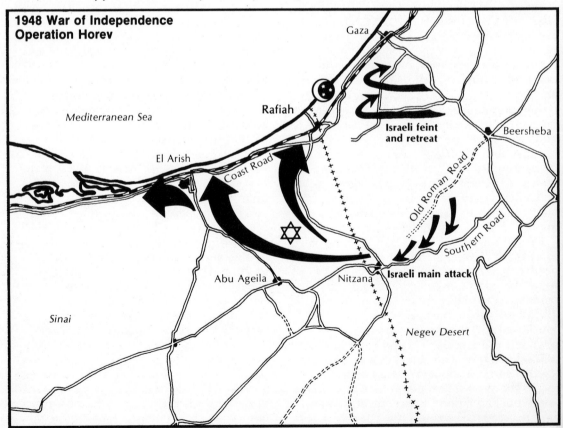

**1948 War of Independence
Operation Horev**

Mediterranean Sea

Gaza

Rafiah

**Israeli feint
and retreat**

Beersheba

El Arish

Coast Road

Old Roman Road

Abu Ageila

Nitzana

Southern Road

Israeli main attack

Sinai

Negev Desert

British military commentator B.H. Liddell-Hart, architect of the strategy of indirect approach.

Below: Palmach forces advancing on Beersheba during Operation Yoav, with inset showing historic photograph of the first Israeli forces to penetrate Sinai. Second from right is Yitzhak Rabin, who was to become Chief of Staff of the IDF and Prime Minister of Israel. [Josef Roth]

military doctrines.

On December 22, while the siege of the Faluja Pocket continued, Operation Horev, the last of the war, began. This offensive, based primarily on mobility rather than frontal attack, resulted in the total rout of the Egyptian Army. Five brigades, including one of armor, participated in the operation. In the beginning, a small force penetrated the enemy rear and secretly moved along one of the mountains that controlled the main road. When it reached the peak, it announced its success by the dispatch of a messenger dove, the signal to begin the at-

tack. While the bulk of the forces were pushing forward, one division moved along an old Roman road which had not been used for hundreds of years. This unit appeared suddenly in the rear, in the Nitzana region, and totally surprised the Egyptians. It was a brilliant application of Liddell-Hart's theory of the indirect offensive.

The main Egyptian positions on the road were taken by the assault. The follow-up was in hand-to-hand battles between the remaining Egyptian forces and a unit of MAHAL volunteers who were veterans of the French under-

Arab refugees leaving homes near Lydda and Ramle in the wake of Israeli advances.

ground in World War II. The road thus cleared, the IDF broke through to the Sinai Peninsula. On December 30, the Army reached Abu Ageila and raiding forces penetrated deep into Sinai.

The Egyptian Command was shaken. The fate of the Egyptian Expeditionary Force in Palestine was nearly sealed when diplomatic circumstances extricated Cairo from total defeat. Calling upon her 1936 Defense Pact with Egypt, Great Britain delivered an ultimatum demanding immediate withdrawal of Israeli forces from Egyptian territory. The ultimatum was delivered through the United States Ambassador in Israel together with a warning from President Truman that it would be wise to heed the English demand. Yigal Allon, the commander in the field, cabled the General Staff: "There is no military reason for retreat!"[9] He then left the front and flew to Tel Aviv, but his efforts to convince Ben-Gurion that withdrawal should be delayed until the Egyptians were destroyed were in vain. His orders were to withdraw within twenty-four hours. A few days later, another ultimatum demanded the removal of IDF forces in Gaza. These forces had driven a wedge into the Gaza Strip by way of Rafiah which effectively prevented the safe retreat of Egyptian forces from Palestine. Diplomatic intervention clearly saved Egypt from total defeat. A day before the Gaza ultimatum, a message radioed to Cairo by the commander of the Egyptian Expeditionary Force had been intercepted by Israel. Its text: "The chances of solving the Palestine problem by military means are nil. Try diplomatic means!"[10]

Allon sent a strong message to the General Staff: "I am shocked by the withdrawal order! This is the second time that we are throwing away a certain chance of inflicting a final defeat on the Egyptian enemy!"[11] Again Ben-Gurion was resolute. He believed that by agreeing to withdraw IDF forces, he would achieve Cairo's agreement to negotiate for an armi-

stice. He ordered the Chief of Staff to inform the commander on the front that he was not entitled to interfere in diplomatic matters and was forbidden to criticize the management of the war. On January 6, 1949 Egypt did indeed announce her willingness for negotiation. Yigal Allon refused to participate as a representative in the Israeli delegation. He later contended that Israel had made a diplomatic mistake in accepting armistice without guarantees instead of demanding a peace treaty.

The last battle on the southern front was not with the Egyptians, but with the British. British fighter planes flew over Israeli territory and

opened fire on IDF forces. Five English planes were shot down in aerial combat with Israeli planes and by ground fire. Among the Israeli pilots who took part in this battle were some who had served in the Royal Air Force during the Second World War and had learned its secrets during their service. The joy of victory was tempered by sorrow over the fate of the pilots who were downed. The Israeli squadron sent a telegram to the British squadron that was stationed in Cyprus: "Comrades, forgive us. But you were on the wrong side of the fence."[12]

The war with Egypt was over. Attention

Badge of the Veterans of the Independence War.

Below: [Frederic Lewis]

turned to the southern Negev as far as the Red Sea, the gateway to Africa, the Indian Ocean and the Persian Gulf. This operation was also primarily based on rapid movement and proceeded almost without a shot being fired. The Jordanians retreated to Aqaba across the Gulf when they saw IDF forces approaching. When the latter reached the place where today stands the town of Eilat, the commander of the Israeli force radioed: "We have reached the end of the map!"[13]

King Abdullah tacitly recognized Israeli rule over this important area. In return, Israel acceded to Arab Legion occupation of all areas of western Palestine that were originally intended by the UN for the Arab state. Ben-Gurion would later regret this agreement. In a conversation with UN Secretary General Hammerskjold, Ben-Gurion said that had he known how relationships with the Arab states would develop, he would not have considered conceding those sectors to Jordan. Nineteen years were to pass before the Six-Day War, when the IDF again conquered this part of Palestine.

"We Won the War, But Lost the Peace"

The IDF's last operations showed considerable progress in the level of strategic planning by the Israeli General Staff. The Israeli forces proved that they excelled in defense. They were not as noteworthy for their offensive tactics, yet they were impressive in maneuvers of large-scale forces and in the creation of operative situations which stymied the enemy. The IDF came out of the War of Independence confident of itself. The feeling was that peace was at hand. Only a few saw otherwise. Yigal Allon, for example, summed up the war to his officers: "We won the war, but lost the peace!"[14]

Following the signing of armistice agreements in February, March and April of 1949, Israeli forces evacuated Lebanese territory south of the Litani; the Syrians evacuated their bridgehead in Upper Galilee; the surrounded Egyptian brigade was allowed to leave the Faluja Pocket; Egypt retained the Gaza Strip which, together with Jordan's takeover of the west bank and the Old City of Jerusalem, prevented the establishment of an Arab state in Palestine as prescribed by the UN partition plan. Israel emerged with more than the original plan had allocated to her. It was, however, much less than was within her military ability to win.

Footnotes

1 Israel Defense Forces, *Toldot Milhemet Hakommiyut* [History of the War of Independence] (Tel Aviv: Maarachot Publishers, 1964), p. 49.
2 For ETZEL's version of the episode, see Menahem Begin, *The Revolt* (Los Angeles: Nash, 1972), pp. 162-5.
3 For Begin's account of the Altalena Affair, see *ibid.*, pp. 154-76.
4 David Ben-Gurion, *Behilahm Am* [A people's struggle] (Tel Aviv: Mapai Publications, 1951), p. 34.
5 *Ibid.*, p. 11.
6 Israel Defense Forces, *op. cit.*, p. 169.
7 Interview with author, originally published in *Ha'aretz*, September 1969.
8 For Allon's account of this period, see *The Making of Israel's Army* (New York: Bantam, 1971), pp. 34-51.
9 Yeruham Cohen, *Leor Hayom Oobemachashach* [By the light of dawn] (Tel Aviv: Amicam Publishers, 1969), pp. 239, 250.
10 Allon, *Keshet Lohamin*, p. 218.
11 Cohen, *op. cit.*, p. 250.
12 *Diary of the First Combat Aviation Squadron*, internal publication, Israel Defense Forces.
13 Cohen, *op. cit.*, 266.
14 Allon, *Making of Israel's Army*, p. 48-9.

3. FIRST YEARS

The Israel Defense Forces emerged from the War of Independence as a victorious army, but one faced with myriad new problems. It had been formed in the heat of battle—a hodge-podge of fighting men quickly organized to respond to the pressing defense needs of the Jewish community—but after the war it was the national defense force of a new state. There was much to be accomplished in those early days. It soon became clear that Israel's defense was a major priority, that readiness for war would always be essential and that the task of the IDF had just begun.

It was a young army lacking in traditions and it occasionally seemed to be little more than a fighting rabble, founded by idealists but totally lacking in form. The immediate problem of operations gave way to peace-time problems— it was necessary to decide what the structure and character of Israel's army would be. But the first order of business was the demobilization of the victorious army and the return of thousands of soldiers to civilian life.

The Standing Army Is Consolidated

The IDF numbered 120,000 soldiers at the end of the Independence War, an immense figure considering that the entire Jewish population of Israel was at that time no more than 600,000. The scope of demobilization depended on how large a standing army would be maintained. David Ben-Gurion, in whose hands the decision lay, was wary of the politicization of the Army. The leftwing parties in particular worried him. They had played a key role in the Haganah and the Palmach, and many senior IDF commanders tended to the political Left. The atmosphere had heated up at the beginning of 1948 when two leftwing parties amalgamated to form Mapam as an alternative to Ben-Gurion's centrist Mapai party. Frictions were evident during the War of Independence, even before the official creation of the IDF.

It was against this background that Ben-Gurion decided to dissolve the Palmach and to reduce the influence of Mapam-linked officers in the IDF. Upon the dissolution of the Palmach, hundreds of its officers left the military, refusing to join the regular army. Those who remained did not at first receive appropriate promotions. The discontent of the former Palmach men adversely influenced the standard and morale of the IDF command—it appeared that politics counted more than ability.

Some military leaders, such as Mordechai Makleff, who became the IDF's third Chief of Staff in 1952, were convinced of a positive side to the exodus of senior Palmach officers:

The bulk of those who resigned were the ones who had political aspirations. The lower echelon of Palmach officers, who were able to contribute to forming the young Army, for the most part remained. Had the senior commanders remained in the IDF, we would have been compelled to waste another two years in disputes over organization. Thus, matters were decided far quicker, and we didn't waste valuable time on sterile discussion.[1]

Ben-Gurion's fears of political deviation among former Palmach and Haganah commanders increased his reliance on those officers who had acquired their experience in the British Army during World War II. In making his early appointments to senior positions, Ben-Gurion chose a large percentage among graduates of the British forces. He felt they were the only ones with formal experience in administration, supply and use of support weaponry. This policy was hotly debated and increased the already serious factionalism within the IDF.

In December 1949, after much consideration, Ben-Gurion finally yielded and decided to transfer the command of the IDF into the hands of the younger generation of officers. The aging Yaakov Dori was replaced as Chief of Staff by thirty-two-year-old Yigal Yadin. Despite his youth, Yadin had served as Chief of Operations

IDF Chiefs of Staff in the first years: Yaakov Dori, 1948-49; Yigal Yadin, 1949-52; Mordechai Makleff, 1952-53; Haim Laskov, 1958-61. [Israeli Army]

in the war-time General Staff and had filled in during the Independence War when Dori was ill. Yadin brought into the command echelons other young officers who participated in vital decisions. Notable was Mordechai Makleff, who was appointed Yadin's deputy and was later to become Chief of Staff. Another future Chief of Staff, Haim Laskov, was among Yadin's brain trust. Yadin emerged as a leader of real stature and a distinguished Chief of Staff. During his tenure the IDF's foundations were laid.

The first problem faced by the General Staff was determining the size of the regular army. It was clear from the outset that Israel's economy could not support a large standing army. The manpower needs in other sectors of national life were too great and the population of the country too small. Nonetheless, the defense requirements of Israel were also important. The threat of future Arab incursions had not been removed by the Independence War and many officers believed that a large army would have to take precedence over the lesser needs of the economy. Suggestions were made that the Army be based on selected volunteers, an approach Yadin described as follows: "Whether to create an army from the 600,000 selected Jews who resided in the country before the War of

Independence, and treat the others as garbage, or to conceive of the problems of the IDF as part of the problems of a state that is absorbing immigrants with all the attendant difficulties and dangers."[2]

The outcome of the debate was the establishment of a small regular army (comprised mostly of the officer corps) and a large reserve army that would include new immigrants. This was in response to Yadin's point that the disadvantaged immigrant population would have to be given a place in Israeli society.

In 1949, Yadin went to Switzerland to study that country's organization of reserve units. He was followed, in 1950, by Generals Makleff and Aharon Remez. The IDF adopted the Swiss system of reserves, but had to alter a number of aspects to suit Israel's needs. For example, Swiss reservists take their weapons home. This could not be done in Israel. Israel's arsenals were not sufficiently rich to risk the loss of such weapons. It was feared that the new immigrant soldiers would not act responsibly as regarded their weapons. Furthermore, Israel's borders were far from safe. Bands of marauding Arabs were, at that time, attacking border settlements and stealing everything they could get their hands on. The IDF command was aware that reservists' weapons could easily come into

The Command insignias of the IDF: Northern, Central and Southern.

Arab hands in that manner. Special arsenals were set up for the reserves. The emergency warehouse system made it possible to keep the weapons secure at the same time as they were readily available when needed.

Once the system of reserves was established, the basic doctrines of the IDF still had to be hammered out. Because the early leaders of the IDF were almost entirely infantrymen, infantry strategy was paramount. It was only later that armored forces became crucial.

The IDF's orginal organization was adopted from the model of the British Army. After a sharp debate, and despite opposition from the Air Force, a common General Staff for all branches was established. Land commands were set up in relation to the surrounding Arab states. The Southern Command was stationed near the Egyptian border; the Northern Command opposed the armies of Syria and Lebanon, and the Central Command faced the Jordanian Legion. The commands were attached

to the General Staff; the territorial brigades, the largest operative formations, were directly subordinate to the commands.

Development of the Israeli Soldier

One of the IDF's critical problems in its early days was officer training. The Army had lost the cream of its officers in the War of Independence, and a survey after that war revealed that only a small percentage of IDF officers had had professional training of any sort and fewer still had completed an officers' course in either the British Army or the Haganah. Thousands of officers, in both the regular army and the reserves, had received their commissions without passing courses.

An immense training operation was launched in the early fifties. Gen. Haim Laskov was placed in charge of the operation whose objective was to train 27,000 officers within eighteen months. Under Laskov's direction, thirty military schools were established and, for the first time in the history of the Israeli fighting force, uniform instruction was instituted. Previously each commander had trained his men his own way, with the methods he considered best. Under the newly designed program, there was a single training base for the absorption of new recruits and a single basic officers' course. After basic training, candidates moved on to specialized training in the various branches.

In these early years, the IDF did not have its own training literature and most of its officers, who had disrupted their high school education for the struggle against the British and the War of Independence, did not know foreign languages. "One of the first things that I did," Laskov relates, "was to teach many officers English so that they could read foreign military literature."[3] Efforts were also made to send officers for advanced training in foreign armies. This was only mildly successful—at first most foreign military officials were reluc-

Boundaries of Israel, 1949

Syria · Haifa · Tel Aviv · Jerusalem · Jordan · Egypt

Emblem of the Druze minorities in service with the IDF.

Bottom: Newly arrived Jewish immigrants. [Frederic Lewis]

tant to accept Israeli soldiers. A course for battalion commanders and a Staff and Command School were developed within the IDF.

Years of Decline

The years immediately following the War of Independence were years of decline for the Israeli Army. The primary reason was that the great immigration of Jews from backward North African and Mideastern nations filled the ranks of the IDF with manpower of the lowest standard. The Army absorbed thousands of illiterate recruits who had to be taught basic grooming, reading and writing, in addition to soldiering. They lacked motivation and saw service in the Army as a punishment. They filled the combat units and thereby reduced the IDF's operational level. *Sabras* and the educated filled the higher ranks. This segregation within the armed forces nurtured the growing alienation between native-born

Israelis and the new immigrants. Mordechai Makleff recalls that he was often approached by officers concerned about the low level of the average Israeli soldier. His reply was that the average enemy soldier, the disadvantaged Arab, was likely to be even more backward.[4]

The problems experienced in absorbing the new immigrants into the IDF, especially those from the Mideastern communities, particularly worried Ben-Gurion. He was driven by a desire to see commanders emerge from the Oriental population. He believed that this would ensure their integration into the Army and Israeli society at large. At Ben-Gurion's instigation, the IDF attempted an ultimately disappointing social experiment. Makleff describes the program:

We decided to try to prove that it was possible to produce good commanders from among new Oriental immigrants with the help of a speeded up process. We selected 150 can-

didates from different countries and we tried to indoctrinate them with the help of the best teachers and officers and the assistance of sociologists and psychologists. The course lasted for ten months and it was the first and last course of its kind. We achieved nothing. Altogether we succeeded in producing fifteen sergeants but not one officer. The disappointment was terrible but we learned that it was impossible to take shortcuts and that progress would have to be slow, over many years.[5]

The decline in level of the IDF was most evident in the small-scale retaliatory actions against fedayeen terrorists that the IDF staged from time to time. Many missions failed because of the low operational abilities of the Israeli soldiers. The IDF was finally shocked out of its lethargy by a disgraceful performance in battle against the Syrians.

In May 1951, Syrian regular and irregular forces crossed the Jordan River where it meets the Sea of Galilee and occupied a hill in Israeli territory. A small IDF force summoned to that point was quickly turned back. A larger force followed. But it was a hot Saturday and difficult to stage an assault at the rocky area of battle. The IDF custom at the time was to feed soldiers on Saturday with a heavy Jewish Sabbath pudding—*cholent*—cooked the preceding day because of the prohibition against cooking on the Sabbath. That day the cholent was bad and many of the soldiers went into battle with upset stomachs and diarrhea. During the assault the soldiers held back in fear of Syrian fire. The assault was pushed back and twenty-seven Israeli soldiers were killed. The Syrians were finally uprooted when additional forces were brought up with the support of heavy artillery.

The IDF viewed the battle as a disaster, a sign that combat units loaded down with new immigrants were not ready for battle. The General Staff convened for a post mortem.

Yigal Yadin, Chief of Staff at the time, later explained the reasons for failure: "In accordance with government directives, the IDF was not then oriented to immediate war. An army that has no combat challenge, that marks time, is faulty. This did not derive from lack of combat willingness in the General Staff or the senior echelons."[6]

One of the reforms effected after the meeting was an immediate move to send *sabras* into combat units. A special effort was made to enhance the quality of junior officers in combat units and a combat school was set up to train junior commanders under battle conditions.

The IDF realized that a broader program was required to improve the standards of its soldiers. Training in combat was not enough. Morale, literacy and a sense of mission had to be part of the approach. Women were assigned to serve as teachers to eliminate illiteracy in immigrant settlements and to assist in the assimilation of the immigrants. The Army began to grow potatoes and tomatoes on its farms to ease the shortage of food.

Yigal Yadin recalls:

New immigrant soldiers would visit their parents in transit camps and find them in leaking tents and degrading deprivation. I saw in this an extreme danger from the viewpoint of national security. I suggested to Ben-Gurion that the IDF adopt the transit camps. We took care of educational, housing and food supply problems. This may possibly have hampered the effort to build the Army and its fighting spirit, but these activities assisted the State of Israel no less than combat actions.[7]

Cutting Back the Peace-Time Defense Budget

The conflict over priorities between IDF tasks on the one hand and Israel's enfeebled economy on the other finally resulted in a bitter dispute between Ben-Gurion, who was both

Israeli paratroops in training, 1950s. [Israeli Army]

New immigrant recruits in the IDF, 1952. [Israeli Army]

Bottom: Israeli soldiers during bivouac at Masada, 1953. [Israeli Army]

Prime Minister and Minister of Defense, and his Chief of Staff. The immediate outcome was the resignation of Yadin, but ultimately a streamlining of the IDF resulted. In the early 1950s, before Egypt began to send fedayeen against Israel, Ben-Gurion estimated that the country would be safe from war for the coming five or six years. He accordingly decided that defense should not be considered Israel's primary task but that the emphasis should be shifted to social and economic development. He ordered a drastic cut in the defense budget and proposed that the IDF withdraw from functions not directly connected with fighting.

Chief of Staff Yadin was unhappy about the plan to reduce the defense budget but was prepared to comply if the government insisted. The pivotal point of conflict was determining by whose authority the cuts would be made. Yadin contended that, as Chief of Staff, it was up to him to decide exactly where cuts would be made; Ben-Gurion, for his part, ordered the arbitrary dismissal of 8,000 regular army men and another 10,000 civilians employed by the IDF. Yadin refused to authorize the dismissals and submitted his resignation.

At the time of Yadin's resignation, the Deputy Chief of Staff, Mordechai Makleff, was in London studying economics in preparation for his demobilization from the Army. He was called home to replace Yadin. Makleff supported Ben-Gurion's position in the dispute. "I realized that if we were released from maintaining military hospitals, laundries, etc., we'd have more funds for purely combat missions."[8]

Makleff reduced the IDF budget by a sixth and dismissed thousands of regular army men and civilian workers. He recalls:

My plan was to trim the administrative fat without harming the fighting force. I rejected a proposal to thin down units and instead we eliminated commands and units that weren't essential. We examined the file of every officer and decided on dismissals. I knew that in the heat generated by our drive to quickly establish a regular army, we had absorbed a high proportion of incompetents. I knew that the money we would save would be directed to important social objectives. Ben-Gurion thought that a weak civilian population would in turn cause the army to be weak and I agreed with him.[9]

Makleff, who was appointed IDF Chief of Staff at age thirty-three, continued the youthful tradition begun by Yadin. Ben-Gurion welcomed Makleff to his new position with these words: "Your life is a tragic model for the young generation . . ."[10]

At the age of nine, Mordechai Makleff had been thrust into the conflict that engulfed Palestine. He lived with his parents and three brothers and sisters in the small *moshava* of Motza near Jerusalem. In the 1929 riots, Arabs from neighboring villages attacked his settlement. Makleff escaped through a window and hid in the branches of a tree. From there he heard the screams of his family. When the attack ended, he found them dead. He was adopted by relatives and at an early age joined Orde Wingate's Night Squads. During World War II, he served in the British Army, where he rose to the rank of major.

There was a tradition of tragedy among the early Chiefs of Staff: Yadin and Moshe Dayan lost brothers in the War of Independence and Haim Laskov's father had been murdered by Arabs in the 1930s.

Having won the budget dispute and secure in the knowledge that the IDF Chief of Staff held views consistent with his own, Ben-Gurion began hinting to friends that he was considering retirement. He was no longer young, and from time to time was subject to depression. Often he spoke of death and the immortality of the soul. He believed that if he went to one of

Chief of Staff Moshe Dayan with Minister of Defense Pinhas Lavon, 1954. [Israeli Army]

Moshe Dayan, Chief of Staff of the IDF from 1953-58. [Israeli Army]

the desert kibbutzim, Israeli youth would follow his example. In 1953, Ben-Gurion did indeed resign as Prime Minister and Minister of Defense. He appointed Pinhas Lavon as Minister of Defense, a move he later regretted. Makleff had finished the year he had agreed to serve as Chief of Staff and, before departing for the Negev kibbutz of Sde Boker, Ben-Gurion appointed Moshe Dayan the fourth man to hold that position.

Reform and Restructure

Moshe Dayan played a highly significant role in the development of the IDF. Along with Ariel "Arik" Sharon, the new Chief of Staff took seriously the challenge facing Israel's Army—reform was essential if a dependable and effective fighting force was to be maintained.

Under Dayan, the IDF adopted a more aggressive stance. In this it is clear that Ben-Gurion and Dayan saw eye-to-eye and it was one of the reasons for Dayan's appointment. After Ben-Gurion's short retirement he was often influenced by Dayan's vigorous retaliatory approach. General E.L.M. Burns, head of the UN Truce Supervisory Team, wrote of the interaction between Ben-Gurion and Dayan in his book, *Between Arab and Israeli*: "One wondered whether in their private enclaves Dayan's aggressiveness may not have turned Ben-Gurion, who is not exactly a dove of peace himself, towards more violent and warlike solutions. At any rate, one can surmise that Dayan's influence with him, which was bound to be considerable, was usually exercised in the direction of solution by force."[11]

Dayan's influence on the IDF was to be felt for many years. Together with Sharon, he raised the Army to a new high combat level. They dragged the Army out of its stagnation by developing crack units. The impetus was pro-

vided by the need to answer the threat of fedayeen terror. Sharon was put in charge of the special commando Unit 101 and later the paratroops, which he developed into an impressive combat force. Dayan infused the whole of the IDF with enthusiasm for battle and victory.

Everybody willingly aspired to the standards set by Sharon and the paratroops he commanded. Sharon had a rule for his paratroops that there would be no return from an action if it had not been carried out. Dayan spoke in more brutal terms. "A commander who returns from an action without having carried it out, and whose men have sustained less than fifty percent losses, will be dismissed!"[12] The paratroop officers made "Follow me" their battle cry and the wounded were never left on the battlefield. This ethic spread through the whole of the IDF, but the paratroops were outstanding in their willingness to sacrifice more and more of their men in order to extract a wounded man from enemy territory. In one case, a soldier taken prisoner by the Jordanians was released only after the IDF carried out many actions in which numerous men were lost in order to seize Jordanian prisoners who could be exchanged for their comrade. General Burns cites the IDF's extreme sensitivity over prisoners. He writes that it is not unlikely that this "captivity complex" derives from the dread of Nazi concentration camps through which many Israelis had passed in World War II.[13]

The paratroops' battle tactic was assault at any price and in any situation. Sharon claimed that it was the only way to overcome the Arab fighter and eliminate his advantage in fire power. In retaliatory actions, fighters clashed face-to-face. To facilitate movement with a minimum of casualties, all operations were carried out under cover of darkness. Sharon's standing order was to withhold fire up to the moment before the assault. Fire was not to be answered even if a unit had been discovered in its approach and fired upon. Everything must be kept in reserve for the moment of attack. This was a combat tactic that overcame the Arabs but the paratroops paid for it with heavy losses. In September 1956, Dayan wrote in his diary: "I do not know whether there are any officers who have not been injured in one of the actions of the paratroops."[14]

Throughout the early fifties, under Dayan's guidance, the IDF developed its combat readiness, improved the quality of the average fighting man and raised the level of morale. The constant threat of Arab insurgency required continued vigilance. But the retaliatory missions of Sharon's paratroops did not succeed in bringing peace to Israel's borders. What had started as sporadic plunder and robbery by the Arabs soon turned into sabotage and murder, under the sponsorship of Cairo. In 1956, when France proposed that Israel take part in a joint action against Egypt, the government of Israel agreed that the time had come for a punitive action and the IDF, having emerged from the difficult first years, was ready to take on the challenge.

Footnotes

1   Previously unpublished interview with author, 1973.
2   Interview with author, originally published in *Davar Hashavva*, 17 March 1972.
3   Previously unpublished interview with author, 1973.
4   Previously unpublished interview with author, 1973.
5   Ibid.
6   Interview in *Davar Hashavva*, ibid.
7   *Ibid.*
8   Previously unpublished interview with author, 1973.
9   Ibid.
10 Letter from David Ben-Gurion to Mordechai Makleff, 1952.
11 E.L.M. Burns, *Between Arab and Israeli* (London: Harrap, 1962), p. 67.
12 Interview with paratroop commanders, 1954.
13 Burns, *op. cit.*, p. 36.
14 Moshe Dayan, *Yoman Maarchat Sinai* [Diary of the Sinai Campaign] (Tel Aviv: Am Hasefer, 1965), p. 29.

4. THE SINAI CAMPAIGN

Israel's second war, the Sinai Campaign, began on October 29, 1956. Known in Israel as Operation Kadesh, the Biblical name for the Sinai Peninsula, it lasted seven days and was waged on the Egyptian front only. Egypt was the target because of her sponsorship of increasingly frequent and effective fedayeen raids against Israel. She had further aggravated Israel by closing the Straits of Tiran in 1951, and Israel saw her chance to free the Gulf of Aqaba and reopen shipping to Eilat. Other Arab states bordering on Israel did not move their forces, despite their military treaties with Egypt.

The 1956 War cannot be understood without a review of the military relationships between Israel and France. Had it not been for these relationships, the war might not have begun when it did, and would certainly have been of a different nature. The IDF's Sinai Campaign was developed to parallel the unsuccessful French and British Suez operation against Nasser's Egypt. The French chapter is an important one in the history of Israel's military power. It began before the Sinai Campaign and continued until the eve of the Six-Day War, when President de Gaulle declared an arms embargo against Israel.

France and Israel Face a Common Enemy

The first military contacts with France were made through the Haganah, before Israel achieved statehood. With Haganah help, representatives of Free France erected a secret radio station in Palestine, without the knowledge of the British Mandatory Authority. During the conquest of Vichy-held Syria and Lebanon, Palmach scouts led the Allied armies. The connections between the Zionist Movement and the generation of the French Resistance were strengthened, and the French Gaullists, Socialists and Communists gave their full assistance to the Haganah and ETZEL during the struggle to establish the Jewish State. They helped the Jewish underground procure weapons and transfer Jewish refugees to Palestine.

French support of the struggle against the British stemmed in part from her bitterness over the British role in reducing French authority in the Mideast. One outcome of the treaties that ended the Second World War was the removal of the French protectorate in Syria and Lebanon.

After the end of the British mandate over Palestine, and upon establishment of the State of Israel, France wanted to play the Arab card but without discarding the Israeli hand. The Quai d'Orsay, the French Foreign Office, dictated the nature of relationships between France and Israel first by withholding recognition of Israel and later by placing restrictions on her policy toward the new State. *De jure* recognition was made as late as May 21, 1949, and after that France kept up perpetual pressures for the internationalization of Jerusalem.

The first signs of change in France's attitude accompanied the growing rift between France and the Arabs over control of the North Sahara countries: the states of Tunisia, Algeria and Morocco. At the end of the 1953, France promised to sell 155mm guns to Israel. This promise was not kept because of internal changes in the French government. A year later, the cabinet of Mendes France made a first gesture to the IDF when it invited Chief of Staff Moshe Dayan to France to receive the Legion d' Honneur for his activities on French behalf in Syria. The Algerian War of Liberation was raging and it was believed that France would rely on Israel in her struggle against the wave of pan-Arabism. Dayan sensed the way the wind was blowing and spoke to the French Chief of Staff. "We face a common enemy, the Arabs," said Dayan. "You are on the home front, while we are in firing lines. Don't you think that, when the front lines are burning, the arms should be transferred from the home front to the forward

Shimon Peres, Director General of the Ministry of Defense, 1958. [Wide World]

Far right: French Premier Pierre Mendes-France, 1954. [Wide World]

Below: Egyptian President Nasser.

positions?"[1]

The first arms transaction, a shipment of Ouragan jet aircraft, was made at the end of 1954. Israel was asked to guarantee that she would not strike at Syria and Lebanon, which France saw as being in her sphere of influence. The Quai d'Orsay was not in favor of the transaction for it still hoped for a thaw in relations with the Arabs. Members of the Foreign Office argued that the supply of weapons to Israel should be coordinated with Great Britain and the United States, but these countries were maintaining a selective embargo against Israel.

The IDF had been compelled to live from hand to mouth and to rely on the generosity of small countries. Israel often had to pay exorbitant prices to private arms dealers. For example, she paid $200,000 for obsolete Messerschmitt fighter planes, the real value of which was $40,000. When Israel realized that the French Foreign Office was hampering her efforts to find a way out of the maze of the embargo, she decided to bypass the Quai d'Orsay. The man in charge of this operation was Shimon Peres, the young and dynamic Director General of the Israeli Defense Ministry. Peres was the man who wove the first web of contacts between the Defense Ministry and the French Armed Forces Ministry, and between the two armies.

The Israeli emissaries found sympathetic ears in the Armed Forces Ministry, the French Army and the Ministry of the Interior. Events in Algeria had convinced the French that Israel and France had a common interest. "The tides of the Mediterranean lap the shores of France and Israel, and murky waters should not be allowed to burst their banks. The two sides can and must cooperate!"[2]

France was convinced that Egyptian President Nasser was the main supplier of arms to the Algerian Liberation Movement and Israel didn't contradict this belief. Whenever she

was in possession of information about Egyptian aid to the Algerian FLN, it was quickly transferred to Paris. Maj. Gen. Yehoshofat Harkabi, Head of Israeli Military Intelligence, became a regular visitor of the French Minister for Algerian Affairs and the director of French espionage services. In retrospect, it is clear that Nasser's share in the Algerian rebellion was exaggerated by Paris and Israel.

The contacts and connections between the defense ministries of the two countries developed in parallel with the worsening of the Algerian situation. In practice, these ministries maintained the foreign relations between the two countries. Although the foreign ministers

The Big Four, 1955. The contenders for a Mideast sphere of influence meet in Geneva: (from left to right) Soviet Premier Nikolai Bulganin, American President Dwight D. Eisenhower, French Premier Edgar Fauré and British Prime Minister Anthony Eden. [Authenticated News]

were in the picture, their ministries, for the most part, did not know most of the details. Neither foreign office willingly accepted the idea that generals and security officers were wearing diplomatic top hats. The French Foreign Office continued to believe that it could find a common language with Nasser. In April 1956 a last effort was made by France to convince Nasser to stop arms shipments to Algiers. The Egyptian ruler promised that he would transfer no more weapons, but a week later the French fleet stopped an Egyptian ship off Algerian shores and found it loaded with arms. This marked the end of French Foreign Office attempts to delay any rapprochement with Israel.

Soviet Arms Pour into the Mideast

Two important events forced the issue and eventually led to war in the Mideast. The decisive date for Israel was October 27, 1955,

when Nasser announced his first arms transaction with the Communist Bloc. For France the decisive date was July 27, 1956, when the Egyptian ruler announced the nationalization of the Suez Canal, in reaction to United States and European refusals to finance the Aswan Dam.

Egypt's first transaction with the Eastern Bloc was made, according to a Soviet decision, with Czechoslovakia. It was believed in Israel that Moscow was making its first tentative steps in what would be an extensive penetration program. Since Russia was then convinced that the Middle East is a Western sphere of influence, she decided that the first transaction with Arabs should not be made directly, but by way of the Czechs.

The weapons transaction caused heavy shock in Israel. It included 530 armored vehicles, of which 230 were tanks; 500 guns; 150 MIG-15 fighter planes; 50 Iluyshin-28 bombers; submarines and other naval craft; and many hun-

Israeli infantry in review, 1955.

dreds of transport vehicles. In one stroke the already shaky balance of power was upset. Until the Czech arms deal, Israel and Egypt had only 200 tanks each. The Egyptians had more than 80 jet aircraft, while Israel had about 50 jet planes.

Israel believed that the new Egyptian acquisition was a preparation for war and that it was only a question of time before Egypt opened an offensive. Israel was compelled to activate her war machine and talk of preemptive war increased.

A sharp debate began as to the date by which the Egyptian Army would have absorbed the masses of Russian equipment. Chief of Staff Moshe Dayan was convinced that the Egyptian Army would be prepared for war in 1956. Maj. Gen. Yehoshofat Harkabi's evaluation was that the Egyptians would not complete the absorption of such quantities of arms before 1957. The outcome of the war at the end of 1956 proved Harkabi correct. Considerable quantities of Russian equipment had not yet reached the various units and, in many cases, the new and modern equipment hampered the Egyptian soldiers.

This reality, which was revealed only after the war, revived the question of whether the

Egyptians had set themselves a date for an overall offensive against Israel. Major General Harkabi said of this, years later, "The Egyptians did not intend to attack us at the time!"[3] Major General Sharon, who commanded the paratroop brigade during the operation, was of the same opinion. "The Egyptians were not about to attack us. When we penetrated Sinai, we did not find an offensive disposition. This contention was only heard after the war, in order to justify the operation."[4] The Head of General Staff Operations Division, Maj. Gen. Meir Amit, said, "We knew of Egyptian planning and preparations and, had he the opportunity, Nasser would certainly have attacked us, but it would be exaggerated to contend that we knew Nasser was on the eve of a tangible operation against us."[5] Shimon Peres balances these opinions to some extent. "I am not convinced now, and I wasn't then, that Nasser had a final date for attack on Israel, but we did have a great deal of evidence, and general logic also indicated that he intended to strike out at us."[6]

France's willingness to supply Israel with considerable quantities of arms undoubtedly also derived from her desire to see Egypt defeated. The French spoke of this in no uncertain terms. French Defense Minister, General Koenig, said: "Israel must be given more arms, so that her excellent soldiers can make use of them."[7] After the nationalization of the Suez Canal by Nasser, the French specifically stated that they would like to see Israel act against Egypt with the help of French arms. At the end of July 1956, Bourgess Monorey, the new Defense Minister, asked Shimon Peres: "Aren't you thinking one day of acting on the southern borders? How long does your army need in order to cross Sinai and reach the Suez Canal?"[8] Shimon Peres understood from this question that the French Government was herself thinking about a military operation against Egypt. His answer was: "Our Suez is Eilat. We will never accept a blockade of the Straits against Israeli shipping."[9]

Operation Musketeer

In September 1956, important decisions were made that resulted in a military alliance between Israel and France and the first joint preparations for military action against Egypt. In July 1956, France had agreed to supply Israel with considerable quantities of weapons. France stopped reporting to the joint committee of the three Western powers and didn't ask its approval for the supply of arms to Israel. On July 7, Maj. Gen. Amit, Head of the General Staff Operations Division, visited Paris. It was known that France and Britain had begun planning a joint military operation, named Musketeer, designed to gain control over the Suez Canal. Amit was sounded out on the possibility of Israeli participation in Operation Musketeer. Amit contended that France and Britain exaggerated Egypt's power; that the IDF could easily overcome the Egyptian Army in Sinai. France was not prepared to make a commitment regarding the Israeli share in the operation, but did want to know whether Israel's airfields would be available to French planes.

As far as Israeli participation in the operation against Egypt was concerned, France was dependent on Great Britain. The difficult memories of the mandatory period and the War of Independence were not the only obstacles to understanding between England and Israel. Britain had mutual defense pacts with Jordan and with Egypt. Ben-Gurion saw this as a conflict of interests and feared that Britain was likely to betray Israel. Nor was London eager for open partnership with Israel, which might damage her status even in Arab countries opposing Nasser. France acted on two separate levels between these conflicting interests.

Dayan and Peres were convinced that Israel had ample and good opportunity for action against Egypt. Joint action with France and Britain, or coordination with them, would, in their evaluation, guarantee Israel against intervention by the Great Powers, and especially the Soviet Union. On the same day that Amit visited Paris, Dayan said in a General Staff session, that "Israel must not find herself in a position where she will be compelled to forego convenient diplomatic opportunities to strike at Egypt."[10] Three days later, Dayan ordered the General Staff to prepare operative plans for the conquest of Sinai, the Sharm-el-Sheikh Straits and the Gaza Strip. He emphasized that Israel was not a party to the dispute over the Suez Canal, but only with regard to Gaza and the Straits.

At the end of September, Ben-Gurion sent a ministerial-level delegation to Paris to coordinate joint military action with the French government. The delegation included Foreign Minister Golda Meir, Transport Minister Moshe Carmel, Chief of Staff Moshe Dayan and Shimon Peres. Mordechai Bar-On, the delegation secretary, wrote after the first day, "It became clear that France much preferred that Israel open an offensive in the Sinai Peninsula, alone and on her own initiative. Against this background, the French would be able to motivate the British into beginning their integrated operation. The IDF offensive is to be used as an excuse to cover military intervention in Egypt."[11] In the event that the Franco-English operation did not take place, France was prepared to guarantee massive military support to Israel. The French unofficially promised that in such an event Britain would not activate its defense pact with Egypt. At the same time, the French transmitted a British warning that, if Israel attacked Jordan, she would be opposed.

The Israeli delegation returned from Paris with mixed feelings. Britain's position aroused suspicions. Less than three weeks later, while Israel was carrying out a retaliation action against Jordan, these suspicions were strengthened. The British Chargé d'Affaires in Israel

Prime Minister David Ben-Gurion. [Authenticated News]

announced to Ben-Gurion that an Iraqi division was about to enter Jordan to defend that country against future IDF actions.

Military contacts with France, however, grew stronger. The two armies established a kind of joint General Staff in preparation for the operation. At the beginning of October, the Commander of the French Air Force arrived in Israel to survey the country's military needs. He was allowed to glance at the IDF operative plans and noted on his return to Paris the simplicity of them. His impression was that the French and English commanders attached greater significance to the Egyptian Army than did the Israelis.

On October 16, Ben-Gurion received an invitation to a secret meeting with representatives of the French and British governments. Ben-Gurion's hesitations about a joint excursion into war were increasing. He assumed that a day would come when Israel would have no alternative but to fight, but he did not want

An IDF command group, including Moshe Dayan (second from right), discusses maneuvers.

France and Britain to accord Israel the role of aggressor while they behaved as saviors of the region. Ben-Gurion worried about the morality of the three-way transaction and wanted a full and more open partnership. He was prepared to take great risks, but only if there were no other alternative; he was not certain that preventive war was the only choice. Dayan and Peres urged him to attend the meeting to seek answers to the two problems that bothered him most: aerial defense of Israel's civilian targets and a French promise that the English would not run out on them at the last minute.

The conference opened on October 22 in a small town near Paris. In that part of the meeting which was attended by the British, the atmosphere was heavy. Fearing betrayal, Ben-Gurion refused to present Israel's operational plan in the presence of the British. He rejected a proposal that Israel's role be solely that of providing an excuse for the French and the English to intervene in the war. The conference was on the verge of breaking up when Dayan made a proposal acceptable to Ben-Gurion as well as to the representatives of France and England. According to this proposal, Israel would not open overall and comprehensive war. The first move would be the dropping of a paratroop unit not far from the Canal zone. Israel would not follow with an aerial attack, nor a general assault along the length of the Egyptian border. Thus, it would appear to the Egyptians to be a large-scale retaliatory action. If the British and French kept their promise by going into action following this opening move, Israel would also continue her operation. If not, the paratroops would be ordered to withdraw.

Ben-Gurion imposed other conditions. He demanded that Israel's allies begin bombing Egyptian airfields no more than thirty-six hours after the beginning of the Israeli operation. He especially feared the bombers that Egypt had received from the Soviet Union. He also insisted that once control over Sinai had been achieved, Israel be permitted to maintain hold over the island of Tiran in the Straits of Tiran leading to the Gulf of Aqaba.

At the end of the conference, France agreed to dispatch sixty planes and pilots to defend Israel's settlements. They were to reach Israel a day before the beginning of the operation. France's agreement calmed Ben-Gurion, but in return, the IDF was asked to change its first operational order. Instead of limiting itself to the conquest of Northern Sinai, the Gaza Strip and the Straits, the IDF was directed, "... to create a threat on the Suez Canal, by the taking of objectives in close proximity."[12] By making this concession, Israel was forced to collude in the French and English conspiracy. It was now clear that the whole Israeli operation was dependent upon and connected with the tripartite action; it was no longer an operation that stood on its own merits.

In his diary, published in 1965, Moshe Dayan admits: "Had it not been for the Franco-British operation, it is doubtful whether Israel would have started the Sinai Campaign, and had she done so, the results would have been entirely different, both militarily and politically."[13] Dayan continued by asserting that Israel would not have taken up arms even if the Canal dispute between Egypt, England and France had become a military conflict had not the Egyptian ruler adopted a hostile policy against Israel. Dayan likened Israel to a bicycle rider who chances upon a car that is climbing the hill. The rider hangs onto the car, but lets go of it as the roads separate.

The Israeli government was not consulted on the decision to go to war. There were ministers like Golda Meir and Knesset member Moshe Carmel who set off for prior clarifications in France, but the full session of the Cabinet heard of the decision to go to war only when the machine was already in high gear. It was October 28, one day before the campaign was to begin, that Ben-Gurion brought the information and the proposal to the government. The commitments he made during the conference in France had already been signed and sealed. Not one member of the government appealed against this method of operation; the government of Israel approved the proposal to go to war.

Israeli Strategy Develops

The operation by Israel's two partners was a total failure because of political helplessness, military delay and command hesitation; the Israeli operation, on the other hand, succeeded. Inside of 100 hours, the IDF approached the Suez Canal and took control over Sinai. The Egyptian Army, which received retreat orders at the peak of the Israeli action, lost some 3,000 men and more than 5,000 Egyptians were taken prisoner. The IDF could have killed many more Egyptian soldiers, but was ordered to limit itself to upsetting the Egyptian Army dispositions.

The strategic plan for the Israeli operation

was brilliant. An indirect approach made what was in fact all-out war appear to be a mere retaliatory action. As a result, the Egyptians were bewildered and, for a full day, did not understand what was happening. The stress was laid not on frontal attacks, but on feints. The planners determined that there should be no assault at all on the Gaza Strip, which was closest to Israel, and that conquest of that area should only be attempted toward the end of the operation, when the Egyptian Army in Sinai would be crumbling.

Dayan depended on the fact that while the Egyptian Army acted schematically, with its command posts sitting to the rear, IDF units could work more flexibly and less routinely. He therefore ordered that every force going into action operate independently and seek to reach its final objective in its first thrust.

Israel prepared a very detailed deception that was successfully activated before the operation. The illusion was created that Israel intended to attack Jordan. In General Staff meetings, the number of people party to the secret was kept to a minimum until the last moment. Senior officers were asked to leave General Staff meetings when secret details were to be discussed. The Director General of the Prime Minister's office sensed suspicious activity and asked Ben-Gurion what it was all about. Ben-Gurion swore him to absolute secrecy and then told him that Israel planned a possible attack on Jordan. On the eve of the operation, while French vessels carrying huge quantities of arms for Israel were offshore near the Kishon Harbor, the ships' captains were asked to tell their crews that they were anchored off the Algerian coast.

The order to mobilize the reserve units was also given only at the last moment. The armored units completed mobilization three days before action, while other units were ready on the second day before the operation. When the scale of mobilization was revealed, many coun-

British Prime Minister Anthony Eden, 1956. [Wide World]

Below: An Israeli officer briefs his troops for action in the Sinai Peninsula, October 31, 1956. [Wide World]

tries were convinced that the objective was Jordan. The head of the UN observer team, General Burns, mentions in his memoirs that up until October 28, he sensed nothing extraordinary, and didn't receive any special reports from the American military attachés, who usually took care to keep him advised. Even when it appeared that Israel was mobilizing a considerable army, it did not occur to Burns that the IDF objective was Egypt.[14]

On October 25, a few days before the action, Egypt, Syria and Jordan announced that they had signed a tripartite military treaty and would establish a Joint Arab Command. Ben-Gurion was finally convinced that the operation was vital to Israel's safety.

On October 27, a planeload of Egyptian officers was lost over the Mediterranean on its return from Syria where the coordination talks had taken place. The Egyptians have always contended that Israel shot down the plane but Israel has never officially confirmed this. Nonetheless, the result was that on the eve of the war Egypt's command capabilities were severely diminished by the loss of these high-ranking military men.

Below: On October 31, 1956, Israeli troops advance into Sinai. [Wide World]

telephone lines in Sinai, thereby hampering Egyptian communications with their command posts.

Israel used nine brigades on the Egyptian front. The remaining IDF force was positioned along the borders with Syria and Jordan in the event that these countries joined the war. But despite the fresh military agreement, Arab solidarity was inoperative.

Of the nine brigades that operated on the Egyptian front, one was armored and two were mechanized. The remaining brigades were of infantry, and one of them was the paratroop brigade commanded by Arik Sharon. The Israeli force was faced by the Egyptian Third Division in northeastern Sinai. The Eighth Division and a few more brigades of Palestinians were in the Gaza Strip. More Egyptian units were stationed to the rear with an armored force in the Canal zone.

In conjunction with the paratroop drop, the IDF carried out two surface penetrations on the edges of the front. The rest of the paratroop force headed by Sharon penetrated Sinai. Their objective was to advance 125 miles and join up with the battalion dropped over the Mitla Pass, under the command of Raphael Eitan, a farmer from one of the Jezreel Valley settlements. Further south near Eilat, the Ninth Infantry Brigade, commanded by another farmer soldier, Abraham Yoffe, began its long march toward Sharm-el-Sheikh. This force was to cross a nearly impassable tract and to advance as quietly as possible till it reached the Straits where the Egyptians were blocking Israeli shipping. At first, it was thought that this march would last forty-eight hours, but the brigade reached its objective only after a week.

The confusion in the Egyptian High Command was great; they did not grasp the scope of the Israeli operation. They made do with activating their aircraft in the Sinai arena and dispatching reinforcements into the peninsula. Ben-Gurion, who was taken ill, rejected every

Israel Makes the First Move

On October 29, at 16:20 hours, Israel's second war with Egypt began. Sixteen Dakota transport planes, one of which was piloted by a woman, dropped a battalion of Israeli paratroops forty-five miles from the Suez Canal. The battalion, which numbered 395 men, grouped and took control of the entrance to the Mitla Pass. A short while earlier, two Mustang fighter planes completed another mission over Sinai. The propeller blades of these two-piston aircraft cut

Armored warfare in the Sinai Peninsula. [Israeli Army]

proposal to activate the Air Force against Egyptian airfields, even after the war began.

According to the plan, the Seventh Brigade, the main armored unit of the IDF, was to begin action on October 31 and to break through the central axis of Sinai towards Ismailia. Two hitches occurred on October 30. The Commander of the Southern Command, Asaf Sim-honi, disobeyed an order and decided to activate the Seventh Armored Brigade a day early. Military needs seemed to him more important, and he did not bother himself with the political background. The second hitch took place when it became clear that the French and English had decided to delay the beginning of their bombing of Egyptian airfields for one day. The

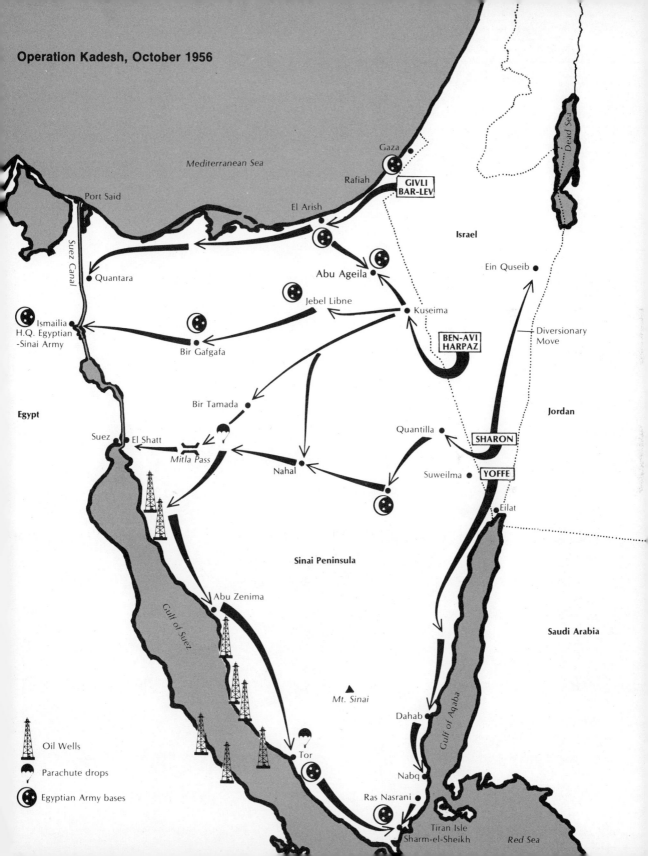

Operation Kadesh, October 1956

Following pages: 155mm artillery unit shelling enemy positions in Sinai.

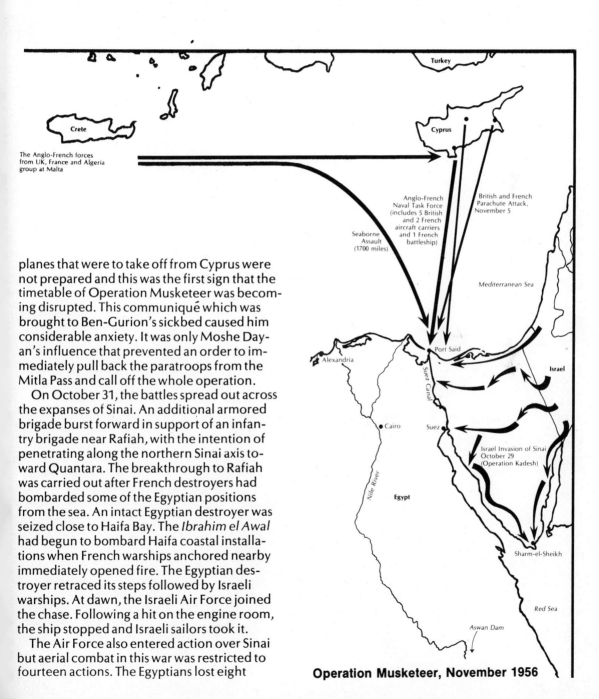

The Anglo-French forces from UK, France and Algeria group at Malta

Anglo-French Naval Task Force (includes 5 British and 2 French aircraft carriers and 1 French battleship)

British and French Parachute Attack, November 5

Seaborne Assault (1700 miles)

Mediterranean Sea

Crete

Turkey

Cyprus

Port Said

Alexandria

Israel

Suez Canal

Cairo

Suez

Israel Invasion of Sinai October 29 (Operation Kadesh)

Nile River

Egypt

Sharm-el-Sheikh

Red Sea

Aswan Dam

Operation Musketeer, November 1956

planes that were to take off from Cyprus were not prepared and this was the first sign that the timetable of Operation Musketeer was becoming disrupted. This communiqué which was brought to Ben-Gurion's sickbed caused him considerable anxiety. It was only Moshe Dayan's influence that prevented an order to immediately pull back the paratroops from the Mitla Pass and call off the whole operation.

On October 31, the battles spread out across the expanses of Sinai. An additional armored brigade burst forward in support of an infantry brigade near Rafiah, with the intention of penetrating along the northern Sinai axis toward Quantara. The breakthrough to Rafiah was carried out after French destroyers had bombarded some of the Egyptian positions from the sea. An intact Egyptian destroyer was seized close to Haifa Bay. The *Ibrahim el Awal* had begun to bombard Haifa coastal installations when French warships anchored nearby immediately opened fire. The Egyptian destroyer retraced its steps followed by Israeli warships. At dawn, the Israeli Air Force joined the chase. Following a hit on the engine room, the ship stopped and Israeli sailors took it.

The Air Force also entered action over Sinai but aerial combat in this war was restricted to fourteen actions. The Egyptians lost eight

Israeli soldiers display photo of Nasser confiscated when they overran an Egyptian position. [Israeli Army]

November 1956: Chief of Staff Moshe Dayan at Sharm-el-Sheikh with Gen. Avraham Yoffe (right), commander of the capturing forces, and Gen. Asaf Simhoni, who was killed two days later. [Israeli Army]

The Egyptian Army Retreats

On November 1, the action was more or less resolved. When it became clear to Nasser that he was also facing France and Britain, whose planes had begun to bomb Egyptian airfields, he ordered his forces in Sinai to withdraw. Within a few hours this withdrawal turned into panic-stricken flight. Air Force planes began to swoop down over Egyptian convoys in the desert. Many hundreds of Egyptian vehicles were hit, and many more abandoned. A train left El Arish carrying only Egyptian officers, while the soldiers retreated on foot toward the Canal.

In the land battles, one of the bloodiest actions took place when the paratroops penetrated into the Mitla Pass. It was Dayan's contention that Sharon disobeyed orders by entering the Pass without permission, while Sharon argued that a reconnaissance force had bogged down and extrication was essential. The Egyptians fought properly from their surrounded positions, and more than forty paratroops were killed in

planes, of which four were MIGs, and four British-made Vampires. Israel lost nine planes, eight of them to ground fire, and one reconnaissance plane which was hit by Egyptian aircraft.

British paratroops patroling streets of Port Said, November 1956. [Wide World]

Aerial view of Dakhaila Airfield near Alexandria, Egypt, after bombardment by British aircraft, November 1956. [Wide World]

taking the Pass.

On November 2, IDF vanguard units approached the Canal in the central and northern sectors. On the same day, one infantry and one armored brigade began an attack on the Gaza Strip. Three days later, Sharm-el-Sheikh was also taken by the Ninth Brigade. This

ended the military part of Operation Kadesh. Israel lost 177 men in battle. Two days after the end of battle, Asaf Simhoni was killed when his plane crashed into Jordanian territory.

International Pressure

Operation Musketeer ran aground from the very beginning. The ships with landing units set off late; too much time was given to preparations and each step was more complex than its predecessor. The hesitations of British Prime Minister Anthony Eden also caused delays in the timetable. French paratroops finally took position in the Canal zone, but the whole operation was doomed to failure. Meanwhile, the Israeli operation drew to a close and with it, to all intents and purposes, the excuse for Anglo-French intervention. Israel announced that she was prepared for a cease-fire and withdrawal from the Canal. The French were shocked by this announcement, and under pressure from them Israel announced that they would agree to a cease-fire only if the Egyptians would declare their willingness to abandon the state of war and enter into peace talks.

On November 5, the day on which Sharm-el-Sheikh was conquered, the campaign of Soviet threats and pressures began. In letters dispatched to the Prime Ministers of Britain and France, Moscow threatened to take steps if their forces would not retreat from Egypt. The Soviet Union was encouraged by the fact that Washington was diverted by her own presidential election campaign and was angry with her allies over the operation in Egypt.

A Russian letter sent to the Prime Minister of Israel threatened the existence of the State of Israel. The following day, France and England expressed their willingness for a cease-fire. That same day, Golda Meir and Shimon Peres left for Paris to check the French position in the event of Russian intervention against Israel. The French Foreign Minister promised that

American President Dwight D. Eisenhower.
[Frederic Lewis]

Below: In June 1957, Soviet destroyers steam
through the Suez Canal, the first Russian warships
to pass through the waterway since World War I.
[Wide World]

France would stand by Israel and would share
military resources with her, but there was no
ignoring the Soviet Union's numerical and military advantage.

Anxiety grew in Israel when reports were received of unidentified planes flying from the direction of Turkey to the Middle East. The
United States increased the panic by spreading
news, later proved incorrect, of Russian military concentrations in Syria. The Head of the
Central Intelligence Institution, Isser Harel,
recommended withdrawal. The United States
had by then opened a campaign of pressures on
Israel. Grants and the sales of food surpluses
were stopped, and negotiations for development loans were suspended. There were also
threats that contributions by American Jews
would be subject to tax payments.

On November 9, Ben-Gurion was compelled
to announce that Israel was ready to withdraw.
His attempt to maintain Israeli jurisdiction over
the Gaza Strip was in vain. On December 22,
the British and French evacuated the Canal
zone. The Israeli withdrawal was slower and
more gradual, as the retreating Israelis destroyed the Egyptian military network of roads
and airfields in Sinai.

In return for her withdrawal from Sinai, Israel was promised that the Gaza Strip would
remain demilitarized. This promise was not
kept for long, but when the Egyptian units returned to the Gaza Strip, Israel did not renew
the war. A UN emergency force was positioned
along the border on the Egyptian side. This
force carried out its function until the eve of
the Six-Day War, when it withdrew on Nasser's
orders.

American President Eisenhower promised
Israel free maritime traffic through the Straits
of Tiran. This promise was kept, but not for
many years. With the opening of the Straits,
Israel took a giant stride toward the African
continent. Her isolation was broken and she
found herself on the international map as

tankers laden with oil began to reach Eilat.
Freedom of navigation continued until 1967,
when Nasser again closed the Straits to Israeli
shipping. But Israel had by then learned her political lesson—guarantees and demilitarization
do not give real security.

The Postwar IDF

The only regrets after the war concerned the
conspiracy between Israel, France and Great
Britain. This conspiracy was uncovered many
months after the war and the feeling among
IDF commanders and the Israeli public was that
Israel should have gone to war alone. "This
partnership caused Israel considerable political
damage. We should have relied on our strength
alone, and we could have beaten the Egyptians
without political involvement with France
and England,"[15] Major General Sharon stated
years later.

From a military viewpoint, Operation Kadesh
brought about a revolution in the structure of
the IDF and gave foundation to new concepts of
combat. On the eve of war, there was a great
fear that the reserve army would not be able to
function on a sufficiently high level. The reserve units were based on a considerable proportion of new immigrants who had come to
Israel after Statehood and among them were

many from the backward Islamic countries. In the course of the war, however, it became clear that the reserve units did not fail, nor were they on a level much lower than that of the regular units.

The war did reveal many faults in the operation of the IDF. The logistics system proved weak, and only various improvisations prevented serious hitches. The artillery arm did not keep up with the rapid rate of advance. And what seemed far more severe, the IDF communications system did not operate properly. The Supreme Command of the IDF found it difficult to draw up a battle picture as it was taking place, and most of the details were in fact received from the Air Force. Chief of Staff Moshe Dayan, who joined the fighting units, vanished during three days and it had been impossible to contact him. But for early and successful planning, it is doubtful whether it would have been possible to change and determine detailed moves in the midst of battle with such a communications system.

After Operation Kadesh, it was decided to put greater energy into strengthening the Air Force, to ensure that in the future the IDF would not be compelled to rely on foreign air forces.

The armored echelons also found their place on the map after the 1956 war. Before the war the question had arisen whether the 250 tanks at the IDF's disposal should be concentrated in armored companies or should be divided into smaller support units within the infantry. The armored corps men, headed by Major Generals Laskov, Zorea and Benari, demanded the concentration of armor in large units. They felt it would strengthen the logistics system and widen communications networks. Moshe Dayan, who still saw the infantry as king of the battlefield, objected and demanded the dispersion of the armor as a support weapon for infantry. He believed that the level of maintenance was low. The debate took place in the presence of Ben-Gurion and the decision was

made in favor of Dayan's concept. He therefore ordered the infantry to break through first with half-tracks and other vehicles, and the tanks to follow behind on transporters. After the tanks carried out their allotted tasks, they were to make way again for transported infantry. In fact, the war was carried out in a different fashion. Haim Laskov and Uri Benari set the rate of advance with the help of the armor that they commanded.

After the war, Dayan admitted that the commanders of the armored corps had been right. The IDF began its transition into a mechanized and armored army. From this standpoint, the Sinai Campaign served as a kind of expensive exercise in preparation for the Six-Day War. Israel's victory in 1956 did not cloud the reformers' view. The Sinai Campaign gave Israel eight years of tranquility which she utilized to develop, refine and strengthen the IDF.

Footnotes

1 Michael Bar-Zohar, *Gesher al Hayam Hatichon* [Bridge over the Mediterranean] (Tel Aviv: Am Hasefer, 1964), p. 59.
2 Shimon Peres, *Kela David* [David's sling] (Tel Aviv: Am Hasefer, 1970), p. 31.
3 Previously unpublished interview with author, 1972.
4 Previously unpublished interview with author, 1972.
5 Interview with author, originally published in *Ha'aretz*, October 1966.
6 Interview with author, originally published in *Ha'aretz*, October 1966.
7 Yosef Evron, *Beyom Sagrir* [On a cold and rainy day] (Tel Aviv: Ot Paz, 1968), p. 18.
8 Peres, *op. cit.*, p. 49.
9 *Ibid.*
10 Dayan, *op. cit.*, p. 25.
11 Mordechai Bar-On in *Maariv*, 5 June 1973.
12 Dayan, *op. cit.*, pp. 180, 182.
13 *Ibid.*, p. 9.
14 Burns, *op. cit.*, p. 117.
15 Previously unpublished interview with author, 1972.

5. ARMY OF FARMERS

The dream that Jews would one day be farmers in the land of Israel was closely tied to the Jewish defense of Palestine. In pre-Statehood days, this was indeed a revolutionary notion since the Jewish people had for centuries possessed neither military capability nor a connection with their homeland. The creation of NAHAL, an acronym for *Noar Halutzi Lohem* —Pioneering, Farming Youth Corps—as an integral part of the IDF reflected this early visionary thinking. The importance of the warrior farmer to the future of Israel was aptly expressed by Yigal Allon, Commander of the Palmach and Deputy Premier in the Golda Meir government: "The true frontier of the State of Israel moves and forms according to the movement and location of Jewish workers of the earth. Without Jewish settlement, defense of the country isn't possible, even if we double the force of the Army."[1]

Ben-Gurion's Dream:
An Army of Farmers

The late David Ben-Gurion, founder of the Israel Defense Forces and Israel's first Defense Minister, dreamed of making the IDF a farmer's army. He saw the IDF as a working army which would combine superior combat ability with an agricultural education to form a brotherhood of pioneer/fighters. Emphasis was to be placed on settling and developing the resources of the Negev Desert, another of Ben-Gurion's cherished dreams. This vision of an army of farmers was influenced by earlier Zionist thinkers who stressed that the redemption of the Jews was to be found in labor for their historic homeland.

The original idea that each soldier devote a year of his military service to agriculture was eventually subsumed by the more urgent demand for specialization and technical training. But NAHAL remains, as a standing unit of the IDF, the embodiment of Ben-Gurion's dream.

Ben-Gurion's original plan was expressed in the Defense Service Act of Israel (1949) which specifically imposed the obligation of agricultural service on every recruit. This law is still on the books in Israel although it is no longer enforced. Theoretically, the IDF can send any recruit for a year of agricultural training. In Article F, the law states: "The first twelve months of regular service of a recruit will be primarily devoted, after preliminary military training, to agricultural preparation as shall be determined in the Regulations, except that for a recruit sent to serve in the Air Force or Navy."

As the great waves of immigration to Israel began after World War II, Ben-Gurion saw the number of new settlers exceed that of native Israelis and veteran settlers. Many came from the nations of Islam, from Yemen and North Africa, from stagnating ghettos and even from primitive cave dwellings. As the sons of the new immigrants entered the ranks of the IDF immediate problems arose. One of the commanders of the IDF at the time, Brig. Gen. Yitzhak Pundak, recalls: "There were boys who didn't know what shoes were. Others had never in their lives seen soap. The first thing we did was put them in a shower."[2]

Ben-Gurion hoped that the encounter between immigrant youth and *sabras* at IDF agricultural settlements would stimulate the process of immigrant absorption. In August 1948 Ben-Gurion submitted the Law for Defense Service to the Knesset saying:

There are fifty-five nations of origin represented in the Army and you have no concept of how great the distances are and how considerable the differences between these national groups. The great majority of our nation is not yet Jewish, but human dust, bereft of a single language, without tradition, with roots, without a bond to national life, with-

Shoulder badge of NAHAL.

out the customs of an independent society. We must mend the rents of the Diaspora and form a united nation. An efficient army will not arise in this country, which is a country of immigration, if the youth, and especially the immigrants, do not first accept the agricultural education which will give them roots in the life of the homeland, will accustom them to physical work, will give them a language, cultural habits and a routine of discipline before they enter the regular army. A year of agricultural preparation is intended in the first rank to build the nation, to crystallize this dust of man collected together from all ends of the earth into one national entity.

An even more immediate rationale for making the IDF an army of farmers could be found in the economic situation of Israel at the end of the 1940s and the beginning of the 1950s. Some three-quarters of Israel's area was wilderness. The agricultural population of the young State was only twelve percent of the nation's total. Israel urgently needed additional farmers to feed the growing population. A shortage of food in Israel during the years of austerity in the 1950s led the General Staff to order the Army to develop agricultural farms on which to grow potatoes for its own needs and that of the civilian public. Two such farms were founded and a company of soldiers was concentrated on each. These soldiers were to work the fields within a military regimen, but under the supervision of veteran farmers from kibbutzim. As the supply of food in Israel improved, the IDF's agricultural farms were disbanded.

1948: NAHAL Is Born

The idea of integrating military service and agricultural settlement appealed to high school students who belonged to youth movements and who worked as volunteers during vacations at kibbutzim to supplement Israel's

meager manpower. A delegation of youth movement leaders, encouraged by the kibbutzim, approached Ben-Gurion in 1948 with a request that rather than being separated and sent to various army units, they be inducted as whole units and assigned to agricultural settlements for the duration of their national service. Ben-Gurion liked the idea and ordered the General Staff to organize the fighting, pioneering youth. It was thus that NAHAL was born.

The first recruits came to the Army in seven homogeneous groups. Most came from the same schools and had spent a few years together in the youth movement. The recruits were accompanied by their youth movement instructors who shared the task of supervision with the regular IDF command. The NAHAL youths entered the Army with a common purpose: to go to an agricultural settlement and adapt to that way of life for at least a few years. This high motivation accounts for the fact that NAHAL members are for the most part superior soldiers with high morale.

NAHAL is, in many respects, the spiritual heir of the Palmach, a connection which was not without its negative aspects, both external and internal. The resemblance that NAHAL bore to the Palmach aroused the suspicions of Ben-Gurion's political opponents who were convinced that following the dissolution of the Palmach in November 1948, Ben-Gurion was merely attempting to mold a new Palmach which would remain loyal to him rather than to the political parties. These opponents misinterpreted Ben-Gurion's actions. His rationale for dissolving the Palmach was not, as they believed, that he was opposed to its aims, rather that he was opposed to the existence of separate armies within the State. He was all too aware of the tendency in Jewish society to splinter into factions over relatively unimportant issues and he knew that the young

"The true frontier of the State of Israel moves and forms according to the movement and location of Jewish workers of the earth. Without Jewish settlement, defense of the country isn't possible . . ."

Below: The two faces of NAHAL—the sword and the plough.

Opposite: A NAHAL settlement in the Negev Desert, 1952.

State's only chance to stand up against the Arabs lay in a unified and concentrated armed force. The Palmach spirit of pioneering and self-sacrifice, however, was worth preserving and Ben-Gurion sought to keep it alive in NAHAL.

There was also internal dissension over the formation of NAHAL. Many members who came from the leftwing youth movement resisted the new framework. They had aspired to an armed force like the Palmach and justified their resistance and resentment for NAHAL on ideological grounds. Desertion and breaches of discipline encouraged by the left-

wing Mapam party and its kibbutz movement plagued NAHAL in its early days.

The continuation of the tradition of the Palmach was further emphasized in the design of the badge for the new unit. The badge of the Palmach had pictured two ears of wheat with a sword lying diagonally across them. The badge of the NAHAL pictured a sword and sickle with a common handle overlaying two ears of wheat. This badge was the continuation of a tradition that had begun in the organization of Hashomer, the first Jewish military organization since the renewal of Jewish settlement in Palestine. The Hashomer badge

showed a plough and a rifle with the slogan: "The way of strength is labor!" The same motifs appeared in all three badges: the blending of arms with agricultural tools or ears of wheat to symbolize labor on the land. The implication is that the arms are intended to protect the achievements of building and labor.

The first NAHAL recruitment in 1948 was known as the "Children's Draft." The IDF was a poor army then living from hand to mouth and vital equipment was earmarked for fighting units. In their first military parade the new NAHAL soldiers looked bedraggled, wearing sandals and slippers and sporting many individual touches in their dress. At first the NAHAL units had to train with sticks instead of rifles.

Discipline and Independence

The feeling of many of its soldiers that NAHAL was the continuation of the Palmach tradition created specific disciplinary problems because they wanted to preserve the democratic feisty spirit of the Palmach commandos. There were those who objected to having to work outside the settlements in addition to military training. The desire to create a special life style of civilian-like camaraderie inside a military camp gave rise to internal conflicts. "We had to prove that we were an army and *not* partisans,"[3] Yitzhak Pundak, the Commander of NAHAL, recalled in a recent interview.

The Palmach had encouraged self-discipline and individualism rather than formal, imposed discipline. Members of NAHAL who wanted to preserve that tradition and attitude sparked a debate over the issue of saluting which arose when rank badges were first distributed to commanders. Despite the general desire to preserve a popular spirit in the IDF, there was no alternative to the use of rank badges as a means of identifying officers. Officers had at first worn red crosses on their shoulders; the permanent ranks were subsequently instituted. It was then that the question of saluting the commander arose. "Doesn't saluting harm the Israeli spirit?" many soldiers asked. Up to that time the custom had been to stand at attention in front of an officer. "What was wrong with standing at attention? Why do we have to imitate foreign armies? We show respect for officers without the external marks of it!" the opponents of saluting insisted. In NAHAL the controversy was even sharper. Soldiers cited the Palmach where officers were not saluted and, claiming NAHAL's spiritual legacy, insisted that the formality be rejected.

It was also widely believed that a NAHAL private should have the right to oppose an officer and to dispute orders given. The Hebrew expression *"Kol Mamzer Hamelech"* —"Every bastard a king"—illustrates the Jewish aversion to authoritarianism. This trait was reflected in other objections to disciplinary formalities raised by the soldiers of NAHAL. They insisted, for instance, that polishing boots should be left to the individual's discretion and not be subject to orders from the commander. Such matters, the NAHAL soldiers believed, had little to do with operational discipline. Similarly, in the matter of dress, the NAHAL members chose to wear their shirttails outside their pants, a gesture in imitation of a custom that began in Palmach. Because each NAHAL unit was jointly supervised by an IDF officer and the NAHAL settlement coordinator, the question arose over who had final authority on such matters as work arrangements, details of kibbutz living and the issuance of passes. The unit coordinator was chosen by the NAHAL unit itself and many felt that he should have precedence over the IDF officer in charge.

USSR Premier Joseph Stalin. [Sovfoto]

Below: Commando techniques are part of NAHAL training.

But NAHAL commanders stood their ground and protected their prerogatives. They did not want to forego such signs of discipline as saluting and a decent military appearance, but they were, on the other hand, prepared to grant many powers to the NAHAL members' own committee, including the power to recommend removal of a soldier from a unit if he should so desire.

An extensive propaganda campaign was not sufficient to enforce discipline. There was a frequent need for arrests and courts martial. One of the severest breaches of discipline in NAHAL was a case of political mutiny which took place in 1952.

IDF regulations forbade the display of photographs of political leaders and personalities in soldiers' rooms, other than pictures of the President of Israel, Prime Minister, Minister of Defense and the Chief of Staff. At the beginning of the 1950s, when the Soviet Union was holding Stalin's show trial against the

Jewish doctors, one of the pro-Russian left-wing parties in Israel was split over the issue of protesting the matter to the Soviet Union. One group separated itself from Mapam and united with the Israeli Communist Party which justified the doctors purge. At a NAHAL settlement comprised of Hashomer Hatzair (Mapam) members in Kibbutz Bet Alpha, pictures of Stalin were hung in a number of soldiers' rooms. When ordered to remove them, the soldiers refused.

The NAHAL commander, Col. Moshe Netzer, met to discuss the matter with members of the Bet Alpha NAHAL unit. The soldiers heatedly justified their refusal to remove Stalin's photos from their rooms in the name of freedom of expression. They insisted that, in a democratic army *and* an independent unit, a soldier should be permitted complete freedom of action and expression outside of training hours. Faith in Stalin and the Soviet Union did not, they contended, conflict with the spirit of the IDF. And again, reference was made to the spirit of Palmach as the past model of independence within the armed forces.

Nor was this an isolated incident. At that time the enormity of Stalinist atrocities and the extent of Soviet anti-semitism had not yet been revealed and Mapam was conducting an extensive pro-Soviet propaganda campaign which included sharp criticism of the Israeli government. Propaganda activity within the IDF was counter to orders of the high command and concern grew about the spread of such insubordination as had occurred at Bet Alpha. Therefore, to prevent the spread to other units of what the army considered mutiny, the NAHAL commanders and the General Staff decided to disband the Bet Alpha unit and reassign its members to other non-NAHAL units.

Those NAHALniks who joined up as members of youth movements were oriented to the

Like a circle of covered wagons, the NAHAL settlement is an important instrument of defense on Israel's vulnerable borders. [Frederic Lewis]

combination of agricultural work and military training, but those soldiers assigned to NAHAL from other units did not always welcome farming. There were those among the new immigrants who regarded physical labor as degrading and did not understand the necessity of farmwork during their military service. In certain cases there was no alternative but to court martial those who refused to go to work.

Organized resistance occurred in 1950 at Kibbutz Nir Am in the Negev when a platoon of soldiers refused to work in the kibbutz. NAHAL commanders sent to quell the mutiny

were told that the dissidents were not afraid of going to military prison. The affair ended when six of the ringleaders were sent to prison and the remainder ordered to return to work.

NAHAL in Transition

During the few years that the program of one-year agricultural training for all soldiers lasted it was NAHAL that organized the training. In November 1949, fifty camps were built in various kibbutzim, intended to absorb the first draft of agricultural soldiers. At the same time, hundreds of youngsters, sons of kibbut-

Agricultural training at a Negev settlement.
[Authenticated News]

zim and *moshavot* (semi-collective agricultural settlements), attended a course for squad commanders which would prepare them to serve as a non-commissioned cadre for the thousands of IDF agricultural workers who would come to the farms. The Defense Ministry prepared a special contract that the kibbutzim were asked to sign when they took in Army units for work. Under the contract's terms the kibbutz undertook to employ each unit for at least nine months with the stipulation that no more than twenty-five percent of each unit would be employed in the kitchen, laundry and other service work. The Army's

intention was that the soldiers not be required to perform menial labor, but would receive proper agricultural training. The kibbutzim agreed that the soldiers would receive military training for five days a month and study and lectures one day a month. The new immigrants among them were entitled to half a day a week to learn Hebrew.

The great dream of converting the IDF entirely into a working army, devoting half of its time to agricultural training, ran aground quickly. By 1950 it was clear that if Israel wanted a progressive army equipped with modern weapons, full-time professional train-

NAHALniks training in small arms.

Bottom: Golan, a NAHAL settlement in the Golan Heights. [Zeev Schiff]

ing for all branches was necessary. Army commanders put pressure on Ben-Gurion to revise the Defense Service Law. And, in 1950, the first amendment was introduced which freed soldiers needed for continued professional service from agricultural training. Soldiers who were recruited into the Army over the age of twenty were also to be exempt from work on the land. Later there were two additional amendments to the Law: At first, the Defense Minister was given permission to defer the period of service intended for agricultural training and devote it to ordinary military service; and finally, the program of universal agricultural training was shelved altogether.

This freeze came into force and remained in effect because Ben-Gurion's program for a large farmers' army could not withstand the pressures of a professional armed force. The great demand for soldiers who could perform tasks that required full-time training took precedence. The years of terrorist infiltration and the skirmishes along the borders were upon Israel. Larger numbers of youngsters were needed in well-trained combat units. After the 1956 Sinai War, the crop of youngsters eligible for call-up had decreased since the birth rate had declined in the difficult years at the beginning of the Second World War. During this time the Army had, of necessity, entered a period of greater specialization in weapons systems which demanded longer training periods. So the universal agricultural training scheme was doomed.

The Contribution of NAHAL

In addition to agricultural work, NAHAL from the outset undertook auxiliary duties. They serviced planes that were bombing Arab positions in the last battles of the War of Independence. In April 1949 all the members of NAHAL were sent to pave a road from Sodom on the banks of the Dead Sea to Ein Gedi,

which was the most distant point the Army had reached along the Dead Sea. Following this, NAHAL turned south to build fortifications around the first houses of Eilat, Israel's new Red Sea port and the southernmost settlement, on the edge of the Sinai Peninsula.

But by far NAHAL's greatest accomplishment was the establishment of a system of fortified settlements in strategic border areas. During the War of Independence, the High Command of the IDF was convinced that the best defense for the young State lay in the agricultural settlements. These settlements, especially the kibbutzim, formed obstacles for

Nahal Mitzpe Shalem in the Jordan Valley, overlooking the Dead Sea. [Zeev Schiff]

Nahal Gilgal, located on the site where Joshua settled after defeating the Canaanites at Jericho. [Zeev Schiff]

the invading armies. Whenever an Arab army ran up against agricultural settlements it had to fight harder and risk heavy losses. After the War of Independence, the IDF tried to continue filling in gaps on the borders with agricultural settlements. The problem was that there was not enough manpower for rapid construction of civilian settlements. It was therefore decided to put up settlements manned by soldiers.

The idea did not originate in Israel, but in imperial Rome. Roman legionnaires who had been released from combat service built settlements along the Empire's borders. Men of the

Palmach had also founded a number of such settlements before the establishment of the State, but the NAHAL was to give this operation an impetus that changed the map of Israel.

These camps are known in Hebrew as *heachzuyot*, "holding settlements," and they are maintained jointly by the Army and civil agencies of the government. The men engage in guard and patrol duty and in the time left over farm and carry on light industry. The women gravitate to the traditionally domestic chores—cooking and cleaning. Many holding settlements have in time become permanent

and self-sufficient civilian settlements. The NAHAL holding settlements played an important role in eliminating fedayeen terrorism in the territories captured in the Six-Day War.

NAHAL soldiers sent to holding settlements are required to remain there for at least a year and they enjoy all the privileges of regular soldiers — wages, leave, etc. At the end of the year they may remain in the holding settlement and if they choose to form a permanent agricultural settlement, all the livestock and equipment remains at their disposal.

On July 23, 1951, the first holding settlement was established facing the Gaza Strip,

which was bursting at the seams with Palestinian refugee camps and battalions of the Egyptian Army. A young commander named Danny Mat, assisted by junior commanders, sons of kibbutzim and *moshavot*, and a company of NAHAL soldiers climbed a small hill and named their settlement Nahal Oz. As darkness fell one of the soldiers read the founding declaration:

Today the twenty-first of the month of Tammuz, the fourth year of independence of Israel, we are planting the first stake in the construction of a soldiers' settlement on the

Top left: NAHAL training in high-speed operations.

Bottom left: Herding sheep at a settlement in the Golan Heights.

Top right: Preparing for patrol at Nahal Gilgal. [Zeev Schiff]

Bottom right: NAHALnik on guard at border settlement.

Moshe Dayan proposed that NAHAL members receive advanced military training at the expense of agricultural duties.

borders of our nation. We, new immigrants and native sons from every corner of our people's exile, have gathered here today and are taking upon ourselves the defense of this tract of land. The supreme, the primary and the most difficult in the tasks of the NAHAL, we set out to do this day: building a settlement of defenders and builders, guards and creators. This vision of the IDF is before our eyes, the vision of a working and fighting army. May the nations around us know that we shall protect this building against all comers and shall defend life at any cost.

A month later, Gonen, the second NAHAL holding settlement, was founded on the Syrian border. Like Nahal Oz, it was also to become a successful kibbutz in the ensuing years. In October 1951, NAHAL went south and founded Yotvata, the third holding settlement, in the Arava Rift Valley on the Jordan border. In the next two decades NAHAL founded or rehabilitated thirty agricultural settlements. By 1973, twenty-four of the holding settlements had become permanent kibbutzim. Fourteen others in various parts of the country and occupied territories were in the process of becoming permanent kibbutzim.

After the Six-Day War, holding settlements took on a clearly political character because they indicated the possibility that Israel would retain large portions of the territories captured from the Arab states. Holding settlements sprang up on the Golan Heights, a strategic point from which the Syrians had bombarded the Israeli settlements of the Hula Valley; a line of NAHAL holding settlements filled the Jordan Valley and others were built in Sinai and the Gaza Strip. Several of these have since become permanent settlements. However, the fact that the holding settlement is, in practice, an Army camp with an agricultural character gives the Army and the government the right to order its dissolution. After the Israeli conquest of the Sinai Peninsula during the 1956 war, Nahal Ophir was set up in Sharm-el-Sheikh. It was dismantled by order when it was decided under American pressure to retreat from Sinai.

Opposition to NAHAL within the IDF

Despite NAHAL's achievements, the opposition of many professional soldiers persisted. This opposition grew more severe as the IDF felt the manpower pinch in the early fifties. In the early days of the IDF, NAHAL was seen as a military bastard with no rightful claim to a portion of the strained defense budget. These officers felt *some* youth settlements should be maintained—but that was all. When Moshe Dayan became Chief of Staff of the IDF he expressed grave doubts about the wisdom of diverting considerable manpower to kibbutzim at a time when the Army needed superior warriors. Dayan proposed that NAHAL members receive advanced military training at the expense of their agricultural duties. He suggested that they be trained as paratroops and be included in a special battalion of the IDF airborne forces. The NAHAL paratroop battalion, who wear the

Both the gun and plough are set aside at Ramat Hagolan. [Zeev Schiff]

A sprinkler assembly plant at Nahal Gilgal. [Zeev Schiff]

NAHAL badge on their sleeves and the paratroops' red beret, took part in many military operations and compiled an exemplary record.

In May 1958, a few months after his release from the Army, Dayan sparked a controversy among kibbutzniks and NAHAL. In his first political appearance as a civilian he stated, "I don't believe in youth going to settlements for two years in NAHAL and from there to university." He continued, "It's a fiction because these youths only go to settlements in the knowledge that they won't stay there. A counterfeit slug in place of the coin of truth destroys and doesn't build."[4]

In the wake of a deluge of attacks, Dayan explained that he did not mean to denigrate NAHAL as a settlement tool, but was attacking those who go into NAHAL knowing they will not remain permanently at kibbutzim. Ten years later, as Minister of Defense, Dayan changed his opinion. At a convention of NAHAL graduates, Dayan praised NAHAL's success and vitality.

NAHAL Today

Dayan's change of mind regarding NAHAL has not yet done away with the opposition of

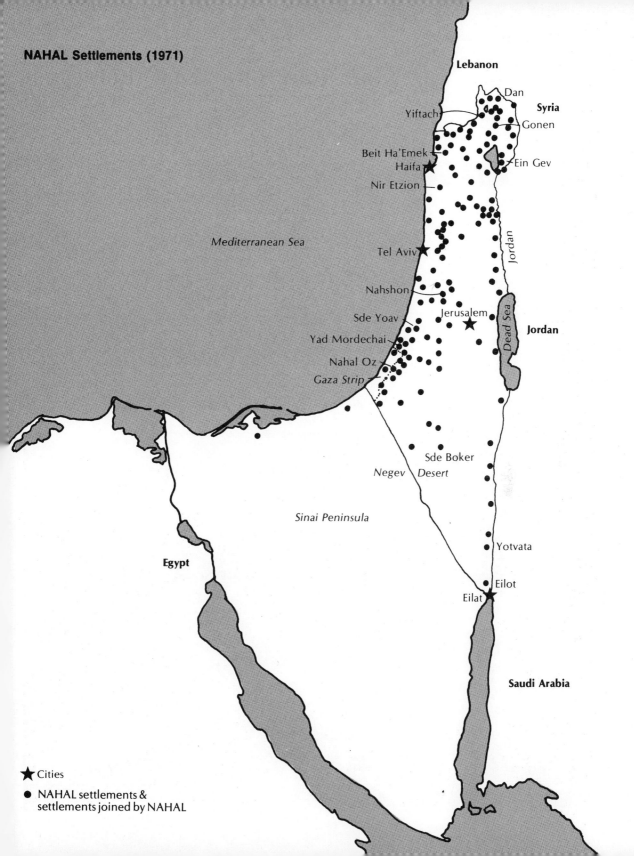

NAHAL Settlements (1971)

Lebanon

Dan

Yiftach

Syria

Gonen

Beit Ha'Emek

Ein Gev

Haifa

Nir Etzion

Mediterranean Sea

Tel Aviv

Nahshon

Sde Yoav

Jerusalem

Yad Mordechai

Jordan

Dead Sea

Jordan

Nahal Oz

Gaza Strip

Sde Boker

Negev Desert

Sinai Peninsula

Yotvata

Egypt

Eilot

Eilat

Saudi Arabia

★ Cities

● NAHAL settlements &
settlements joined by NAHAL

"We must mend the rents of the Diaspora and form
a united nation"—David Ben-Gurion. [Nancy Reese]

Living quarters at Nahal Sinai. [Paul Hosefros]

military men who feel that in periods when the IDF is starved for superior manpower the cream of the recruits is often directed to NAHAL. And it is true that many of the privates in NAHAL could have become fine officers had they gone to other units in the Army. The IDF thereby loses many officers, not only during the period of compulsory service, but also during the years they would serve in the active reserve.

NAHAL fights for its continued existence, but also adapts itself to reality and to pressures from within the Army. After the Six-Day War, when the IDF needed additional tank

crews to man the greatly increased number of armored units, NAHAL agreed to divert some of its men to armored training.

The routine of service in NAHAL has been changed considerably. Of the thirty-six months of compulsory service, only sixteen are now devoted to agricultural preparation and settlement in a kibbutz. The remaining time is given to regular military training and operational employment. Those who are not in perfect health volunteer for combat units on the second line as, for example, long-range gunners and combat engineers. NAHAL women volunteer to serve two years instead

of the twenty months required of other IDF women.

NAHAL has made a name for itself abroad. Many developing countries have taken the NAHAL as a model and created similar units to train and develop their youth. Many Asian, African and South American countries send students to Israel to attend NAHAL-organized courses for instructors. NAHAL emissaries have been welcomed in such places as Ghana, Tanzania, Ecuador, Bolivia, Thailand and the Philippines.

The existence of NAHAL is a source of pride for Israelis and Jews who still cherish the return to the land as an essential element of Zionism. NAHAL has cemented the bond between agriculture and the obligation of Jewish defense. Although its inspiration was the Palmach, NAHAL's roots go back to the earliest days of the Zionist enterprise and contribute a sense of continuity and idealistic commitment to the modern IDF.

Footnotes

1   Yigal Allon, *Masach shel Hol* [Sand screen] (Tel Aviv: Hotzaat Hakibbutz Hameuchad, 1959), p. 233.
2   Previously unpublished interview with author, 1973.
3   Ibid.
4   Speech at Haifa Technion, 1958.

6. THE MAKING OF THE ISRAELI SOLDIER

Opposite: [Israeli Army]
Right: Shoulder badge of GADNA.
Below: GADNA youth are trained to use machines of peace and war.

Although the Israel Defense Forces is by necessity similar to other armies in recruitment, training and operations structures, it differs markedly from most other fighting forces in its attitude toward discipline and its high sense of purpose and camaraderie. The Army holds a uniquely central position in Israeli society and as such is the repository of the nation's hopes as well as fears, its commonality and its differences, its past and its future.

"IDF Commanders have to deal with Jews," an IDF Education officer, Colonel Yeshayahu Tadmor, once wrote. "We have considerable awareness of events, a tendency toward skepticism and criticism. We are given to debate and dissertation. Our leadership is given no latitude unless it proves its capability. It can only succeed by constant persuasion, encouragement of thought and criticism and by safeguarding the soldier's dignity."[1]

Brigadier General Yitzhak Arad, former Chief Education Officer of the IDF, writes "We are an army that asks many questions. We encourage the soldiers to ask questions too. In the weekly unit discussions it is clear that IDF soldiers think. They ask about the government's diplomatic positions, the chances of peace or war in the future, in short, our daily reality."[2]

Israeli society is fundamentally a small, intimate society. Everybody seems to know each other. This familiarity makes it difficult for the officers to create what would be an artificial distance between themselves and subordinates. The familial feeling is good for morale but it makes the imposition of discipline and command somewhat difficult. The IDF officer must win his men's esteem; he cannot achieve it by title alone. Officers are selected from the ranks of enlisted men and their comrades participate in the selection process—they are asked by questionnaire to name those in their unit who they believe are best suited to be officers.

An Israeli grows up in a society closely identified with the Army. Military news is of foremost importance. In contrast to traditional European Jewish societies which revered intellectual achievement, Israel awards high social status to the man who rises in the ranks of the IDF. The Israeli's inclination to handle weapons and to excel in military tactics and actual combat are not only responses to the reality of his nation's precarious circumstance. These tendencies also represent a reaction to the image of the Jew in previous generations—the eternal student, the merchant, the money lender and the cosmopolitan intellectual to whom fighting was anathema. For modern Israel, the historical example of the Diaspora Jew, afraid or unwilling to fight for his life, is a baffling and shameful one.

In her wars with the Arabs, Israel has fash-

Again, after millennia, a Jewish fighter of superior quality . . .

Bottom: GADNA educational hike near the border with Jordan. [Israeli Army]

ioned a fighting Jew of superior quality who is at once a source of pride and an example to Jews throughout the world, notably those in the Soviet Union. In Israel the Jew became a fighter when he finally accepted that existence is as important as faith, that risking one's life in battle to preserve the Jewish state is equal to honoring the religious tradition of prayer, observance and study.

The pioneers who immigrated to Israel at the end of the last century came from generations of small businessmen and rabbis, as well as some scientists, writers and musicians. These early settlers proved they could return to the land and succeed as farmers. Their sons and grandsons became the fighters. The continuing condition of Arab hostility necessitates that the current and future generations of young Israelis also learn the skills of war.

GADNA: The Youth Battalions

Most Israeli boys and girls are required, at the age of fourteen, to join a paramilitary organization called GADNA (Hebrew acronym for Youth Battalions). GADNA youngsters engage in military drills, are given rudimentary instruction in arms and map-reading, and tour Israel on frequent camping excursions.

GADNA members at a training camp.

In some instances GADNA units undertake projects at Arab villages such as constructing recreation centers. When they meet after school and on weekends GADNA members wear khaki uniforms but do not have ranks. The movement does, however, have an emblem — a bow and arrow.

Organizing the younger generation into special youth battalions is not unique to Israel, but it seems that no Western society has organized its youth in such a fundamental and all-encompassing manner. GADNA is not simply an Israeli version of the Boy Scouts. For a large segment of Israeli youth, GADNA membership is considered a normal obligation, much like the study of mathematics, literature, the Bible, etc.

Some social critics wonder if the existence of GADNA and the introduction of a military stimulus during adolescence is not a sign of militarism. The Israeli experience suggests that rather than militarism it reflects a predilection of the nation to direct the younger generation toward the military organization that has safeguarded the country's existence. GADNA commanders indicate that in recent years the emphasis has passed from the use of weapons to sports and physical training. Israeli educators often worry that GADNA imposes the harsh reality of Israel's military situation at too early an age when, after all, there will be no escape from this reality at a later age. IDF and civilian educators often ponder if in GADNA there is not a blurring of the independent identity of Israeli youngsters.

Colonel Baruch Levy, a former Commanding Officer of GADNA, was asked these questions in an extensive interview. He posed yet another question:

What will be the face of the coming generation? A generation that will breathe the air of war, defense procedures, gun powder, casualties and tragedies of war? After considering this problem I think we can help adjust our youth to these unpleasant realities if we try to make life as normal as possible in other ways.

This means that the activities of GADNA should not only include training directly connected with military needs, but should emphasize social activity on marches and walks as well as cultural activities while strengthening the bond with the land of Israel and the nation's heritage. [3]

GADNA officers and many of the older generation of youth specialists and parents are convinced that recruitment of young Israelis into GADNA eases the eventual entry into the full-time military framework. Before he is called up for national service, the young Israeli has already spent time in an army camp, has met officers and sergeants and has taken orders from them. He has slept in a scout tent away from home and gone on daily hikes for distances of twenty miles. The boys and girls know what it is to be away from home and have even learned to use a carbine.

Nevertheless, preparation of Israeli youth for army life is not the primary purpose of

Five stages of NAHAL instruction and training.
[Two left photos: Israeli Army]

Basic military
training

Agricultural
training

History and natural
history courses

Advanced military
training

Operational tasks

36 months

GADNA. It provides nationalistic inspiration
and indoctrination into Israel's special security situation. GADNA members hear lectures
designed to strengthen their security consciousness. The younger generation is found
to be inquisitive and argumentative, but generally does not tend to formulate a dissident
or opposition sentiment to Israel's security
policies. It has been found that the GADNA
experience confirms a sense of responsibility
toward Israel's plight and stimulates the
youngsters to serve willingly and courageously.

GADNA was founded in 1940 as a part of
the Haganah. The sixteen year olds who were
inducted into the Haganah youth branch took
an oath of loyalty with a Bible and a revolver
as was customary in the Jewish underground.
The members were employed to clandestinely
distribute propaganda posters and gather in-

formation on British activities and movements. By 1948, when the War of Independence began, GADNA numbered thousands
of youth and some of its units took part in the
battles for Jerusalem and Haifa. When the IDF
was formed, GADNA became part of the military establishment. In 1954, it was structured
as a nationwide command with six special
training camps for members. The Ministry of
Education is responsible for the GADNA units
in the schools and the IDF officers serve as
advisers to the Ministry. GADNA instructors
are paid by the Ministry and there is an overall supervisor for GADNA programs.

GADNA instruction accounts for about eight
to ten percent of the curriculum in the first
three years of secondary school. The GADNA
school programs also embrace Arab high
school pupils and members of Israel's other
ethnic minority communities such as the

Fitness training at a GADNA camp. [Frederic Lewis]

Druze and the Circassians. Training in arms begins in the last year of high school when GADNA members are sent to army training camps for extended periods of time. The Arab boys and girls are not included in this later stage of GADNA training. However, the Druze youth, who are eligible for military service, join their Jewish friends at army training camp.

About 75,000 secondary school boys and girls are included in the GADNA program and an additional 30,000 youth are drawn for recruitment at institutions for delinquent youth, wayward girls and disadvantaged children. GADNA works with young delinquents serving sentences in reform schools in response to a basic complaint of young offenders that without military service they could not find employment. The IDF has altered its policy of excluding youths with police records and has entrusted GADNA with early rehabilitation

counseling and military training prior to call-up for national service. GADNA commanders feel that by giving delinquents an opportunity to serve in the Army they are, in effect, restoring them to society. In some cases a number of young inmates, already beyond the call-up age of eighteen, have been released from prison to enlist in an Army GADNA program.

The IDF has achieved a high degree of success with integrating one-time misfits into regular service. It has broadened their training to include vocational instruction so they can leave active duty with a trade.

The contribution of tens of thousands of GADNA youth to the security network is considerable. An emergency plan calls for the integration of GADNA into the mobilized manpower system. During the Six-Day and Yom Kippur Wars, GADNA members served as orderlies in hospitals, replaced postal workers called up to service and helped out in essential civilian industries.

National Service Is a Passport to Society

After completion of secondary school, Israeli youths are eligible for national service in the IDF, an indispensable credential. The young man who lacks discharge papers is treated with suspicion by prospective employers; these papers are a kind of certificate of honesty and morality. The number of those who try to evade military service is small because of the social stigma attached to those who do not fulfill this prime obligation. In fact, youngsters excused from military service for medical reasons often try to bring pressure upon authorities to permit them to serve and are willing to personally assume responsibility for any health risks.

Compulsory service for men is three years, for women twenty months. There are some exceptions to this rule. A man over twenty-three

The IDF Training Command insignia.

who is married and the father of at least two children need serve only six months. Men over twenty-six serve three months of active duty and are then transferred to the reserves. The compulsory service law does not apply to those over twenty-nine. If he desires, an older man can train for six weeks and then serve in the reserve force.

The willingness to serve in the IDF is great; few ask for and fewer are granted exemptions. The conscientious objector is not generally recognized in the IDF. The number fluctuates around ten a year. They are not excused from service but each case is handled separately and if their reasons are found to be sincere, an effort is made to assign these soldiers to hospitals or border settlements where they can serve in noncombat roles.

Release for reasons of conscience is permitted for women only. Requests for exemption usually indicate religious conviction, very rarely pacifist beliefs. The request for exemption for women is submitted to a public committee and must contain a sworn declaration and the signature of two guarantors—not close relations—who testify that the girl has a deep religious conviction. Approximately forty percent of women reporting to recruiting offices receive exemption from military service for various reasons.

There is also a special arrangement for *yeshiva* students, based on agreements between the labor and religious parties. A *yeshiva* student who can prove that all his time is devoted to religious learning can be temporarily excused from service. He must be enrolled in a recognized *yeshiva*, and upon completion of his studies must report for military service as the law requires.

Malingerers, or "artistes" as they are called in Israel, are not a problem in the Israeli Army. In many foreign armies they constitute a difficult problem for military doctors who strive to

unmask them. A former Chief Medical Officer of the IDF, Brigadier Dr. Reuven Eldar, says: "Contrary to other armies the number of malingerers in the Israeli Army is very small. They use such amateurish methods that it is easy to spot them. On the other hand, those who suffer from defects and do not declare them at the time of recruitment in order to join volunteer units are a problem."[4]

Classification

The restricted manpower resources of Israel as compared with the unlimited quantities of manpower in the Arab countries makes the classification and preparation of the Israeli soldier all the more crucial. The aim is to achieve maximal utilization of this manpower. Of those eligible for service, a mere 3.5 percent are turned away by recruiting centers as unsuited to serve. But recruiting a vast proportion of the population is only half the battle; the next aim is to properly allocate each soldier to an active role which takes best advantage of his individual talents and qualities. Like other progressive armies, the IDF conducts numerous tests to aid classification. Unlike other armies, the results of psychological tests are the most influential in the actual assignment decision.

The first task of the classification system is to determine which recruits are suited to command positions and which are likely to cause problems. The process extends over the recruits' first year in the Army and includes intensive personal interviews. Army psychologists believe that their work is easier than that of their colleagues in other armies since, on the whole, the Israeli youth is extremely frank about his personal ambitions and problems. The examiner seeks to determine motivation, devotion, independence and the degree of sociability of the candidate.

The thrust of the selection process is directed

IDF recruiting posters: (left) "The best ones fly";
(middle) "Learn a trade in the Air Force"; and (right)
"Your place is with us"—the submarine service.
[Israeli Government Printing Office]

toward placing superior manpower in field and
combat units, an almost holy principle in the
IDF. When Moshe Dayan was appointed Army
Chief of Staff in 1953, the classification system
was changed. Previously, more educated
youngsters found their way to staff offices
while the others went to field units where service was tougher. At present, it is the fighting
units that receive the cream of the manpower.
A youngster with a superior medical profile has
every chance of being sent to a fighting unit.

these may reach noncommissioned rank. The
other gradings are destined for lower enlisted
ranks. Quality ranking in the IDF is determined
on the basis of a number of facts: the results of
the intake interview; IQ; education; knowledge
of the Hebrew language and health status.
Upon completion of the primary classification
stages, candidates are dispatched to volunteer
units. Pilots and aircrew receive first preference in the division of the manpower cake,
followed by submariners and frogmen, para-

There are few exceptions to this rule. Only sons
are not posted to fighting units unless they volunteer and receive the approval of both parents. The parents' signatures must be notarized
by an attorney to prevent forgery. Youngsters
from families that have lost one of their sons
in war require parental agreement and approval by the military authorities.
    Soldiers are divided into fourteen classifica-
tions. Only those included in one of the six
high-quality groups can reach commissioned
rank. Soldiers from the four groups beneath

troops and volunteers to special reconnaissance units.
    Each volunteer unit maintains its own tests
for candidates. Some of the methods in these
tests, particularly in the Air Force, are secret.
It is known that candidates for service in the
Navy Commandos are taken on a ninety-five-
mile march along the length of the coast. An
Army psychologist is attached to this hard route
march to examine candidates' reactions. Not
all who show a good physical tolerance and
reach the final line are necessarily accepted

into the Navy Commandos and not all who fall by the wayside are necessarily disqualified. The true test is not endurance but the reactions of men to different situations. For example, eight food rations might be prepared for a group of ten men, and the reactions of the men to this circumstance observed and analyzed. These tests, and others, assist in spotting those who are not prepared to cooperate with their fellow soldiers and assist them in time of need.

Heavy reliance is placed on such psychological evaluations. Teams of field psychologists are stationed in each unit. With their help IDF commanders can achieve maximum efficiency in organizing combat groups and teams. For example, a psychologist might suggest which individuals are most suited to serve as tank gunners and which as tank drivers. In infantry units, the psychologists might indicate who is likely to be a good mortarman or machine gunner. Special emphasis is placed on the composition of tank, submarine or mobile artillery teams. This system has also influenced the composition of teams in platoons of infantry. It is based on a survey of professions carried out by the IDF to determine what personality characteristics are suitable for the operation of specific weapons.

Education

Israel's disadvantaged Oriental Jewish population is a problem for both society at large and for the IDF. Social pressure has been brought upon the Army to absorb the poor, uneducated youngsters and to teach them a profession. The hardcore poor in Israel remain so largely because of educational deficiencies. The system of education in Israel has undergone reform and the situation of the Oriental Jews is gradually improving. The IDF plays a part in this. More and more officers from the Oriental community can be seen in the IDF. The number is much greater than it was in the fifties

and sixties but it is still low in terms of their proportion to the total population—more than fifty percent.

For the IDF the question has been how much to invest in the training of new soldiers from the "deprived" strata. An easy solution would be to place them in such nonspecialized jobs as kitchen or guard duty. The harder solution, which the Army chose, is to raise their performance and capabilities through education. It is a long-term process but the IDF today does provide the opportunity for any soldier to complete his grade-school education.

The IDF is perhaps the only army that must teach the language of the country to thousands of its soldiers. Upon induction, each new recruit is examined for his proficiency, written and spoken, in Hebrew. Some 5,000 soldiers are taught Hebrew every year. Of these, twenty percent are born in the country, and the rest are new immigrants. At least a half of those who learn Hebrew in the Army come from the countries of North Africa and the Middle East. They must continue their studies until they receive a passing mark and cannot be promoted without a suitable fluency in Hebrew.

The general rule is that an IDF soldier is not permitted to complete his service until he has received a certificate of elementary education. Nearly 1,200 soldiers undergo these elementary studies every year. The IDF educational system in elementary studies, language and secondary education encompasses over 17,000 soldiers. This is in addition to the many thousands more who learn technical professions during their military service.

The IDF's educational system makes an important contribution to the problem of the Oriental Jews' educational lag. Before release from service, selected members of the Oriental communities with a partial secondary education are given many months of intensive preparation for university studies as civilians.

Paratroop trainees. [Israeli Army]

Training

A unique characteristic of the system of training and guidance in the Israeli Army is the multiplicity of exercises under live fire. The purpose is to bring the soldier as close as possible to real combat situations, and to prepare the reserve soldier to adapt to the sharp transition from the life of a civilian to that of a fighting soldier.

Another program peculiar to the IDF is instruction for soldiers in noncommissioned ranks. The squad commanders' course is such a program. Few armies have a similar combat course. One of its primary objectives is the development of initiative in the noncommissioned officer. The stress is on development of independent thought, which will permit improvisation under battle conditions rather than dependence on orders from above. Every noncommissioned officer is drilled in solving battle problems in unorthodox ways. At IDF Staff College—unlike similar schools in other armies

—there are no prepared solutions to exercises and problems. The general principles are taught and students are encouraged to search for their own specific solutions. The idea is to prevent the Israeli commander from ending up in the rut of uniform military solutions.

Although the Israeli Army depends primarily on mechanized and armored units, its commanders feel that it is the infantry officer who holds the greatest obligation to think in battle. Therefore, all future Israeli officers are taught management of an infantry unit. Armor, artillery and engineering officers afterwards continue in specialized studies in other courses.

The highest combat course in the IDF is for company commanders. Above this, there is only an irregular series of refresher courses for battalion commanders, primarily in armor, and for battalion commanders from reserve units of the IDF. The Israeli Army General Staff attempts to bridge a part of this gap by sending many officers to the Staff College, where ad-

IDF training methods are of great interest to other emerging nations. An Israeli instructor works with Joseph Mobutu, President of Zaire, during paratroop training. [Israeli Army]

ministrative and command instruction is integrated into academic studies. The length of the course is one year and participants are officers of the rank of major and lieutenant colonel.

The Command Echelon

The IDF differs from other armies in the constant mobility of its command echelons. This mobility derives partly from the general rule that in order to enrich the experience of IDF officers, they are replaced in most positions every two years. There is also a constant flow from the ranks of the Army to civilian life.

Every IDF officer knows in advance that the number of years he can serve in the Army is limited. In the 1950s, Chief of Staff Dayan wanted to ensure that the IDF would always be a young army. He ruled that the majority of officers should retire at forty. This is further encouraged by Israeli law which provides a partial pension for military men from age forty. Other government service positions do not allow for retirement with pension until age sixty-five.

Because of the early retirement age, ninety-nine percent of all IDF officers have left the service by age fifty.

Even the most talented officer knows that as he approaches his fortieth year he must think of leaving the Army and plan his second career in civilian life. Even if he were exceptionally successful in his job and reached the rank of major general, he could not hold more than two positions at that rank, unless he were a candidate for IDF Chief of Staff.

The Chief of Staff himself, upon his appointment, knows more or less the date on which he must retire from the Army; the period of service of a Chief of Staff in the IDF is three years and any extension must be approved by the government. Until now, all the Chiefs of Staff have retired before reaching the age of fifty. If we examine the famous photograph of the Israeli generals who directed the Six-Day War, we see that all are now civilians.

However, in the wake of growing utilization of sophisticated weapons systems that necessitate specialization, the Israeli General Staff is convinced that retirement at forty is too early and is likely to harm the professional standards of the Army. No formal change has occurred in the rules laid down in Dayan's time, but every year the average age of senior commanders rises. This process will most likely continue. The average age of the Chief of Staff is currently thirty-eight, but the trend is toward

The generals of the IDF posing with President
Zalman Shazar after the Six-Day War. Directly to
Shazar's right can be seen Lt. Gen. Yitzhak Rabin,
Chief of Staff at the time. On Shazar's left is Lt. Gen.
David Elazar and behind him former Air Force Chief
of Staff Ezer Weizman. [Israeli Army]

appointing older men.

However, at the same time, there is an effort
to promote young and talented officers over
those with seniority. In field and combat commands the stress is on young commanders.

The selection process in the upper command
echelon of the IDF is complex because of the
small size of the standing army. The number
of senior positions is further limited because
the Army is based primarily on reserve units.

Each officer is summoned to the Manpower
Division and told of his chances for promotion.
A number of officers who have passed the age
of thirty-five are told that it would be worth

their while to think of retirement. Others are
told that though they have no chance of promotion, the IDF is nevertheless interested in
them and asks them to continue their military
service.

This process of elimination has caused the
generation of Israel's War of Independence to
vanish from the ranks of the IDF. The new generation has acquired all of its military education in Israel, although some have attended
advanced courses in European and American
military colleges. This generation found a military framework already in existence and did
not undergo the transition that had been neces-

Insignias of the IDF General Staff HQ and the Naval Command.

sary for those who had come from the ranks of underground armies and guerrilla forces.

One result of this development is that the up-and-coming generation of commanders is comprised of military technocrats, seemingly less individualistic and colorful, but in some ways preferable to their predecessors. These are professional soldiers without complexes. Their grandfathers may have been great scholars and their fathers farmers who came to Palestine, but this generation has a different mission: to provide Israel with a sophisticated, first-rate army.

The formal education of the new generation is at a higher level than that of the earlier fighters who rarely had time to pursue their studies in an organized way, having enlisted in the Haganah or other forces upon graduation from high school or even earlier. The commanders of the future benefit from an IDF program which gives them leave for two years with pay to complete B.A. or B.S. degrees that normally require three years at Israeli universities.

Israel has no pre-induction officers' courses like those offered at West Point or through ROTC, so officers of the IDF are commissioned upon completion of an officers' training course given after entrance into the armed forces. Israel's two military schools are two-year secondary institutions and have only been mildly successful in developing officer material. They do not offer commissions.

Recruits who successfully complete the officer course can sign on for two or three additional years beyond their national service requirement, depending on their area of specialization and the current situation. Most Israeli youth who sign on do so initially to save money for school or because they have acquired a taste for leading men and feel a sense of national responsibility. They rarely aim for a military career at the outset.

Among the young officers I interviewed, most reject any notion of having a mission.

They take a pragmatic, unsentimental view. "Why talk Zionism," one said. "It's a fact that the Army is an important thing and I feel it. Outside, I could have earned much more, but here I am doing an important job. Were we like Switzerland or Holland from the point of view of security, I would not stay in the regular army another minute."[5]

Young officers from kibbutzim and agricultural cooperatives usually sign on for short periods and then muster out. These young men are considered among the best soldiers in the IDF. The collective framework of their upbringing and idealistic education, as well as a closeness to nature and a developed sense of responsibility toward the group seem to suit them to army life.

Political Consciousness within the Command Echelon

Until the controversy following the Yom Kippur War, the young generation of officers tended to agree with diplomatic and security principles determined by Israel's leaders. Criticism tended to be more on social and economic matters. But even in this respect, the young officers of the IDF are no more rebellious than other Israeli youth. In comparison with the younger generations of various countries in the Western world, the Israeli youth is obedient and traditional. Radical political phenomena like the New Left are only felt on the margins of young Israeli society.

The young officers are more serious-minded than their peer group outside the ranks of the Army. Not because they are more intelligent, but because the responsibility imposed on them of necessity makes them more mature. The army equips them with more information than the average civilian youngster. Care is taken to keep them supplied with booklets on various internationally important subjects. They are required to hear lectures on these subjects and participate in educational preparation courses

Yitzhak Rabin during paratroop course. In the 1950s, the IDF passed a regulation requiring all senior officers to qualify as paratroopers. [Josef Roth]

General Ariel Sharon, Commander of the paratroops, presenting wings to Chief of Staff Dayan upon his completion of the compulsory training course, 1956. [Israeli Army]

for commanders.

The Israeli Army does not play at soldiering. Little emphasis is given to spit and polish; yet there is discipline. It is based on common sense, and the over-riding purpose of the Israeli Army is to be ready at a moment's notice to defend the nation. The new generation of officers are professionals; they concentrate on the Army's ultimate purpose and work constantly to enhance their battle readiness. But they are not militarists seeking to set the Army apart from the people as a distinct class with broad powers over the civil sector as has happened so often in the Middle East.

The absence of militarism is reflected in the attitude toward discipline. It is necessary only insofar as it aids in carrying out the security mission. Thus, there is little cant in Israel about the importance of blind obedience in shaping a soldier's character. Every officer in the IDF can question exceptional orders and demand to know their purpose. There have been occasions when soldiers who have refused to obey what seemed to them unlawful orders have been exonerated. The excuse, "I only carried out orders," has been heard too often from the lips of Nazi War criminals to have any validity in the Army of the Jewish nation.

Nevertheless, when operational orders are issued they are carried out explicitly. Whenever there are deviations there is no possibility of concealment because there is always an officer or soldier who will take care to report it to the senior ranks. This is the way of the IDF.

A cross-section of the IDF reveals few young officers who relish military life, yet there is a noticeable ambition to serve with distinguished combat records. Israeli soldiers all say they desire peace, yet the majority do not want to miss combat action. A brigade commander explained it this way: "There may possibly be some [war-hungry officers] but they are few and far between. Most wait for the moment of their baptism under fire and want it, but they

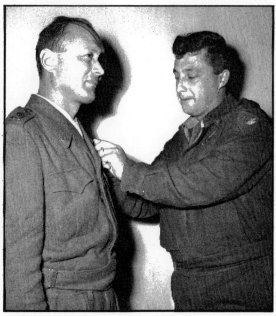

Informality is one distinctive feature of the IDF. Here
Maj. Gen. Bren Aden consults with commando on
the Egyptian front during the Yom Kippur War.

[Israeli Army]

will not provoke the enemy without orders. There are among them those who could be compared to disciplined hunting dogs who the moment they are released will leap on the enemy ferociously."[6]

Comparison between the new generation of officers and their counterparts in the War of Independence and during the salad days of the IDF is inevitable. Senior officers who remember their own generation's officers in 1948 and who have commanded many cycles of recruits and junior officers are able to comment on the generational change. Maj. Gen. Shmuel Gonen, former Director of the Training Division of the General Staff, told me: "Each generation surpasses the one before it. In the past, we had no standards for comparison. Now the demands made of them are greater and the criteria different. The willingness in the ranks to volunteer for combat units and the low rate of desertion are positive indications of the quality of today's officers. The junior officers are better professionals, their experience is considerable and they face more severe crises."[7]

Today's high standards were set by those who served, before the IDF was organized, in the Haganah and the other underground organizations which were based solely on volunteers. It was in that period that a tradition of sacrifice and leadership was established. The officers' watchword became: "Follow me!" In many other armies, the order is often "Forward!" It is reasonable to assume that in such a situation, the lives of many officers are saved, but the spirit of the assault and the manner in which it is carried out are different. The IDF still perpetuates the tradition of "Follow me!" despite the high rate of casualties among officers.

The IDF fulfills an important social role. It contributes to the integration of the disparate groups making up the Israeli nation. The IDF is a gigantic school for the population and a melting pot for the different cultures and national backgrounds merged in Israel. New immigrants meet *sabras* of their own age for the first time in the IDF. Perhaps the most realistic work of absorption is done in the Army, the only place where all are equal according to their talents. Here democratic, cultural and traditional Jewish values are dispensed.

Footnotes

1 Israel Defense Forces, internal publication, 1970.
2 Briefing for military correspondents, 1971.
3 Previously unpublished interview with author, 1972.
4 Previously unpublished interview with author, 1972.
5 Previously unpublished interview with author, 1968.
6 Previously unpublished interview with author, 1968.
7 Previously unpublished interview with author, 1973.

7. WOMEN IN THE ISRAEL DEFENSE FORCES

Opposite: [Frederic Lewis]

Right: The Emblem of CHEN.

Below: Graduation ceremony for guards at civilian installations.

One of the most publicized and least understood aspects of the IDF is the Women's Army, known by its Hebrew acronym—CHEN. The image seen throughout Israel of miniskirted soldiers conjures up the sexuality of women in uniform as a theme of literature and films. The erotic fantasy of stern and cruel lust-arousing women is particularly associated with the Nazi era and the image of stalags and Hitlerian love camps. Perhaps it is somewhat ironic that Israel, a state born of the Nazi holocaust, should have its own *mädchen* in uniform. But the Mediterranean has softened the Prussian hard edges and the Lily Palmer milieu of barely concealed lesbianism and chilly barracks. The Israeli Women's Army is noted for its easygoing camaraderie and wholesomeness.

Why a Women's Armed Force

Although women often fought with men in the partisan military units of pre-Statehood days, today the women soldiers carry out non-combat functions. They are trained in the use of light arms for self-defense, but are not assigned to forward battle areas. During the Yom Kippur War, for example, female soldiers were immediately evacuated from the Golan Heights on the Syrian front and from camps near the Suez Canal. Nevertheless, one woman was killed by Syrian shells while she operated a radio and two were killed by shelling in Sinai.

The shift from actual front-line assignments to rear-echelon work was accompanied by a change in the image and style of CHEN. From baggy, shapeless khaki drill pants and government-issue brassieres, the women soldiers have moved on to the bare-leg look, tapered blouses and personalized lingerie.

As the Women's Army evolves into a kind of auxiliary, the question of its necessity is increasingly raised. Is the Women's Army's contribution to the military power of the State worth the problems it creates?

Israel is the only state in which there is com-

pulsory military service for women and this, of course, makes the IDF unique. There are women in many other armies but they are volunteers. In Israel, the law requires every unmarried woman to register for military service when she reaches the age of eighteen. The law sets women's service at two years, but the period is shortened if conditions permit. It is now twenty months. To avoid conflict with strictly religious Jews who regard military service as incongruent with the traditional concept of womanhood, the IDF exempts women who claim to be observant. Exemptions are also granted to women whose educational level or

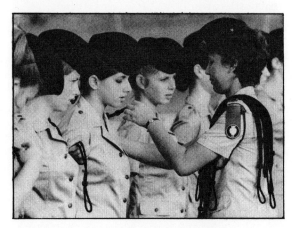

IQ is extremely low. Upon completion of service, very few women are obliged to do reserve duty. The Army is entitled to call women for reserve duty up to the age of thirty-four (men up to forty-nine), if they have no children.

The recruitment of women in the Jewish society of Palestine stemmed from the pressure of circumstances, rather than an ideological impulse to achieve full equality between men and women. The constant shortage of manpower forced the leaders of the community to seek ways to fully utilize its human resources—be they male or female. This situation remained unchanged from the time of the establishment

Right: Sarah Aharonson, who worked with the Nili spies, the World War I espionage network that operated against the Turks. [Haganah Archives]

Far right: Hanna Senesh, who served British Intelligence during World War II and was executed for spying in Budapest. [Haganah Archives]

Bottom: Woman on watch at fence-and-watchtower settlement, 1936. [Haganah Archives]

of the Haganah up to the present day. The population of Israel has grown, albeit gradually, but the reality of its precarious position as a small enclave surrounded by populous Arab states prevails.

Fighting Women in Israel's History

The history of Jewish self-defense and the armed forces of the Jewish community of Palestine are full of examples of feminine courage. In 1920, when the settlement Tel Hai fell, there were two women—Devorah Drachler and Sarah Chizik—among the ten defenders who, led by Joseph Trumpeldor, finally perished in that northern outpost. A few years earlier, when the Jewish Legion was established in General Allenby's expeditionary force, Rachel Yanait (later the wife of Yitzhak Ben Tzvi, the second President of Israel) demanded that women be included in those new battalions of the British Army.

Sarah Aharonson, one of the settlers of Zichron Yaakov, was a leader of the Nili Organization, a World War I espionage network which assisted the British forces against the Turks. In 1917, Sarah was captured and tortured by the Turks and finally took her own life.

Women played a key role after the establishment of the Haganah. Volunteering by women for military functions reached its peak in World War II. In 1942, the number of women members of the Haganah was in the tens of thousands. The number of women in the Palmach increased until they were about a third of the total in that commando force. Some 4,000 women were recruited into the auxiliary arms of the British Army, and most were sent to Egypt and Italy where, at the end of the war, they assisted Jewish survivors of the Nazi extermination camps.

One of the chapters of supreme bravery in that period was the participation of young Palestinian women in a group of Jewish para-

troops trained by British Intelligence. The paratroops were dropped into Europe behind enemy lines for the purposes of espionage, sabotage and assistance to partisans in the various countries. Two of the women, Hanna Senesh and Haviva Reich, were caught by the Germans and executed. Both were members of kibbutzim and Haviva Reich was in the Palmach. Hanna Senesh, who was twenty-three when she died, had come to Palestine from Hungary at the age of eighteen. She returned to that country with two other paratroopers, but was caught in action. She was put on trial and executed in Budapest Central Prison, when the

Group of Palmach women during induction into the
IDF, July 1948. At far left is Yitzhak Rabin's wife,
Leah. [Haganah Archives]

guns of the Red Army could already be heard
in the suburbs of the city. Six years later, after
the independence of Israel, her remains
were brought home for reinterment. Settlements in Israel were named for the two women, who are remembered as heroines and
martyrs to the cause of independence.

The tradition of courage by women volunteers continued during the underground period
and the War of Independence, the only Israeli
war in which women actually fought. Twelve
thousand women soldiers served in the IDF during the War of Independence. They escorted
convoys, fought in isolated settlements and
many were killed or captured. Women were in
every command and some served as pilots.
Even as late as the Sinai War of 1956, a female
pilot dropped paratroops over the Mitla Pass
in Sinai.

IDF women soldiers served during the Sinai
War as radio operators and medical orderlies
and many found themselves at the firing lines.
(One who was in the armored regiment that
broke through the Suez even won a mention in
dispatches.) The same was true during the
Six-Day War and the War of Attrition that followed it. Although they were forbidden to engage in combat and were removed from the
front lines, there were always women who
found themselves in the battle areas and were
even wounded.

The Present: Noncombat Service

Today the emphasis in women's service is
placed on auxiliary military tasks and non-
combat activities. Hundreds of women soldiers
are sent to immigrant settlements to teach Hebrew to adults or to run youth clubs. Others
assist in the absorption of new immigrants and
do social work among poor youth in urban
slums.

The military exercises of a CHEN soldier
last five weeks only and include physical training, parade ground drill, training in weapon
handling and a series of lectures. Afterwards
the trainees are sent for a week's agricultural
work to one of the NAHAL border settlements.
Those who want to remain in the border settlements may volunteer to do so. The others are
sent to various vocational courses and afterwards are assigned to military units.

At one time paratroop training was forbidden
for CHEN women because the Army doctors
believed the impact of landing could damage
the reproductive organs. Nonetheless, some ad-
venturous trainees acted against orders and
jumped anyway. Many others expressed an interest in doing so and the doctors have reconsidered. Parachute jumping is now permitted
for women under certain controlled conditions.

The vocational options for IDF women are
varied: clerk, driver, welfare worker, nurse,
entertainer, sports organizer, radio operator,
parachute handler, flight supervisor, psycho-
technical examiner, computer operator and
more. As the IDF gets more involved in the
operation of sophisticated weapons systems,
so the women get more involved in technical
vocations.

Women carry out important tasks in Operations and Intelligence, and in the regular army
women have reached senior ranks in various
key positions. Many acquire a useful profession
during their military service, but for all of them
the Army is a kind of finishing school. And mar-
riage in the ranks of the Army is common.

Bottom: Paratroop training.

Top: Target practice.

Middle: IDF lieutenant and CHEN soldiers at settlement in Sinai. [Israeli Army]

Bottom: Desert patrol during basic training. [Israeli Army]

The Army profits from the service of the IDF woman. In every place and every unit where women are to be found, they contribute to improved operations and morale. The IDF does not have the look of an austere armed force. A former CHEN commander, Col. Devorah Tomer, says "The IDF would not maintain its present force without the girls. The girls hold important positions and thereby release soldiers and officers for combat duties."[1]

Israel's small but vocal women's liberation movement has attacked the Army for placing women in noncombatant desk jobs, but their criticisms have elicited little response on the part of the women soldiers. Although some Israeli women are nostalgic for the pre-Statehood days when women fought alongside men, most accept the present structure of the IDF.

At the present time, active feminists in Israel number only a few hundred and they have not succeeded in gaining broad-based

A mixed signal corps unit in 1973 Independence Day
Parade. [Israeli Army]

Mixed combat training in the early fifties.

Top: A CHEN soldier helps men at the front write letters home. [Israeli Army]

Bottom: CHEN field communications training.

support from Israeli women. Some sociologists feel that the reality of Israel's embattled existence relegates to a secondary place the concerns of women's liberation which, they say, emerge in societies in which leisure, material abundance and boredom nurture middle-class discontent.

All in all, the argument for retaining a women's armed force wins.

Sex and Social Life in the IDF

Entering the Army at eighteen, for most young women, means their first experience away from home and their introduction to sexual intercourse. As is true for men, Army life serves as a rite of passage for the women. It is widely believed that most women come of age sexually at some time during their military service. Strict separation of the sexes is the rule during training, but permanent postings bring many of the women into daily and close contact

At the front during the Yom Kippur War. [Israeli Army]

with men. At headquarters units there is much socializing, encouraged by regular army officers. Frequent parties are held and the easy-going familiarity promotes an eroticism that is distinctly Jewish: matter-of-fact and controlled. Without alcohol or drugs, pleasure in the Israeli Army is more on the sensible side than the ecstatic. On the whole, the experiment works well and the women seem satisfied with their status and role in the Israeli military. Women grow during their Army service and their personalities crystallize. There are also many religiously observant young women recruited into the IDF, and they apparently retain their religious ways.

Nevertheless, the Army authorities are careful not to encourage promiscuity. They do not recruit young girls with criminal files. Only very occasionally does a recruiting examiner, after careful personal investigation, recommend a young woman who has been involved in a moral transgression. A soldier who becomes pregnant, even by her fiancé, is immediately released from the IDF. A special clause in the Army regulations permits discharge of a pregnant soldier within twenty-four hours. Generally speaking, the Army does not make use of this clause arbitrarily. The au-

thorities are cautious about abandoning such a young woman for fear that her family will disown her. The commander will often contact the pregnant soldier's parents, and if a rift develops between parents and daughter, they will seek a place for her outside the IDF.

Although procedures exist for assistance after the fact, the Army vigorously rejects proposals that birth control pills be given to women who ask for them. "We do *not* engage in preventive medicine of this kind," the commander of CHEN says. "We do, however, provide sex education. Army doctors lecture the women and everyone is entitled to turn to a civilian doctor; a list of names is available in every unit and can be consulted without the knowledge of her comrades and her commanders."[2]

Special Problems

If the Army is unwilling to arouse public debate and criticism from religious sectors of the population by keeping up with the times as regards birth control, it is ready to protect the femininity of its soldiers in other areas. A lot of the women justifiably complain that they put on weight because of the heavy and rich diet served in military camps. The IDF has responded to this by substituting a number of starchy items on the Army menu with fresh fruit and vegetables. It is impossible to do this everywhere, however, since in most units there is a much greater concentration of men than women, and the menu must be adapted to the needs of the men. The women say they diet and keep away from candy sold in the PX.

What is difficult to accomplish in the field of nutrition is much easier in the area of dress and cosmetics. For many years young women recruited into the IDF received coarse khaki uniforms with no consideration for cut and style. Occasionally items of clothing were contributed by European and American Jews. In the 1950s, for example, Fred Monosson, a wealthy American Jew, donated nylon stockings and raincoats to all women soldiers. In the 1970s, the Army no longer relies on the taste and generosity of donors. The uniforms have been fashionably designed with miniskirts five inches above the knee. CHEN women are permitted to grow long hair if it is plaited or pinned up. Furthermore, IDF women no longer have to accept the underwear issued by the quartermaster's store. Instead, they receive an allowance to choose and buy underwear for themselves. Women who serve as drivers receive an additional allowance for gloves to protect their hands. Army camps are opened to cosmetic consultants from various companies who give free advice and teach skin and body care. Studies have found that during their army service the women spend more money on lipstick, eye makeup and other cosmetics than they did when they were civilians.

CHEN in Hebrew also means grace or loveliness. Israelis are fond of saying that this word epitomizes Israel's Women's Army. Its structure has been copied by several African and Asian nations, and its success proves the viability of a women's military corps.

Footnotes

1   Previously unpublished interview with author, 1972.
2   Ibid.

CHEN women today: combat-trained technicians
and entertainers.

Top left: [Israeli Army]

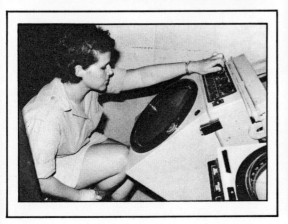

8. INTELLIGENCE

Opposite: Soviet SAM missile captured during
Six-Day War. [Israeli Army]

Badge of Modeyin.

Captain Mortaji's MIG swallowed up the
distances of Sinai at immense speed. Were it
not for the bombs hanging beneath its belly,
his aircraft could have reached its target even
faster. Five minutes earlier, Mortaji had taken
off from an airfield near the Suez Canal, and
he was now penetrating the battlefield of northern Sinai. His mission: to hit the Israeli tanks
which were relentlessly advancing into Egyptian lines on the second day of the Six-Day
War. Suddenly, he heard a voice call his name
on the radio. For a second, he thought he had
heard wrong, but the voice in his earphones
repeated: "Captain Mortaji! Captain Mortaji!
Do you hear?" It was strange; ground control
stations do not call pilots by name during
operations. Mortaji let his curiosity get the
better of him: "I hear you! This is Captain
Mortaji! I hear you!"

Two or three seconds passed, and then the
voice said in a clear, Egyptian-accented Arabic:
"Your game is lost, Mortaji! We know you took
off from Bilbis airfield. The field has been
destroyed. If you want to return to your wife
Neima and to your children, Samy and Fuad,
drop your bombs into the sea. Then abandon
your plane and jump near the Canal. This is
your only chance! Your only chance!"

Mortaji was astounded. How did an unknown voice know the names of his wife and
children? At that point, he turned his plane
northward and moved away from his target
and toward the sea.

Mortaji was thinking: "If they know the
names of my children and my wife, then they
must know everything." A few minutes later
he released his bombs, turned eastward and
pulled the lever of his ejection seat. Mortaji
parachuted down to the Canal and his plane
crashed into the sand dunes. He was taken
prisoner and exchanged after the Six-Day
War.

This story is not the fruit of the imagination

of Arab commanders who tried to make ex-
cuses for their defeat in the Six-Day War. It
was a Soviet paper, Neva, that reported it
while describing the operations of Israeli Intelligence. It was Israeli Intelligence that succeeded in sowing confusion among the Arabs,
the Russian publication related. The Israelis
were able to monitor and at times control the
communications and radio network of the
Arab armies. The paper later added another
story about an Egyptian fedayeen sergeant in
the Gaza Strip who, following the Israeli conquest, reported to an IDF officer and informed
him that he was an Israeli agent who had
penetrated the fedayeen.

Other reports of penetrations by Israeli Intelligence were leaked for the first time after
the Six-Day War. The head of Military Intelligence during the Six-Day War, Maj. Gen.
Aharon Yariv, revealed the story of one of Israel's most successful agents. He had climbed
the ladder of rank in the Egyptian Army and
had reached a senior post. Over the years, he
had made an immense contribution to Israeli
Intelligence, but during the Six-Day War,
when IDF armor attacked one of the Egyptian
Army camps in the heart of the Sinai, he
was wounded and died before he was able
to identify himself. His name was never
revealed.

The Egyptians themselves uncovered various affairs of this sort. Among others, they
told of an Israeli agent, an Armenian named
Antonio Kanalisi, who lived for years next to
the Alexandria port, and from there reported
all the movements of the Egyptian Fleet and
Russian warships that reached the port. He
also reported those that unloaded weapons for
the Egyptians. The Egyptians claimed that on
the basis of Kanalisi's reports, Israeli frogmen
penetrated into Alexandria Harbor during the
war. The frogmen were not notably successful
and some of them were captured. Kanalisi

Maj. Gen. Aharon Yariv, head of Modeyin during the Six-Day War. [David Rubinger]

Bottom: Frogmen, important tools of Israeli Intelligence. [Israeli Army]

was caught after the war and was executed by the Egyptians.

Israel's Secret Weapon

Israeli Intelligence in the Israel-Arab conflict has had far greater impact than many other weapons. Over the years the Arab press has pictured Israeli Intelligence as an omnipotent monster.

"The sovereign state of the Israeli enemy is the Intelligence," the editor of an Arab newspaper, *El Sabua el Araby*, explained. "Intelligence preceded the State, and in order to understand one, we must learn the second."[1] The Arab writer explained that because Israeli society is composed of the members of various nationalities, the choice of Intelligence agents is greatly facilitated. The former editor of the semi-official Egyptian newspaper, *El Ahram*, Hassenein Heykal, wrote, "Israel has complete knowledge of Egypt. They even knew

Isser Harel, principal architect of Israeli Intelligence.

Below: Rare photo of Tzvi Zamir, head of Mosad, Israel's Central Intelligence and Security Agency.

the names of our pilots and the secret codes for our planes."[2]

The international press adds to the mystique. Thus, for example, the Middle Eastern correspondent of *Le Figaro*, Yves Cuau, wrote on November 24, 1967 that the Israelis monitor and decode every Arab broadcast with the use of computers. Israeli Intelligence, he claims, owes its achievements to the Jewish native intellect and electronic genius, and to its ability to plant agents in the most unlikely places.

Eli Cohen, an Israeli agent in Damascus, was being considered for a Syrian cabinet post when he was discovered in January 1965. The well-publicized kidnapping of the Nazi criminal Adolf Eichmann from Argentina in 1960 was also typical of the type of exploits that had made Israeli Intelligence legendary until the Yom Kippur War.

Makeup of the Intelligence Network

Spying in the Holy Land began when Joshua sent forth agents to report on the land of Canaan. The information they brought back enabled him to plan his strategy. Modern Israel began building its Intelligence apparatus at the end of World War I. During the war the Nili spies, a group of Palestinian Jews, had done Intelligence work for the British against the Turks.

Within the Haganah, an espionage branch called SHAI (Hebrew acronym for Intelligence Service) was established. It developed procedures and techniques for espionage and counterespionage. SHAI was able to infiltrate both British military and Arab political circles and advise the Haganah command of British planning and Arab thinking. When the IDF was organized, SHAI served as the basis of *Modeyin* (Information), as IDF Military Intelligence is popularly known.

Israel's Intelligence services consist of three main divisions: the Central Intelligence and Security Agency, known as the Mosad (Hebrew for Institute); IDF Intelligence, which works closely with the Mosad and became preeminent under Maj. Gen. Aharon Yariv's brilliant direction; and the internal security services known as the Shin Bet, similar in scope and function to the FBI and, in recent years, notable for eradicating fedayeen terrorist activity inside the occupied territories.

Israel is understandably reticent about her Intelligence agencies and the names of the head of the Mosad and the Shin Bet are never published.

The uniqueness of Israeli Intelligence, in the eyes of one of its founders, Isser Harel, derives both from Israel's national traits and from the lack of alternative that the war for survival has imposed on Israeli society. Harel's approach perhaps appears chauvinistic, but the majority of Israeli Intelligence commanders are convinced that the Jewish predilection for scholarship has given Jews an outstanding analytical ability. Israeli Intelligence benefits from this advantage and from the knowledge of many languages common among the Jews. One of the former commanders of Military Intelligence, Maj. Gen. Yehoshofat Harkabi, says that the uniqueness of Israeli Intelligence lies in its greater intuitive ability as compared to other Intelligence services. This ability derives from an innovative flair and from the relatively limited territory in which it operates—Israeli Intelligence concentrates on the Middle East and is not compelled to engage in global problems.

Another past commander of Israeli Intelligence, Haim Herzog, is convinced that Israeli Intelligence is the best in the world in its knowledge of the Middle East. Herzog recalls the debate that took place in the summer of 1970 between Israel and the Nixon Administration. One day after the cease-fire took effect on the Suez Canal, Israeli Intelligence contended that the Egyptians, assisted by Russians, had broken the cease-fire by moving missile batteries forward. The Pentagon, despite its satellite surveillance, claimed that there was no proof and refused to accept the photographs and other material offered by Israel. More than two weeks were to pass before the CIA confirmed that Israeli Intelligence had indeed been right about missile movement.

Herzog says that Israeli Intelligence is also outstanding in that its commanders have freedom of thought and are not dependent on evaluations by operational and political echelons. The records of Israeli Intelligence are indeed full of stories about heads of Intelligence who obstinately stood by their evaluations and insisted that they were closer to the target than were the Chief of Staff and political leaders. There are two cases which deserve mention.

After the Egyptian-Czech arms deal in 1955, the central question in the IDF was: How long would it take the Egyptian Army to absorb the new weapons and be ready to attack Israel? The Chief of Staff, Moshe Dayan, was convinced that the arms would be absorbed rapidly and that by 1956, Nasser would be ready for war. Military Intelligence, headed by Harkabi, was convinced otherwise. After the 1956 Sinai War, which Israel started, it became clear that Harkabi's evaluation had been correct.

In the second case, internal differences of opinion spilled over into a public political debate at the height of which Ben-Gurion resigned from the government. In the summer of 1962, Israel was surprised by a show put on by Nasser. On Revolution Day, celebrating the 1954 overthrow of King Farouk, the Egyptians displayed a number of missiles and declared that they had medium-range land-to-land missiles that could reach Israel's cities. Israel was shocked and blamed the Intelligence Services for not knowing what was going on in Egypt. The contention of Isser Harel, who was head of Mosad and overall supervisor of Intelligence Services, was that there had been information on the Egyptian plans, but the evaluation of the information had not been done properly. He sought to put the blame on Military Intelligence, where the work of research and evaluation had been done. Harel pointed out that his people had obtained information that the Egyptians were testing missiles in a wind tunnel in Switzerland. The Israeli experts who received this information estimated that the tests related to an early stage in the planning of missiles. This type of faulty evaluation was characteristic of what happened during the Yom Kippur War.

Egyptian King Farouk, 1953. [Frederic Lewis]

Bottom: Wolfgang Lotz, the Israeli operative who, disguised as a German, penetrated Egypt's defense establishment and conducted a campaign of terror against West German scientists doing missile research there. [Black Star]

After the unveiling of the Egyptian missiles, Harel ordered the Intelligence services to devote themselves to this development. Within a few months Intelligence came up with some new and amazing facts. It emerged that the focal point of the missile affair was not in Egypt but in West Germany, in a Stuttgart research institute. German scientists, some of whom worked for the Nazis in developing missiles and aircraft, were working under a scientist named Wolfgang Pilz. In 1962 and 1963, a number of the scientists visited Egypt and served there as paid advisers to Nasser's missile industry. Israel protested to Bonn but got no satisfactory response. It took a campaign of terror against the scientists — the dispatch of exploding parcels, intimidation and even kidnapping — to put an end to the scientists' activity and stop, for the time being, Egypt's threat.

The German scientists' affair jeopardized Ben-Gurion's policy of rapprochement with West Germany and led to a Knesset debate in which Ben-Gurion's policy came under heavy attack. Seeking to avert a total collapse of relationships between Israel and Germany, Ben-Gurion tried to downplay the affair of the German scientists. To do this he needed the assistance of the Supervisor of Intelligence Services. But Harel refused to cooperate, insisting that the scientists had to be put out of action. The dispute ended with Harel's resignation.

This was not the first time that one of the heads of Israeli Intelligence had been compelled to resign his post. The first commander of Israeli Intelligence, Isser Be'eri, resigned after being placed on trial for wrongly executing an Israeli citizen suspected of espionage. His successor in Military Intelligence, Benjamin Gibli, was also compelled to leave his job after getting involved in the "Unfortunate Affair," in which Egyptian-based Jewish agents attacked American installations in a misguided effort to sour relations between Cairo and Washington. The ramifications of the episode haunted Israeli politics for many years. Yehoshofat Harkabi was also removed from his post because he mistakenly approved a large-scale reserve call-up that caused panic in Israel, and Eli Zeira, head of IDF Intelligence during the Yom Kippur War, resigned in the wake of the investigation into Intelligence mishandling that followed that war.

Early Days

When the IDF was founded, the Intelligence staff was located in Tel Aviv in a corner house disguised as a publishing firm. An early IDF commander considered to be the major architect of Israeli Military Intelligence was Haim Herzog, who acquired experience in the Intelligence services of another army. Son of the Chief Rabbi of Israel, Herzog reached the rank of lieutenant colonel as a field Intelligence officer in the British Army during the Second World War. After the war, he took part in the interrogation of Nazi war criminals and in the uncovering of Russian espionage networks in Germany. He resigned his commission and openly joined the Haganah, in which he had previously served clandestinely. He was named head of Military Intelligence on Ben-Gurion's recommendation and submitted his proposal for the structure of a regular Intelligence service.

It was August 1948 when Herzog asked that 1,500 men be placed at the disposal of Military Intelligence. The Intelligence service was then still a branch of the Operations Division. His demand seemed extravagant but he prevailed.

At first, Intelligence commanders had to make do with makeshift transport and equipment, and departmental heads recruited their own men. There were many dropouts, but there were also some who would develop into experts of international standing.

In the early years, Intelligence operations were loosely organized, methods were primitive and the atmosphere was generally chaotic. Isser Be'eri, head of Intelligence for the IDF from 1947 until 1949, had a small army of

his own; only he knew the details of their missions. Their operations involved little more than finding enemy agents, beating them and throwing them in prison. Arab double agents were captured and summarily executed by Be'eri's men.

The Tubiansky Affair of 1948 put an end to Be'eri's career. Meir Tubiansky, a Jew suspected of having given information to both the Arabs and the British, was arrested by Be'eri's men and executed after a trial by a kangaroo court. It was later discovered that he had been wrongly accused and Be'eri was removed from command of the Army Intelligence Service in January 1949.

1950s: Reform and Reorganization

In the early fifties, the Intelligence Services were reorganized and operations became more sophisticated. Counterespionage was removed from the jurisdiction of Military Intelligence and transferred to the Shin Bet. Early in 1950, Ben-Gurion approved a $200,000 budget allocated for acquisition of electronic transmitters and surveillance equipment from the United States and West Germany.

A Central Committee of all heads of the Intelligence services was set up along lines similar to those in England. The first chairman of the Committee was Reuven Shiloach, an Arabist. He was later followed by the tough former head of the Shin Bet, Isser Harel. The Committee was composed of representatives of the Mosad, Military Intelligence, the Shin Bet, the Inspector-General of Police and the Ministry of Foreign Affairs. In fact, only the Mosad, Military Intelligence and the Shin Bet carried on actual spying and counterespionage.

The status of Military Intelligence within this system increased from year to year. In the beginning of 1953, Chief of Staff Dayan ordered Intelligence separated from Operations, and elevated to a division of the General Staff. Al-

Amin el Husseini, the Grand Mufti of Palestine (white hat and beard), the chief sponsor of fedayeen activity against Israel in the fifties.

though the Mosad was the oldest Intelligence agency, the power of Military Intelligence grew. Its research department developed so rapidly that its authority soon exceeded that of the Foreign Ministry The definitive research on the Arab states was eventually done in the IDF. While the Mosad concentrated more and more in the field of gathering information, Military Intelligence both gathered and evaluated data. The Head of the Intelligence Division in the General Staff became the man to submit the national Intelligence evaluation to the Prime Minister and Minister of Defense. In this way Israel's Military Intelligence differs from most military Intelligence services in the world.

Up until the 1956 Sinai War, the operational counterespionage efforts of Israeli Military Intelligence centered on Palestinian and other Arab fedayeen terrorists and their sponsors. In 1952, for example, IDF Intelligence agents were credited with blowing up the Beirut building

that housed the Arab Higher Command, the supreme organization of Palestinian Arabs in which the Mufti, Amin el Husseini, planned sabotage activities against Israel. IDF Intelligence played an important role in Israel's retaliation actions but details of most of its activities are still classified.

The files of Egyptian Intelligence itself, confiscated during the Sinai War, give details of another action against the head of Egyptian Intelligence in the Gaza Strip, Col. Mustafa Hafez. Also the head of a fedayeen organization operating against Israel, Hafez was a clever Intelligence officer who was responsible for taking the lives of many Israelis. The Egyptian file claimed that in the 1950s, Israel employed an Arab agent who occasionally crossed the border of the Gaza Strip and met with his Israeli contacts. He was, in fact, a double agent, used by Hafez to plant false information. Egyptian Intelligence believed he was leading Israeli

P-3 Orion patrol aircraft flies over a Soviet Z-class missile submarine near Gibraltar. [Walter J. Dumbek, U.S. Navy]

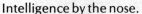

Intelligence by the nose.

In the kind of turnabout so common in espionage, Israeli Intelligence was playing a double game. Its personnel knew that their "agent" was really an Egyptian agent. They waited for the right opportunity to use him for their own ends. Hafez was the target, but it was known that he would be too cautious to fall for a simple ruse. It was decided to trap him by exploiting his suspicions. A booby-trapped package, wrapped as a present, was given by the Israelis to the double agent. It was addressed to the commandant of the Gaza police, a sworn enemy of Hafez. The Israeli assumption was that the double agent would not deliver the package to the police chief, but would rush with it to his boss, Hafez. Everything worked according to plan. Hafez seized the parcel, thinking that he had trapped the commandant in espionage contacts with the Israelis. Mustafa Hafez and his deputy were killed as they opened the package.

A Russian-built TU-16 Badger long-range reconnaissance plane with Egyptian markings shadowing the aircraft carrier USS *Shangri-la* during maneuvers in the Mediterranean. [NATO]

Israeli Intelligence in the World Espionage Community

The Intelligence services of Western nations were suspicious of Israeli Intelligence in its formative years. In the 1950s, many suspected that Jews were involved in espionage for the Communist bloc. The fact that Israel had absorbed a large immigration from Eastern Europe only strengthened the suspicions of the Western Intelligence community.

At the same time, the Iron-Curtain nations made repeated efforts to infiltrate all sections of Israeli Intelligence. In addition to the Russians and some of their satellites, the

United States tried it, too. Many of these agents were caught and sentenced to long periods of imprisonment.

In 1956, with stepped-up Soviet penetration of the Middle East, the stature of Israeli Intelligence increased in the West. The United States and her allies were eager to hear Israel's evaluations of regional developments. Israel became the major source of evaluations on the situation in the Middle East, replacing the British who had by then left the region. The accuracy of the information given by Israeli Intelligence won it a special status.

At first, Israeli Intelligence concerned it-

self only with the Arabs. After the mid-1950s, Soviet penetration in the Middle East and the Kremlin's support for the Arabs began to preoccupy IDF Intelligence. Soviet warships lay at anchor in Arab ports and Soviet instructors and advisors guided the Arab armies. It became essential that the IDF learn about Russian weapons, Soviet doctrines of warfare and the Kremlin's intentions. The problem reached its peak at the beginning of 1970, when units of the Russian Army entered the region to aid in the defense of Egypt. A large share of IDF Intelligence's concern has been devoted to the Russians and there is an ever-growing stress on the recruitment of agents in Arab nations who can report on Soviet as well as Arab activities. A large number of these agents are Arabs.

Israeli Intelligence Services have chalked up impressive achievements. Examples range from reports of Israeli military assistance to the Iraqi Kurdish rebels to the capture of Adolf Eichmann in Argentina. One great Intelligence coup involved the capture of a Russian MIG-21 fighter in full working order. An Iraqi pilot flew the valuable plane to Israel in 1966. Training on this advanced aircraft gave an important advantage to Israeli pilots in the Six-Day War.

Failures of Israeli Intelligence

Israeli Intelligence has had many grand successes, but has also experienced failure. The surprise of Egyptian success in producing missiles; the failure to foresee the events that led to the Six-Day War in 1967; the overestimation of Egyptian military power in the same period; the lack of information on the activities of Palestinian terrorists, including their recruitment of hired assassins from other countries; as well as the lack of preparedness before the Yom Kippur War in 1973, are among the serious shortcomings of the Intelligence services.

Perhaps the most bitter failure was the down-

Minister of Defense Pinhas Lavon inspecting troops, 1954. [Israeli Army]

Field Security poster: Chatter Helps the Enemy's Objective. [Israeli Government Printing Office]

fall of the Intelligence network engaged in espionage and sabotage in Egypt. This "Unfortunate Affair," mentioned earlier in connection with the scandal that led to the removal of Minister of Defense Pinhas Lavon, began when an Israeli agent, Aubrey Elad, was sent to Egypt. Elad had operated successfully as a lone wolf and had even established himself as a house-guest of a German-born Egyptian military advisor. IDF Intelligence hatched a profoundly misguided plan which would make use of Elad to help sour American-Egyptian relations. The plan involved a network of Alexandrian and Cairo Jews who attacked the U.S.I.A. Central Library and the American Consulate, hoping to provoke the Americans into severing relations with Cairo. The plan was amateurish and the entire network, with the exception of Elad, was captured.

An investigation into the matter in Israel revealed that the operation had not been properly authorized. When details of the affair were exposed, a number of senior members of IDF Intelligence forged letters and orders and instructed Elad to falsify his testimony in the inquiry. Pinhas Lavon became the fall-guy and Elad, released from service, went to Germany. Elad was eventually sentenced to twelve years imprisonment for retaining classified documents and establishing contact with Egyptian agents in Europe. There is still much that is not known about the "Unfortunate Affair" and Elad's role in the whole matter, but there are suspicions that Elad was a double agent for Egypt.

Fighting Terror

The 1970s brought IDF Intelligence new tasks and new problems. The terrorist organizations extended their activities against Israeli and Jewish targets throughout the world. Intelligence warfare spread beyond the Middle East.

פטפוט
מספק
למטרת לאויב
!

בטחון שדה

A Palestinian guerrilla carrying a 20mm artillery piece, near Mt. Hermon on the Israeli-Lebanese border. [Ha'aretz]

Rare photo of Black September leader Salah Halaf, also known as Abu Ayad.

Israeli embassies and institutions everywhere became targets for such groups as Black September. Israeli delegations and even tourists were threatened. The Munich Olympics murders are a tragic example of the danger posed by the fedayeen. In the battle against worldwide Arab terrorism, IDF Intelligence shared the responsibility with Mosad, Shin Bet and the Intelligence services of European countries.

As the Arab-Israeli conflict continues, IDF Intelligence must employ increasingly sophisticated techniques and equipment for espionage and counterespionage. The errors of the past must be studied and each new development must be analyzed with an eye toward staying on top of the Mideast situation and, wherever possible, turning it to Israel's advantage.

Footnotes
1 George Issa in *El-Sabua el Araby*, 25 October 1971.
2 *Al Ahram*, 1967.

9. PRELUDE TO THE SIX-DAY WAR

Opposite: May 1967—Nasser threatens total war in the event of any Israeli aggression [UPI] and (below) Nasser and Egyptian Chief of Staff Amer after closing the Straits of Tiran.

Egyptian Vice President Marshal Amer visits Aleksei Kosygin in Moscow, 1966. [Wide World]

June 1967: The Russians at the United Nations. Aleksei Kosygin is greeted by Secretary General Thant as Foreign Minister Andrei Gromyko (center) looks on. [Authenticated News]

The warriors saw with their own eyes, not only the glory of victory, but also its price. I know that the terrible price paid by the enemy also struck deep into their hearts. The Jewish people were not educated nor accustomed to feeling the joy of the victor and conqueror, and this thing was therefore received with mixed feelings.

—Chief of Staff Lt. Gen. Yitzhak Rabin upon receiving an honorary degree from the Hebrew University, Mount Scopus, June 1967.

The Soviet Union in Arab Politics

On March 29, 1967, Soviet Foreign Minister Andrei Gromyko arrived in Cairo for talks with the Egyptian leadership. Gromyko had accompanied Premier Aleksei Kosygin when he had visited Egypt the previous summer and now had returned alone for a four-day visit. Israel wondered why.

No official statement was released about the Russian's discussions with Egyptian officials, but the Yugoslav press agency reported a detail which, though significant, went unnoticed at the time. "Gromyko discussed with his Egyptian host," the agency report stated, "the future of the United Nations Emergency Force stationed on the Egyptian-Israeli border."[1]

On the face of it, the report made little sense. Why should the Soviet Foreign Minister bother with such a marginal subject? Many months later, when the Soviet Union's role in the Six-Day War became clear, that detail suddenly took on importance. Today, various Western Intelligence services are convinced that it was during Gromyko's March visit to Cairo that the Soviet-inspired strategy of pressure on Israel preceding the Six-Day War was planned.

Soviet participation in the political life of the Arab bloc has its origins in Moscow's global strategy. The Russians were interested in preserving Nasser's regime as a Soviet sphere of influence. The Soviet Union manipulated Nasser into a game of brinksmanship with Israel. The Soviet risk was calculated and included the possibility of a limited, short-term war. It certainly did *not* anticipate the debacle subsequently suffered by the Arabs.

The Kremlin believed that bringing Egypt into confrontation with Israel would underscore Nasser's dependence on his Soviet ally. For his part, the Egyptian President seized the opportunity to revamp his image as leader of the Arab world by facing down Israel. He did *not* want war and was, reliable information suggests, quite surprised by the inexorable speed of the sequence of events he touched off when

Soviet Foreign Minister Andrei Gromyko.
[Authenticated News]

Bottom: Abdel Hamid Nasser, the Egyptian
President's sixteen-year-old son, at rifle
practice, May 1967. [UPI]

he blockaded the Straits of Tiran and called
for the withdrawal of the United Nations Emergency Force from Sinai. Nasser was a trapped
actor in history, a victim of his own rhetoric
and militance. The time had come for him to
pay the piper or relinquish his crown as the
unifying spirit of the Arab world. Nasser also
brought disaster for King Hussein of Jordan by
entangling him in his dangerous plan. Hussein
was actually co-opted and drawn into a war
which resulted in the loss of a large portion of
his kingdom.

The Soviet Middle East plan hinged on fabricated reports that Israel was concentrating
forces against Syria—a Russian bluff that precipitated the war and resulted in far-reaching
changes in the Middle East.

In the early spring of 1967, the Kremlin was
concerned about the extremism of the left wing
of the Socialist Baath Party in power in Syria.
Although close relations existed between Damascus and Moscow, the latter worried about
the Syrian regime's open espousal of war
against Israel. Such blatant militance was not
part of Soviet strategy. Damascus supported
Fatah, the Palestinian terror organization, and
gave backing to its infiltration operations in
Israel. Damascus was also the driving force behind abortive plans to divert the headwaters of

the Jordan River and thereby deprive Israel of
necessary water for irrigation. It was clear
that sooner or later Israel would react forcefully against Syrian provocation.

The Soviet Union did not, however, even try
to restrain Damascus, either because it believed
such an attempt could not succeed or because it
feared that such action would irritate relations
between the two countries. Instead of curbing
Damascus, Moscow sought to prevent Israel
from reacting to Syria's meddling. The Russians created a web of pressures and threats
designed to persuade Israel that if action were
taken against Syria the result would be total
war with the Arabs who enjoyed Russia's pa-
tronage.

The Soviet policy of consolidating her sphere
of influence in the Arab crescent and the Mediterranean basin was thus being implemented.
The continuation, without interference, of the
status quo of no-peace, no-war between Israel
and the Arabs was essential to the Soviet design. War in the region would undermine the
consolidation effort and strengthen American
influence anew.

Israel's irritation over Syrian intransigence
increased. Her entreaties to the United Nations Security Council went unanswered,
thanks to the Soviet veto. The Israeli Chief of
Staff, Lt. Gen. Yitzhak Rabin, declared finally
that Israel would have to act against the Damascus regime because of its support of saboteurs and infiltrators who attacked Israeli settlements and irrigation installations.

In response, the Kremlin dispensed with the
usual diplomatic notes warning Israel against
operations on the Syrian front and devised instead a more dramatic deterrent: They decided
to demonstrate the validity of existing Egypt-
ian-Syrian mutual defense agreements. Gromyko's mysterious March visit marked the implementation of that deterrent. He arrived in Cairo
with a plan for concentrating *Egyptian* forces
on Israel's southern border in response to Is-

Eric Johnston, the American special ambassador who devised the 1954 plan for diversion of the waters of the Jordan River, the Pandora's box that held at its bottom the Six-Day War.

rael's alleged threat to *Syria*. President Nasser of Egypt, persuaded to come to Syria's defense, demanded the removal of the UN buffer force. Subsequent events moved rapidly and unavoidably toward war.

The potential for war between Israel and the Arabs had long existed; the hostility was evident. Still, since the Israeli victory in the 1956 Suez War, the region had enjoyed a period of relative tranquility. The hostility had been primarily manifested in various declarations and occasional incidents on Israel's borders with Syria and Jordan. The frontier between Israel and Egypt had been generally quiet.

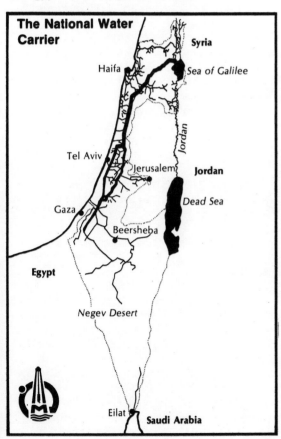

The National Water Carrier

Syria
Haifa
Sea of Galilee
Jordan
Tel Aviv
Jerusalem
Jordan
Dead Sea
Gaza
Beersheba
Egypt
Negev Desert
Eilat
Saudi Arabia

Summer 1961: The Issue Is Water

A Pandora's Box was opened in 1953 and the Six-Day War lurked at its bottom. Israel had first tried to divert part of the Jordan waters to the Negev in 1953, but under pressure from the United States she had been obliged to postpone the plan. President Eisenhower had sent Eric Johnston as special ambassador to the region. Johnston's mission was to formulate a plan for the division of water resources between Israel and the riparian Arab countries, and to coordinate the development programs to be financed for the most part by American aid.

In 1954, Johnston submitted his plan in which Israel's share of the Jordan waters was allocated. Israel felt discriminated against by the Johnston scheme. Jordan, however, was satisfied and King Hussein began to implement the plan by diverting waters from the Yarmuk River that flows into the Jordan. In response, Israel announced plans for a National Water Carrier to pump water from the Sea of Galilee to the arid Negev, but said she would not pump more from the Jordan than had been allocated by Johnston. In June 1961, the Arab Defense Council declared that the project would compel united Arab military action against Israel. As the construction of Israel's project continued, Nasser realized he was not prepared for the war he perpetually promised the Arabs. To forestall the storm of protest Nasser anticipated in response to the Israeli accomplishment, Egypt conceived a new scheme: Instead of attacking Israeli pumping stations, the Arabs would themselves divert the Jordan's sources. In this way, Nasser believed, the onus would be on Israel to retaliate. Nasser convened the first Arab summit conference in January 1964 to discuss the overall conflict with Israel and to unite the Arab states behind his scheme of provocation. Resolutions were passed to divert the Jordan sources located in Arab states; to establish a Joint Arab Command to defend diversionary operations; and, in a bid to assuage

Chief of Staff Tzvi Tzur, 1961-1964. [Israeli Army]
Bottom: Section of the National Water Carrier, between the Jordan River and the Sea of Galilee.

Palestinian agitation, to create the Palestine Liberation Organization.

Provocation and Retaliation

When Israel, in the face of Arab declarations, activated the irrigation project in June 1964, Palestinian extremists, convinced that neither Israel nor the Arab states wanted war, realized that they themselves would have to escalate tension to the point of war in order to liberate what they claimed was their homeland. In early 1965, Fatah, one of the first fedayeen groups, began sabotage activities in Israel.

Yasir Arafat, head of Fatah, soon found a patron in Syria. The Damascus regime, in constant conflict with Nasser, was anxious to prove that it was the sole defender of Arab interests and the champion of the Palestinians. Damascus promoted the notion of a "popular war" against Israel and gave its total support to the new fedayeen organization. At the same time, the Syrians were the only ones to continue di-

version of the Jordan River's sources. Israel reacted with determined military attacks, using both artillery and aerial bombardment against the ambitious Arab hydraulic scheme. Armed clashes grew steadily worse.

On April 7, 1967, a major aerial battle took place between Israeli and Syrian jets. The Syrian defeat was absolute. Seven of their Soviet-made MIG aircraft were shot down and in the course of the sky battle Israel's French-manufactured Mirages circled over Damascus. In response, Arab guerrillas from Syria mined the main northern road in Israel, and Fatah, whose headquarters were in the Syrian capital, bombarded with mortars an Israeli settlement on the Lebanese border. An Arab captured close to the Syrian border confessed to his interrogators that the Syrians had sent him to plant explosives in public places timed to go off during the May 15 Israeli Independence Day celebrations.

The downing of the Syrian MIGs and the

An Israeli soldier searches captured fedayeen.
[Zeev Schiff]

penetration of Israeli aircraft as far as Damascus infuriated Nasser. A few months earlier, on November 13, 1966, he had been censured for not sending help to Jordan. At that time, an Israeli armored force had invaded the Jordanian village of Samua and demolished forty houses in reprisal for the activities of Fatah members from the same village. The contingency plans of the Joint Arab Command called for the Egyptian Air Force to aid the Jordanians in their southern territories whenever so requested. At the time of the Samua attack, Jordan had asked in vain for Egyptian assistance. That story repeated itself following the April 7 aerial battle. The Egyptians, reluctant to engage in battle until they felt ready, contended that Damascus had not asked for assistance. Nevertheless, it was becoming clear to Nasser that his credibility in the Arab world would be seriously diminished unless he made some show of action. It was thus that he put

Gromyko's plan into effect.

Nasser was ostensibly able to justify belligerent action with false information provided by Soviet military Intelligence. The reports claimed that Israel intended to attack Syria on May 17 and that she had already massed troops along the Syrian frontier. Following the April 7 air battle, Radio Moscow's Arabic service added further fuel to the fire by broadcasting the following fictitious dispatch: "American pilots participated in the aerial battle on Israel's side and one of them was taken prisoner by the Syrians when his plane was shot down."

Yet another element in the big bluff was next introduced. With the intent of whipping up a folk frenzy among the Arabs, the Russians announced that Israel was planning a "gas attack on Syria with the assistance of West German experts." The Big Lie technique was escalating in accordance with the scheme of Soviet Intelligence and experts in psychological warfare. Writing in the New York Times, June 23, 1967, James Reston called it the "biggest fish story since Jonah and the whale."

Israel tried to combat the Russian campaign of false propaganda. Premier Levi Eshkol invited the Russian Ambassador in Tel Aviv to visit the border area himself but was refused. Israel then invited UN observers to check the Russian claim and UN Secretary General U Thant announced that as far as he was informed by the observers' reports there were no Israeli military concentrations on the Syrian frontier. Nonetheless, the situation continued to deteriorate and even Eshkol's assurances, communicated to Nasser through intermediaries, that Israel was not massing forces on her border with Syria did not help. Nasser apparently was convinced that Israel was hesitant and weak and that he could safely risk a show of military determination.

The itineraries of several prominent Egyptians during this period held clues to the ur-

Emblem of the Artillery Corps.

gency of the situation but it is doubtful that Israeli Intelligence correctly assessed them. Meetings of the Egyptian General Staff took place frequently. On May 3, the Egyptian Premier, Sudki Suleiman, and the Egyptian Air Force Chief, Mahmoud Sidki, took off for Damascus. On May 14, the Egyptian Chief of Staff Mahmoud Fawzi also left for Damascus, and that same day in Cairo the order for mobilization was given. Yet during this same period, Israeli Chief of Staff Rabin paid a short visit to England. Apparently the Israeli command did not realize in the early part of May that the Egyptian war machine, lacking both brakes and a steering wheel, had been set into motion.

As details of Egyptian strategy and tactics have emerged in the years since the war, Nasser's behavior is better understood. He apparently wanted to prove to the Arab world that he was powerful, but at the same time he believed he could stop short of an all-out war. He reasoned that the entry of the Egyptian Army into the Sinai Peninsula might deter Israel if she really intended to attack Syria, as Egypt's Soviet-guided Intelligence seemed to think was the case. And if it turned out that Israel did not attack, Nasser would have achieved a victory by virtue of his deterrent power. Concentrating the Egyptian Army on the frontier, Nasser believed, would strain Israel's defense capacities. If she did attack, she would have to restrict herself to small-scale operations, whereupon Egypt could react immediately in force and prove herself to the Arab nations.

Nasser had carried out a similar maneuver in the past; why should he not succeed a second time? On February 18, 1960, Egypt had moved three divisions, including one armored, into Sinai. They had deployed near the frontier, with the purpose of restraining Israel from attacking Syria. In those days the atmosphere at the border between Israel and Syria was potentially explosive—Syrian Army provocations and Israeli reprisals were rife. But neither side

wanted war. Israel had responded coolly to Egypt's maneuver and Nasser, satisfied that his show of muscle had been sufficient to save face, had ordered his units to return to their previous stations west of Suez.

Faulty Soviet Intelligence

What happened in February 1960 could not in fact be repeated in May 1967. A number of things had changed. Both Russian and Egyptian Intelligence services assumed that the Israel of 1967, led by Levi Eshkol, was weaker than the Israel of 1960 under David Ben-Gurion. They assumed there was a reasonable chance

Israel: Frontiers and Distances

Lebanon

Safed
←31 miles→

Haifa

←11→

Natania
←9→

Tel Aviv
←15→

Mediterranean Sea

Jerusalem

Gaza Strip
←22 miles→

Beersheba
←65 miles→

Syria

Jordan

Jordan

Dead Sea

Egypt

Sinai Peninsula

←34 miles→

Length of Borders of Enemy Territory:

Lebanon: 49 miles
Syria: 47 miles
Jordan: 330 miles
Egypt: 128 miles
Gaza Strip: 37 miles

←7←

Golda Meir greets Soviet Ambassador Dimitri Zhubakhin.

to pressure Israel into making significant concessions by deploying troops along her borders.

The architect of this concept of Israeli weakness was the Soviet Ambassador to Israel, Dimitri Zhubakhin, a KGB officer. His reports, more than anything else, produced a picture of an Israel which, although militarily strengthened over the years, was unstable. On the face of it, Zhubakhin had reasons for his assessment. For two years Israel had been in the throes of an economic recession and the general atmosphere was troubled. The ruling labor party was torn by squabbles and the leadership of Eshkol, who had succeeded Ben-Gurion, was in doubt. It was easy to conclude that Eshkol's government, even with a strong army, could be easily intimidated, brought to panic and ultimately to far-reaching concessions.

It was a facile conclusion but a faulty one and represented a serious error of Soviet Intelligence, which, in turn, misled Egyptian Intelligence. (Zhubakhin was punished for his incompetence. After the Six-Day War, he returned to his country to be deprived of his high position in the KGB and the Foreign Service.) The Soviet evaluation was superficial because it failed to take into account the social and spiritual background of Israel. The Russians did not understand that just as a strong man like Ben-Gurion could impose his will on the Army, a weak leader like Eshkol, faced with domestic problems, was likely to take drastic steps to assert his political leadership.

The flaw in the Russian plan was its foundation: the mistaken assumption that Israel would react to all Egyptian moves exactly as the Russians and Egyptians wanted. No other possible reaction was taken into account. The condition for success of the Russian plan was that Israel would not open fire.

Egyptian Intelligence was partner to these mistakes and added some serious errors of its own. It underestimated the military power and ability of Israel, most gravely in its assessment

of the "first-strike" potential of the Israeli Air Force. The Egyptian General Staff assumed that even if Israel were to start a war, Egypt could easily recover from the opening strike, and deliver the second and decisive blow.

Israeli Intelligence also made mistakes, but luckily for Israel, they were errors of overassessment. After the 1956 Sinai War, there had been social progress in Egypt: Universities had opened and the number of students grew rapidly; Egyptian industry had also developed at an impressive pace. A new military doctrine was instituted based on Soviet concepts of warfare especially suited to an army with massive resources of uneducated manpower. Israeli analysts tended to overemphasize these developments and concluded that the gap in quality of military manpower between Israel and Egypt had narrowed since the 1956 war. Israel also overestimated the value of the contributions made by foreign military experts who had been instructing the Egyptian Army.

Shoulder badge of the Armor Corps.

It was only natural and certainly seemed logical to be impressed by the quantities of armaments flowing to Egypt from the Soviet Union. This new weaponry was rated as though it were in the hands of a more advanced army than that which was defeated in Sinai and Gaza in 1956.

May 15, 1967: Troop Buildup

The Six-Day War, the third major conflict between Israel and the Arabs, broke out because, in a deteriorating political situation, both sides lost control of events. Events precipitated decisions instead of the other way around. It was a war which neither side really wanted: Nasser, whose army was largely bogged down in Yemen, was drawn into a policy of threats and hoped to defeat Israel without a fight; Israel hoped to prevent war and did not expect 1967 to be a year of total conflict. Her Intelligence evaluations indicated that 1967 would be a relatively quiet year and that

the Egyptians were building up their strength for war in 1970.

On May 15, Israel's Independence Day, the phase known in Israel as "the waiting period" began. It lasted twenty-one days and during that time the UN and the Super Powers displayed total helplessness. A situation leading to war developed before their very eyes but they could do nothing to prevent it.

On May 15, the semi-official Egyptian newspaper, *Al Ahram,* published a terse report: "In accordance with the defense pact between Egypt and Syria appropriate measures have been taken in the light of the concentration of Israeli forces close to the border." The appropriate measures referred to was the mobilization of Egyptian forces into the Sinai Peninsula.

That afternoon a modest military display was held in a stadium in Jerusalem. Before the standard-bearers entered the stadium, General Rabin told Eshkol, who at the time held the portfolio of Defense Minister as well as the premiership, that information had been received that an Egyptian division had begun to cross the Suez Canal bridges into Sinai.

At the same hour, a parade of a different kind was taking place in the Gaza Strip. Hundreds of Palestinian fighters passed in review in front of a wooden platform where Ahmed Shukairy, head of the Palestine Liberation Organization, was sitting with the Communist Chinese Ambassador to Egypt and an Egyptian general, Munaim Husseini. (Husseini was to sign the surrender of Egyptian forces in the Gaza Strip a few weeks thence.)

The Egyptian troop buildup in Sinai was carried out in unmilitary openness, rather like a parade intended to attract attention. Egyptian propaganda offices distributed photos of tanks crossing over the Nile and Suez bridges; armored columns moved through Cairo's streets in broad daylight. It seemed that the Egyptians were trying to raise their own morale and pres-

The Strength of Middle East Armies (Regular Troops) 1966-1967

10,000 men

Egyptian Gen. Abdul Moneim Riad. [Wide World]

Bottom: Saudi Arabian King Faisal conferring with U Thant at the UN. [Authenticated News]

tige in the Arab world.

On the second day of troop movement into Sinai there were still those in Israel who were convinced that it was no more than a show of force. Nevertheless, Israel cautiously decided to mobilize an armored reserve brigade.

UN Troops Withdraw

On the evening of May 16, Nasser made a move which was to set off a chain reaction that inevitably led to war. The Egyptian Chief of Staff sent a message to the UN Emergency Force Commander in the Gaza Strip and Sinai, the Indian General Rikiah, in which he requested withdrawal of the UN forces from the border area.

For years Nasser's opponents in the Arab world had contended he was hiding behind the international peace-keeping troops. Even within the Egyptian Army, senior officers had suggested more than once to Nasser that he demand withdrawal of the UN troops. By sending the message to General Rikiah, Nasser evidently wanted to prove that he would not recoil from war with Israel. The demand was not at first for total withdrawal. Rather, the UN troops were requested to be stationed in three places only—the Gaza Strip, Quantilla on the

Israel-Sinai border, and Sharm-el-Sheikh, the outpost commanding the Straits of Tiran at the entrance to the Gulf of Aqaba.

On the advice of his assistant, Ralph Bunche, who was known to be conversant in Middle East affairs, U Thant committed a monumental blunder. Without conferring with member nations he replied, "All or nothing. The United Nations is not prepared for partial withdrawal of its forces. Either they stay where they are or there will be total withdrawal."

This public response challenged Nasser's pride and forced his hand. The Egyptian ruler felt he had no alternative but to demand total withdrawal. Thant's action was precipitous; he took seriously and acted on a request that Egypt only intended as a gesture. He was thus responsible for bringing a volatile situation to the point of no return.

In Syria, military preparations were noticeable and troop movements took place in Jordan. Two armored brigades that had been stationed far from the Israeli frontier were moved in from the desert. The Israeli command perceived a serious danger in the stationing of Jordanian tanks close to particularly vulnerable borders. The United States had been aware of this danger. When it gave modern tanks to Jordan it stipulated that they be kept far from the Israeli border.

The Straits of Tiran Are Closed

As soon as the UN force withdrew, Egyptian troops took their place in large numbers. The UN flag was lowered in the Gaza Strip and soldiers of the PLO moved into position. The Egyptian High Command began to pour every available unit into Sinai. Instructions were sent to Yemen to return men and equipment to Egypt quickly. In fact, Egyptian preparations were so hasty that tanks were brought to Sinai on their own tracks rather than on tank transporters. Thus the engines were needlessly taxed and es-

Emblem of the Armor Corps.

sential parts worn down during the long trip. Armored battle readiness and operational efficiency were reduced to a minimum.

The Israeli government began to ponder strategic and Intelligence evaluations. If no one had foreseen Nasser's action in Sinai, how accurate were the evaluations concerning the ratio of forces? This and other questions preoccupied Israeli strategists. Their attention was drawn to the Straits of Tiran, the narrow water passage through which oil tankers passed en route to the Israeli port of Eilat at the mouth of the Gulf of Aqaba.

On May 20, the Egyptians had dropped an airborne battalion at Sharm-el-Sheikh to replace a Yugoslav UN contingent. Israel wondered if Nasser would next block the Straits to Israeli shipping or if he would be satisfied with the threat implied by Egyptian presence at the strategic spot. He chose the former course. As he had done in the matter of the withdrawal of UN troops, Nasser again gave in to external pressures and the demands of pride regarding the Straits. Jordanian radio, which might have been expected to espouse a moderate view in order to preserve the region's tranquility, began to call on Egypt to close the Straits. "Nasser would not dare do so," the Jordanians taunted publicly. Nasser responded with a blockade that saved face but precipitated war.

Had he not blockaded the Straits he could have avoided war while at the same time exerting pressure on Israel. Concentration of forces in Sinai, however menacing, would not have sufficed to raise a majority in the Israeli Cabinet in favor of going to war. Israel would certainly not have received international support for a war over troop buildups in Sinai. But the Egyptian blockade was seen as a *casus belli*, a reason to go to war that would be at least understood by many nations, if not directly supported.

On May 22, Nasser, his deputy and his army commanders went to visit the units in Sinai. By that time, some 70,000 soldiers and hundreds of tanks and artillery pieces were lined up in the vast desert peninsula. At the forward air bases newly assigned fighter squadrons augmented the existing air wings. The initiative was entirely in Egypt's hands. Israel waited.

Cairo began to speak of its "rights" over the Gulf of Aqaba. At an army camp in Sinai, in the presence of troops as well as pilots and senior military commanders, Nasser announced the closing of the Straits of Tiran to Israeli shipping. "Israel does not today have Britain and France as she did in 1956. We stand face to face with Israel. The Jews threaten war and we say to them, *Ahalan wasahalan!* (Welcome! Come forth!)"

The official photo (p. 140) of the May 22 declaration shows Nasser and his deputy, Marshal Amer, laughing. The photo was carried in the Israeli press and had a profoundly shocking effect.

A few hours before the morning papers hit the street on May 23, Prime Minister Levi Eshkol was awakened and told of the blockade. Israel was forced to confront the reality of war. The Arabs had not taken seriously Israeli declarations that a blockade in the Straits of Tiran would mean armed conflict. Nasser was scornful of the commitment given Israel eleven years earlier by the United States that freedom of navigation of the Straits would be protected. The Egyptians understood that closing the Straits was provocative but perhaps they hoped for a compromise. It is possible they sought to humiliate Israel but to stop short of fighting. Nevertheless, on May 26, Mohammed Hassanin Heykal wrote in his paper, *Al Ahram:* "There is no alternative to armed clash between the United Arab Republic and the Israeli enemy. . . . In Israel's defense philosophy the blocking of the Straits is the Achilles' Heel on which Israel's existence depends."

British Prime Minister Harold Wilson—
"Any action on the part of Great Britain is conditional
on the United States and other nations."
[Authenticated News]

Bottom: May 28, 1967—Soldiers of the Palestine
Liberation Army at a former UN outpost on the
Egyptian-Israeli border. [UPI]

The Allies Desert

Discouraging signs came from the world
capitals. In London and Paris announcements
were made that the Great Powers Declaration
of 1950 guaranteeing peace in the Mideast was
no longer binding. International guarantees of
freedom of shipping turned out to be meaning-
less as well. Israel's isolation increased daily.
In Bonn, a West German government spokesman said that since his government was not a
member of the United Nations the closing of
the Straits of Tiran to shipping did not concern
it. France, considered a good friend of Israel,
said the question of shipping in the Straits was
a complicated international legal matter and
declined to endorse Israel's right of unimpeded
navigation.

Foreign Minister Abba Eban left Israel on a
mission to seek international sympathy and
support for Israel's position as a means of preventing war in the Mideast. He was to meet

Charles de Gaulle, Harold Wilson and Lyndon
Johnson. The results of these meetings recon-
firmed Israel's isolation and convinced her it
was necessary to take matters into her own
hands.

Eban was given a lesson in the value of international guarantees during his meeting with
de Gaulle. France, more than any other Western
country, was tied by commitments to Israel. A
few years earlier, during Ben-Gurion's visit to
Paris, de Gaulle had ceremoniously declared,
"Israel is our friend and ally." When he came
to collect on this promissory note, Eban was
told by de Gaulle that international circumstances had changed since France first committed herself to Israel's well-being. Israel had to
understand that no guarantee is eternal. De
Gaulle suggesting putting the matter into the
hands of the four Great Powers. The plan was
self-serving since it would permit France to
enter the exclusive club of Super Powers and

French President Charles de Gaulle—"Don't make war. Don't be the first to shoot."

Bottom left: Foreign Minister Abba Eban returning to Israel after his eleventh-hour quest for support from Israel's allies.

Bottom right: David Ben-Gurion visits an IDF base on the eve of the Six-Day War. [Israeli Army]

to play a role in the affairs of other nations. The condition for this arrangement, however, was that the dispute not deteriorate into war, for then France and England would be forced off the panel of "judges" and the United States and the Soviet Union would become the sole arbiters of the conflict. De Gaulle felt he could ask Israel, whom he had aided in the past, to assist him in this plan, even if it were at the expense of her own vital interests. After expressing doubts over Israel's prospects for victory, de Gaulle cautioned Eban, "Don't make war. Don't be the first to shoot."

De Gaulle was not content merely to give advice. He suspected that Israel was not ready to relinquish her legitimate rights of defense for the sake of the French leader's personal ambitions. So, on June 3, two days before war broke out, France imposed an arms embargo on the Middle East. Inasmuch as Israel was the chief buyer of French weapons and the Arabs

were generously supplied by the Russians, the embargo worked to Israel's detriment. Most of Israel's armaments and her entire air force were based on French supply and Jerusalem regarded the embargo as an act of treachery and a threat to her existence.

Eban found the meeting with Harold Wilson more cordial. But the British Prime Minister made it clear that any action on the part of Britain was conditional on the steps taken by the United States and other nations.

The crucial talk took place in Washington. The United States did not deny its commitment to freedom of shipping in the Straits of Tiran but, American sympathy notwithstanding, it soon was clear that Israel would have to stand alone in a military conflict. All Israel could achieve in Washington was a promise that the Russians would be restrained and the United States would remain neutral in the event of war. This was a significant and reas-

May 1967: Egyptian troops dig in at a front-line position near the Israeli border. [UPI]

Bottom: A Cairo poster on the eve of the Six-Day War depicting an Israeli in a stars-and-stripes hat being crushed by an Arab boot. It reads: "With armed force we shall thwart conspiracies of American imperialism and Zionism." [UPI]

suring promise in view of Washington's position during the 1956 Sinai War. At that time, President Eisenhower had joined the Russians in pressuring Israel to withdraw from the Sinai Peninsula.

President Johnson asked Israel to wait until an international naval force could be established to run the blockade. Few in Israel believed in the chances of such an effort succeeding and some even saw danger in the proposal. Israel could not, they contended, live on the benevolence of other countries who were already formulating compromise measures such as lifting the blockade on the condition that ships flying the Israeli flag would not navigate the Straits. There were those in the United States who proposed reaching an agreement under which Israel's losses resulting from the increased cost of transporting fuel and other commodities through Mediterranean ports instead of Eilat would be covered by the United States. Israel dismissed this as unrealistic.

The sea blockade remained a provocative, warlike act but it was eclipsed momentarily by another, more immediate threat developing in Sinai where some 100,000 Egyptian soldiers and 1,000 tanks were concentrated menacingly near the Israeli border. Token forces from Algeria, Sudan and Kuwait had also arrived in Egypt.

In response to the Arab buildup, Israel mobilized most of her reserve army. Some industries shut down and others shifted to lower production. The country could not long remain in such a state—if war did not break out Israel would be hurt economically, but as long as Egyptian units were deployed on the border threatening imminent attack, it would be dangerous to release the reserve units.

While Eban was in Washington, he received a cable from Israel describing the Egyptian troop concentrations and the possibility of a sudden Egyptian attack. The cable asked Eban to examine possibilities of receiving American

aid in the event of an Egyptian attack. Rabin has subsequently described this cable as follows:

After the closing of the Straits, in order to examine where Israel stood and to what degree she need not depend solely on herself, the late Director General of the Prime Minister's Office [Yaakov Herzog] suggested in a conversation with me that he send a cable to the Foreign Minister, then in Washington, in which we would state that according to information in our hands there was likely to be aggressive initiative on the part of the Egyptians. It was to be incumbent on the Foreign Minister to clarify

Prime Minister Levi Eshkol.

to what extent the United States would maintain commitments given in the past to Israeli leaders concerning positive assistance in such an event. The Prime Minister, Levi Eshkol, was finally convinced that this cable was essential to clarify for ourselves to what extent we were isolated, and to what extent responsibility for the continued existence of Israel was placed solely on our shoulders without any outside assistance. The purpose of the cable was not military, but to clarify definitively that Israel was alone in her fate and to establish the basis for an independent decision. [2]

So directed, Eban asked the American President to spell out his country's commitment. The import of Johnson's reply to Eban, later confirmed by highly placed American sources, was, "You are by yourselves! You are responsible for your fate!"

The Brink of War

Israeli representatives heard that the Pentagon's Intelligence appraisal was that Israel would defeat the Egyptians. The Chairman of the Joint Chiefs of Staff, Gen. Earl Wheeler, told Eban that the threatening massing of Egyptian troops in Sinai was a "serious matter," but that in his view Israel would be victorious in any circumstance. Even if the Egyptian Air Force were to attack first, Wheeler said, Israel would eventually prevail.

As it turned out, the American Intelligence evaluation was correct, while the Russians and the French, as well as most military commentators, were wrong in their estimates. To a large extent, the American evaluation was even more exact than Israel's.

The Israeli government was having difficulty reaching a decision to go to war. Upon Eban's return on May 27, the Cabinet was divided nine against nine over going to war. The following day, the government decided to accede to President Johnson's request that Israel wait until it became possible to organize an international convoy to run the sea blockade.

Meanwhile, Nasser became more audacious. He told Egyptians that the coming war would be "total" and that Egypt's primary objective was the "destruction of Israel." At a news conference he said Israel would have to withdraw from Eilat and from Nitzana, an Israeli settlement on the Egyptian border. Shortly thereafter, in an act affirming Nasser's proclamation, Palestinian forces bombarded an Israeli settlement near Gaza.

In Israel, a feeling of imminent extermination was growing. A large number of Israel's citizens had come from Nazi death camps of the Second World War and others had been taught from infancy of the terrible tragedy that overcame European Jewry while none lifted a finger to help. A rope was once again around the necks of the Jewish people, but this time it was

The IDF escalates its preparations for war: Israeli commando unit in practice raid [Israeli Army] and (below) infantry unit marches toward its battle position [UPI].

felt something would have to be done immediately and forcefully without waiting for the rest of the world. Israelis were angry with their hesitant and muddle-minded government. Pressure mounted to remove Eshkol because of his indecisiveness. Criticism came from all sides, including Mapai, Eshkol's own party.

The late David Ben-Gurion, then a former Prime Minister in semi-retirement, told Rabin that in the current situation it would be better for Israel to forego any idea of war. Without the support of one of the Super Powers, Ben-Gurion said, Israel should not go to war. He criticized Rabin for mobilizing the reserves, which he said could lead to war.

Meanwhile factionalsim within the Arab bloc was coming to a head. The most significant conflict existed between Egypt and Jordan, whose proximity to Israel engendered an ambiguous position vis-à-vis united Arab interests. King Hussein was not anxious to fight but

Below: Egyptian President Nasser greets Jordan's King Hussein in Cairo. [Wide World]

Marshal Amer greets commander of the eastern front during his mid-May inspection tour of advance posts along the Egyptian-Israeli border. [UPI]

Bottom: Two lions doze peacefully at the feet of their royal master. They were captured by Hussein personally during a hunting trip in Ethiopia.

Israel's indecisiveness disturbed him. More than Israel, Hussein feared Nasser's designs on his kingdom. Uninvited, Hussein flew his private plane to Cairo in a desperate attempt to come to an understanding with the Egyptian leader.

Hussein's Chief of Staff had just been rebuffed by the Egyptian leadership and Hussein concluded he had no choice but to humble himself. For years the young King had been maligned by Egypt as an enemy of the Arabs and a friend of Israel. Nasserist agents continually worked to subvert the Palestinian middle class in Jordan against Hashemite rule. It was not easy for Hussein to swallow his pride and show up in Cairo hoping for an audience with Nasser. The latter was quick to exploit the situation and signed a joint military pact with the King that provided for an Egyptian general, Abdul Moneim Riad, to assume command of the Jordanian Army. As an added insult, Nasser sent

Emblems of the Signal Corps and the Engineer Corps.

Ahmed Shukairy, head of PLO, back to Amman on Hussein's plane. For years Shukairy had been calling Hussein an enemy of the Palestinian people and had urged his deposition.

Soon Egyptian commando units were flown to Jordan and worrisome information came from Iraq. Iraqi fighter aircraft were deployed to airfields close to the Jordanian border and Iraqi infantry units began to move into Jordan.

June 1, 1967: Israel Takes the Initiative

The camel's back had been broken. Israel's border with Jordan was its longest and most sensitive because it was within reach of many strategically important targets. From this border it was possible to bombard Jerusalem, Tel Aviv and most Israeli airfields. Over the years, Israel had contended that she would never tolerate a foreign army in Jordan. When it was reported that Iraqi and Egyptian units were en route to Jordan, a tense situation became a national crisis.

Discord among Israel's political and military leaders was acute. In meetings between Prime Minister and Defense Minister Eshkol and other cabinet ministers and generals of the General Staff there was a breakdown of communication. The generals accused the government of lacking a clear plan and of losing the initiative through hesitation. They pressed for immediate war since every delay could only increase eventual losses.

They finally prevailed. On June 1, a "National Unity" government was established. Three new ministers from opposition parties were added to the Cabinet, including Moshe Dayan, who was appointed Minister of Defense, replacing Eshkol in that post. The nation was ready for war. Dayan visited the front lines and reviewed the carefully drawn battle plans. The time of hesitation and muddling was over.

The Russians, too, sensed that the moment of decision had come. A few nights before the war began, the Soviet Ambassador insisted on waking Eshkol. At three in the morning the Prime Minister, dressed in his pajamas, received Zhubakhin, who gave him a Soviet note warning against going to war. Zhubakhin then asked diffidently, "Will you be the first to open fire?" Eshkol, alluding to the blockade of the Straits of Tiran, answered tersely, "The Egyptians have already opened fire."[3]

An Israeli emissary left for Washington. His orders were to clarify, once and for all, the chances of American assistance and to ascertain whether there was any point in additional delay. He cabled from Washington that there was no purpose in waiting any longer. The United States no longer believed in the possibility of serious international action. So far, such action had been limited to a joint declaration by the United States and Great Britain on the principle of the freedom of shipping. In Jerusalem it was felt that if Israel did not act quickly, the Americans were likely to withdraw even their tacit support. Eban drove to army headquarters in Tel Aviv and informed the generals that diplomatic efforts had been exhausted. Now it was up to the IDF to defend the nation.

On June 4, the government decided to go to war. At 7:10 the following morning Israeli aircraft took off for targets in Egypt. Fifty-five minutes later Israeli armor crossed the border into Sinai and the Gaza Strip. The Six-Day War had begun.

Footnotes

1   Taniyug, 1 April 1967.
2   Yitzhak Rabin, in *Maariv*, 2 June 1972.
3   Previously unpublished interview between author and Adi Yaffe of Eshkol's office, 1967.

10. THE SIX-DAY WAR

Opposite: [Authenticated News]

Russian monitoring vessel in the Mediterranean at the time of the Six-Day War. [U.S. Navy]

June 1967: Foreign Intervention Is Anticipated

From the beginning, Israel's preparation for war anticipated foreign intervention of some sort, be it UN action or Soviet defense of the Arabs.

The Sinai Campaign of 1956 had taken place against a background of American-Russian collusion in which threats of economic and political sanctions were used against Israel to force a cessation of fighting and Israel's eventual withdrawal. So in June 1967 the Israeli General Staff wondered how much time they would have before similar intervention occurred.

The assumption was that the IDF would be able to act freely and forcefully for two or three days before outside restraints were imposed. The operation would, therefore, have to be mounted in such a way that most of the military achievements could be made in the first days of battle.

As the waiting period before the war lengthened, it became clear that this time there was no danger of American-Russian cooperation and that the prospect of American pressure was minimal. It was believed that, though Washington would not commend Israel on its decision to go to war, it would, after it recognized the closing of the Gulf of Aqaba as an aggressive act, maintain a neutral stance and restrain the Russians from intervening.

In the 1956 war, Russia had threatened Israel in blunt language and had even hinted that she might activate her military forces. Israel had analyzed that affair a number of times since 1956 and concluded that at the time the true danger had been exaggerated. This evaluation was expressed in the risks Israel was prepared to take in 1967.

Furthermore, the Army Command was convinced that because of the distances involved, the Russians would be unable to react quickly and efficiently. By the time they could mobilize, it was believed, conflict on the battlefield would be resolved. At worst, the Russian Navy might move some of its ships in the Mediterranean toward the coasts of Israel as a show of intent.

After the war, Israelis debated why the Soviet Union had refrained from giving direct and rapid assistance to the Arabs to prevent such a total rout. Chief of Staff Yitzhak Rabin said:

The order to the U.S. Sixth Fleet to move to the east of the Mediterranean was only given on June 10, when the war was already over. By then the Soviet Union had no chance of inter-

vening physically in the battle, other than by the use of nuclear missiles. What prevented the Russians from intervening in the war was the fact that the Arab armies were overcome rapidly, within six days. [1]

The fear of Russian intervention gave birth to Moshe Dayan's "great befuddle" plan. The assumption was that pressures on Israel would increase the moment it became clear that the IDF was victorious. By banning announcements of Israeli victories and otherwise withholding or obscuring news from the battlefronts, Dayan hoped to stave off that pressure, even if it meant causing confusion inside Israel and

Yitzhak Rabin, IDF Chief of Staff from 1964 to 1968.

among Jews and friends of Israel abroad.

The plan was assisted by the Arabs who announced victories that never in fact took place. The Arabs fell into the Israeli trap and drew the Russians in with them. It was eight hours after the Egyptian Air Force had been destroyed before Egyptian commanders notified Nasser. When Israeli forces were already deep into Sinai, the Arabs declared their conquest of Israeli areas. These announcements confused their Communist and Third World friends and even the Soviet Union. In the United Nations Security Council, the Egyptian representative vigorously opposed a proposal to declare a cease-fire, convinced that Egyptian forces were racing toward Tel Aviv. When he learned the truth several hours later, he broke into tears and agreed to an immediate cease-fire.

Israel Assesses the Enemy

Israeli war plans focused principally on the Egyptian front. IDF forces on the Syrian front and the Jordanian border were given a defensive role. There was a question whether Jordan would intervene in the war but IDF troops stood ready against that eventuality.

As the waiting period before the war stretched out, King Hussein became entangled in warlike commitments to Nasser. Egyptian commando battalions reached Jordan and an Iraqi division began to move toward that country. An Egyptian general came to Amman to coordinate military operations against Israel. Israel became concerned about these troop movements and responded with some movements of her own: The armored brigade of the Central Command was placed in reserve for a counterattack, and two armored brigades were moved up to the Northern Command, which in the south bordered on the Jordanian front. Even at the outbreak of war on the Egyptian front, the hope still prevailed that Hussein would refrain from extensive involvement.

Gen. Uzi Narkis, commander of the Central Command, said, "We assumed Hussein would make do with something like a salutatory salvo and would thereby fulfill his obligations to inter-Arab unity and the defense agreement with Egypt."[2]

Israel assumed that this time the Syrians would come to the assistance of the Egyptians, though they had not in 1956. The IDF concentrated its major effort on the Egyptian front and was prepared to deal with the other fronts if necessary during a second stage. By exploiting her relatively short communication lines, Israel was able to rapidly transfer units from one front to another, deploying them efficiently to surprise the Arabs who were stunned at the size of advancing forces not previously seen on the front.

Israeli Strategy

No prior thought was given to grabbing Arab territories and holding them. There is no better proof of this than the two chief war plans of the Israeli General Staff. The first, the "small plan," was presented to the Prime Minister in the War Room at Army Headquarters in Tel Aviv on May 23. The scope of the plan was modest and indicated a desire to fight a limited war. It reflected Israel's determination to keep casualties to a minimum.

According to this plan, Israel intended to break through into Egyptian territory at only one point, to contain the battle in northern Sinai, and to advance only as far as El Arish. While the Israeli armored units moved into the Gaza Strip and then proceeded toward El Arish, infantry was to be landed from the sea and paratroops dropped from the air. The sole objective was to overcome Palestinian units in the Gaza Strip and Egyptian forces in northern Sinai. Occupying this small amount of territory was to be a sort of countermeasure for the closing of the Gulf of Aqaba and the

Israel hung in effigy, Cairo 1967. [Tim Page]

Armored Division **Armored Brigade** **Armored Battalion**

Disposition of Egyptian Forces, June 5, 1967

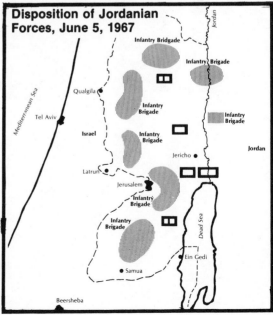

Disposition of Syrian Forces, June 5, 1967

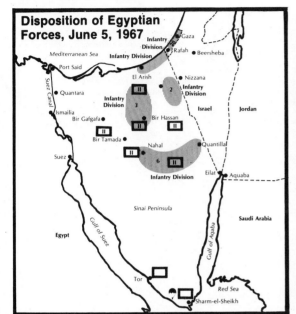

Disposition of Jordanian Forces, June 5, 1967

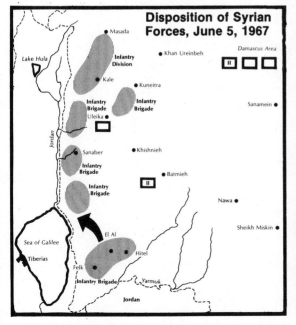

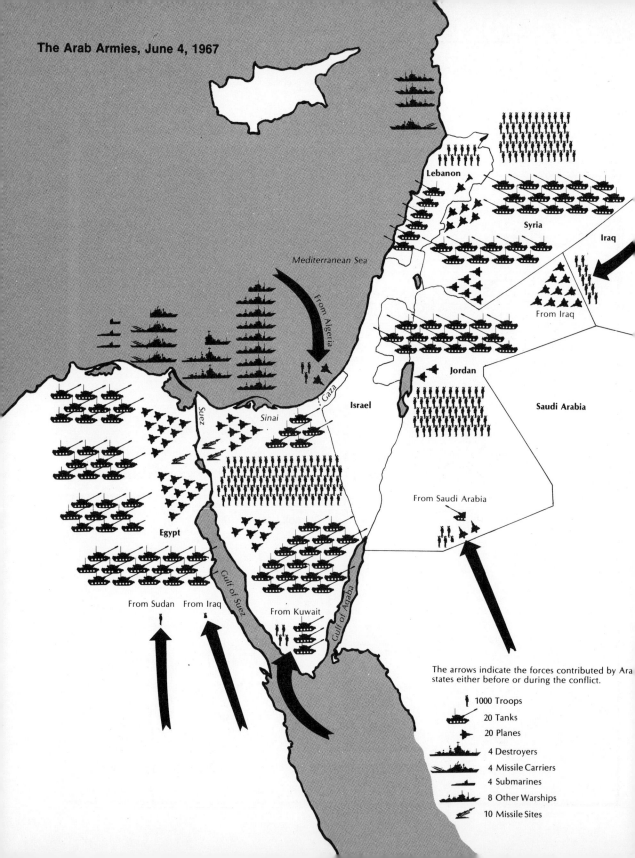

The Arab Armies, June 4, 1967

Mediterranean Sea

From Algeria

Lebanon

Syria

Iraq

From Iraq

Jordan

Saudi Arabia

Gaza

Israel

Suez

Sinai

Egypt

Gulf of Suez

Gulf of Aqaba

From Saudi Arabia

From Sudan   From Iraq

From Kuwait

The arrows indicate the forces contributed by Ara
states either before or during the conflict.

	1000 Troops
	20 Tanks
	20 Planes
	4 Destroyers
	4 Missile Carriers
	4 Submarines
	8 Other Warships
	10 Missile Sites

Top: The Sinai Desert, 1967. [Authenticated News]

Bottom: Centurion tank advancing across Sinai in desert battle. [Authenticated News]

Armored column races toward the Suez Canal.
[Authenticated News]

removal of UN Forces from Sharm-el-Sheikh.

As the waiting period lengthened and the concentrations of Egyptian forces increased, the "small" operational plan was discussed less. The corps commanders on the Egyptian front pressured for bolder aims and, with the appointment of Moshe Dayan as Minister of Defense, support grew for a wider operational plan.

As the number of Egyptian soldiers and tanks in Sinai increased, it became clear that the Straits of Tiran could not be opened until the Egyptian Army was defeated in Sinai. From a political standpoint, it was better to show the world unequivocally that Israel started war only in response to the aggressive act of blocking an international waterway. From a military standpoint, however, such a limited approach presented tactical difficulties. Preference, therefore, was given to opening the Straits by means of smashing the Egyptian Army in the whole of Sinai. Afterwards, it would be possible to pluck Sharm-el-Sheikh like a ripe peach.

This "large" plan involved conquest of the whole of Sinai. The object was to penetrate to the center of Sinai (to the area between Jebel Libne, Bir Gafgafa and Bir Tamada) and there to engage and destroy the Egyptian Army. Moshe Dayan specifically instructed commanders not to reach the Suez Canal. Recalling the international pressures brought to bear on Israel to retreat from Sinai in 1956, he believed that taking the internal waterway would again provoke the Great Powers and other countries to put pressure on Israel.

Sinai and the Egyptian Front

The reconnaissance forces that moved along the northern axis in Sinai reached the Canal but were ordered to return. Dayan's order was eventually rescinded because the defeat of the

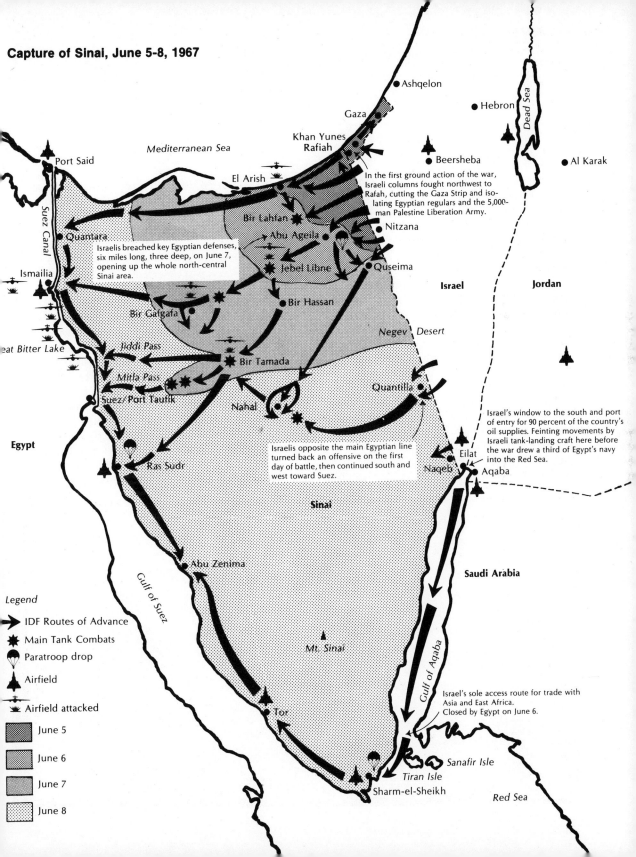

Capture of Sinai, June 5-8, 1967

Mediterranean Sea

Port Said

Suez Canal

Quantara

Ismailia

Great Bitter Lake

Jiddi Pass

Bir Gafgafa

Mitla Pass

Suez/Port Taufik

Egypt

Ras Sudr

Abu Zenima

Gulf of Suez

El Arish

Bir Lahfan

Abu Ageila

Jebel Libne

Bir Hassan

Bir Tamada

Nahal

Gaza

Khan Yunes
Rafiah

Nitzana

Quseima

Negev Desert

Quantilla

Eilat
Naqeb
Aqaba

Ashqelon

Hebron

Beersheba

Al Karak

Dead Sea

Israel

Jordan

Mt. Sinai

Sinai

Saudi Arabia

Gulf of Aqaba

Tor

Sanafir Isle
Tiran Isle
Sharm-el-Sheikh

Red Sea

In the first ground action of the war,
Israeli columns fought northwest to
Rafah, cutting the Gaza Strip and iso-
lating Egyptian regulars and the 5,000-
man Palestine Liberation Army.

Israelis breached key Egyptian defenses,
six miles long, three deep, on June 7,
opening up the whole north-central
Sinai area.

Israelis opposite the main Egyptian line
turned back an offensive on the first
day of battle, then continued south and
west toward Suez.

Israel's window to the south and port
of entry for 90 percent of the country's
oil supplies. Feinting movements by
Israeli tank-landing craft here before
the war drew a third of Egypt's navy
into the Red Sea.

Israel's sole access route for trade with
Asia and East Africa.
Closed by Egypt on June 6.

Legend

➤ IDF Routes of Advance

✹ Main Tank Combats

Paratroop drop

Airfield

Airfield attacked

June 5

June 6

June 7

June 8

El Arish, June 8, 1967: Israeli troops move to the front as Egyptian prisoners, herded in a truck in their underwear, are transported behind the lines. [UPI]

Egyptian Army was so rapid and total that in the absence of resistance Israeli tanks reached the Canal before they could be stopped. The Canal was taken in a hasty, disorganized manner and the IDF did not reach as many places as it could have. In the north, at the entry to the Canal from the Mediterranean, the town of Port Fuad was not taken and was the only point (a six-mile sector) at which the Egyptians were able to gain control of both banks of the Canal. Later, in 1969, this permitted the Russian Navy to bring warships into the harbor of Port Said, which faces Port Fuad at the northern entrance of the Suez Canal.

Three IDF armored corps, under the commands of General Tal in the north, General Yoffe in the center and General Sharon in the southern sector, broke into Egyptian territory at two points. Tal's forces entered Rafiah Salient between Gaza and Sinai and moved toward El Arish and from there to the center of

Sinai. Another secondary force took control of the Gaza Strip. Sharon's forces made a second breakthrough at Abu Ageila. Some of Yoffe's forces moved through this passage leading to the center of Sinai. The plan to drop paratroops near El Arish was cancelled and the paratroop unit was afterwards diverted to action in Jerusalem on the Jordanian front. An additional force was stationed on the more southerly sector facing Quantilla for the purposes of deception. This force was supplemented by dummy wooden tanks and the ruse succeeded beyond all anticipation. Just before the war the Egyptians had transferred a large tank force to face the dummy Israeli force because they mistakenly thought that was where the IDF would attempt its major breakthrough.

Although the Israeli breakthrough plan was based on a frontal attack, the IDF nevertheless achieved surprise at some points by means of an indirect approach. An armored brigade

Top left: MSA1 White half-track personnel transporter with mortar launcher and Browning machine gun. [Authenticated News]

Below right: 105mm self-propelled artillery unit. [Authenticated News]

Below left: The capture of the Suez Canal near Qantara.

Bottom: Paratroop vanguard in southern Sinai.

under General Yoffe infiltrated Sinai by night along Wadi Hardin, an obscure ancient Roman road. They met with no resistance and constituted the first thrust into the heart of enemy territory. Yoffe's second armored brigade broke into Sinai by way of Abu Ageila. While Sharon's forces were hammering the main defenses of Abu Ageila, Yoffe's men surprised the Egyptian rear-guard forces. This stunned the Egyptians and aided in their collapse.

Israeli tanks penetrated to the heart of Sinai along three axes, the same by which they had driven toward the Suez Canal in the 1956 war. The rate of advance was speeded up by parachuting fuel and water ahead. In fact, the advance was so rapid that most of the missions fell primarily on two armored brigades which moved in the classic armored breakthrough pattern: pressing straight forward without taking notice of what happened on the flanks.

While fighting continued along the first Egyptian line of defense, orders were given to proceed to the Mitla and Jiddi Passes to cut off the retreat of the Egyptian forces. A convoy of Israeli tanks drove forward and frequently ran into Egyptian convoys traveling along the same road, but the Egyptians did not open fire because they wanted to retreat unhampered. The Israeli tanks refrained from engaging the enemy in any skirmish not connected with the urgent task imposed on them.

The force that moved toward the Mitla Pass consisted of nine tanks, but four of them broke down and were towed by the others. On arrival at the Pass the disabled tanks were stationed in dug-in emplacements and exposed on an open field. Had the Egyptians hastened to bombard them with their artillery, they might have caused the IDF many casualties.

The capture and holding of the Mitla Pass by General Yoffe's forces was representative of the combination of classic armored patterns and daring improvisation that characterized the Israeli campaign.

Israel's thrust ceased on the banks of Suez. It would not have been difficult to penetrate another sixty miles to Cairo, but when the commander of the armored brigade that had reached the Canal appealed for permission to cross and continue the advance, his request went unanswered.

Summing Up the Israeli Victory in Sinai

For the Egyptians, the great quantity of modern equipment at their disposal was an impediment. They had a hard time extracting the full

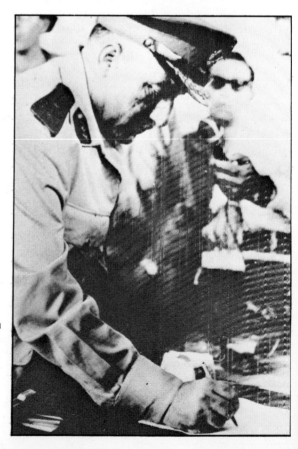

June 7, 1967: Egyptian General Munaim Husseini signing unconditional surrender of Egyptian forces in Gaza. [UPI]

Major Generals Yoffe (left) and Sharon, commanders on the Egyptian front.

benefit and advantage the equipment offered, and in the end they were defeated by it. These weapons grant their users greater speed, a greater rate of fire and greater mobility. But this speed necessitates that command decisions be made at a rate faster than the movement of the weapons on the battlefield. A high degree of integration and exactitude in staff work is required and this the Egyptians lacked. The Israeli commanders estimated this in advance and they knew they would have to do everything to bring the Egyptian units into a battle of rapid movement.

The Russians did not make things easier for the Egyptians, who were burdened with Soviet doctrines of warfare unsuitable for the Egyptian Army. Equipment and weapons were transferred to Egypt according to the table of organization of Soviet divisions without checking whether this equipment, which was prepared for Europe, was appropriate for operation in desert conditions. Among the considerable loot abandoned in the Sinai desert, Israeli experts were surprised to find amphibious tanks and equipment for chemical warfare, which weighed down the Egyptian units. They were supplied to Egypt only because they formed a part of the established equipment of a Soviet division. All this the Egyptians dragged to the desert.

The defeat of the Egyptians was inevitable the moment Israeli armor succeeded in breaking through to the heart of their deployment. The only questions were how long would the battle take and what price would Israel have to pay. Even if the Egyptians had attacked first, it is doubtful that their columns would have succeeded in penetrating, in the best possible event, to a depth greater than the town of Beersheba in the Negev.

The Egyptians left behind some 15,000 dead and almost all their equipment on the sands of Sinai. More than 12,000 soldiers were taken

prisoner (among them nine generals) and the remainder were permitted by the IDF to cross the Canal. For her part, Israel lost 275 of her land forces.

From a numerical point of view, the two armies confronting each other on the Egyptian front were almost equal; each was about 100,000 strong. The Egyptian Army was organized in five infantry divisions, each with its own tank unit, as well as two additional armored divisions. The fighting force of the IDF was organized in three corps (roughly equivalent to a division) and a few secondary units. Egypt had the advantage in weapons, primarily in artillery, but she did not make proper use of it even in defense. The Israeli artillery was outnumbered but had the advantage of self-propelled pieces, while the Egyptian guns had to be towed. In the final analysis, however, the decisive factors were not weapons and their number but better organization, bolder tactics and superior war plans.

The Israeli commanders knew how to engage only part of the Egyptian Army while avoiding the whole reservoir of Egyptian weaponry. Immediately following the initial Israeli breakthrough of the front lines, the attack centered on the Egyptian rear. The pressure, which can be understood in terms of the domino theory, compelled Egyptian units to retreat without fighting and without causing any losses to the Israeli forces. After the war, Egyptian generals complained that they were withdrawn from battle without having fought. The Russians blamed the Egyptians and said that if every Egyptian tank and gun had fired only once the results of the war would have been different.

From the outset, fictitious reporting, the traditional bugaboo of Arab armies, was present. For eight hours, the Egyptian General Staff did not report to Nasser the results of the Israeli air attack. False reports multiplied and the

operational reporting system broke down. Commanders in the field fabricated successes or, in order to justify failure, exaggerated the size of the Israeli forces and their movements. From experience, Israeli Intelligence knew that the longer the battles continued, the worse the Arab Command would entangle itself in a vicious circle. The principle of this circle is simple: Field commanders do not obey orders from higher up because they know that these are based on fanciful misinformation received originally from field officers. Officers avoid carrying out the orders and try to act indepen-

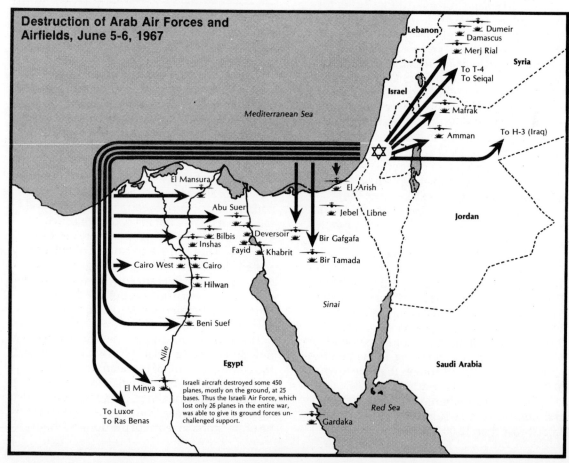

Destruction of Arab Air Forces and Airfields, June 5-6, 1967

Lebanon

Dumeir
Damascus
Merj Rial
To T-4
To Seiqal
Syria
Israel
Mediterranean Sea
Mafrak
Amman
To H-3 (Iraq)
El Mansura
El Arish
Jordan
Abu Suer
Jebel Libne
Bilbis
Deversoir
Bir Gafgafa
Inshas
Fayid Khabrit
Cairo West   Cairo
Bir Tamada
Hilwan
Sinai
Beni Suef
Nile
Egypt
Saudi Arabia
El Minya

Israeli aircraft destroyed some 450 planes, mostly on the ground, at 25 bases. Thus the Israeli Air Force, which lost only 26 planes in the entire war, was able to give its ground forces unchallenged support.

Red Sea
To Luxor
To Ras Benas
Gardaka

Below left: Egyptian MIGs destroyed on the ground by the Israeli Air Force.

Top: Egyptian MIG shot down during Six-Day War. [Authenticated News]

Bottom: The mauve and white *wadis* were specked by burning convoys, Sinai, 1967. [Authenticated News]

dently according to information that seems to them to be correct. Incompetent reporting and inept reconnaissance precluded effective Egyptian measures.

In summing up the elements of victory against Egypt, Gen. Yishayahu Gavish, who was overall commander of the southern front, numbered the following:

(a) Concentration of our forces, speed of movement and maintenance of the impetus. We concentrated most of our force in places where we wanted to concentrate them, and created favorable balances of force in all the

arenas of the battle, in places and at times that suited us. We maintained the constant impetus and fought by day and night without cease. We did not give the enemy rest, and we did not break off contact with him for even an hour.

(b) The Command led in battle. A high proportion of our casualties were commanders who moved at the head of their units.

(c) The morale of the fighters derived from the recognition that this was for the existence of the nation.

(d) Unconventional tactics. We made unconventional penetrations to bring about rapid decision, to isolate the enemy and to restrict his ability to maneuver and to reinforce his besieged forces.

(e) A rapid and flexible maintenance system. This gave the Army corps independence for at least seventy-two hours, and they needed reinforcement only at the end of the battle.

(f) The decisive contribution of the Air Force. [3]

The Air War

The Israeli attack on Egypt was led by the Air Force, which caught most of the Egyptian planes on the ground. Not one of their airfields escaped the surprise Israeli bombings and the runways were destroyed by special bombs. The Israeli Air Force carried out a plan it had rehearsed for many years and when the first wave of aircraft returned, it was clear that the blow sustained by the Egyptians was devastating. After the second and third waves there was no doubt that the air battle had been resolved and that the Egyptian land forces had lost their aerial assistance.

One of the most notable aspects of the Israeli air strike was the rapid turnaround of the aircraft. The time devoted to arming and refueling a plane from the moment it returns from one sortie until it takes off for the second sortie is an important factor. The operational output of each aircraft is expressed in the number of sorties carried out by the Air Force during the war. Turnaround efficiency reached its peak when, within seven minutes, aircraft were ready to take off for a second sortie with a freshly briefed pilot in the cockpit. Frequently pilots were ordered while in the air to alter a combat mission from one front to another. Rapid turnaround and split-second decisions led the Arabs to believe that Israel was oper-

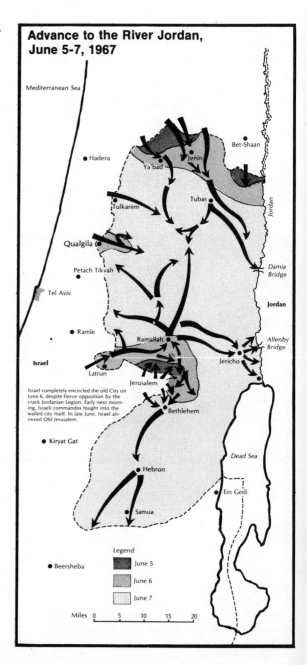

Advance to the River Jordan, June 5-7, 1967

Mediterranean Sea

Hadera

Bet-Shaan

Ya'bad

Jenin

Tulkarem

Tubas

Jordan

Qualgila

Damia Bridge

Petach Tikvah

Tel Aviv

Jordan

Ramle

Ramallah

Allenby Bridge

Israel

Jericho

Latrun

Jerusalem

Israel completely encircled the old City on June 6, despite fierce opposition by the crack Jordanian Legion. Early next morning, Israeli commandos fought into the walled city itself. In late June, Israel annexed Old Jerusalem.

Bethlehem

Kiryat Gat

Dead Sea

Hebron

Ein Gedi

Samua

Legend

June 5

June 6

June 7

Beersheba

Miles 0 5 10 15 20

Fighting for the Rockefeller Museum in Jerusalem.
[Shimon Fuchs]

ating many more than the 200 planes she actually had.

On the first day of war, the Israeli Air Force destroyed some 350 Arab aircraft. The Egyptian Air Force alone lost 300 planes at seventeen airfields. Five airfields were attacked in Syria, two in Jordan and one in Iraq. In all, the Arab air forces lost 452 aircraft, seventy-nine of them in aerial combat. The Israeli Air Force lost a total of fifty aircraft of various types, mostly from ground fire. Twenty Israeli pilots were killed.

In the short space of two hours and fifty minutes, the Egyptian Air Force ceased to exist. For another hour, the Israeli Air Force worked over Jordan and Syria and by noon Israel had gained aerial supremacy in the Middle East. Most of the aircraft were then directed to ground-support missions.

Over the exposed expanses of Sinai and the roads between the sand dunes this task was exceptionally easy. Egyptian armored and transport vehicles were a convenient prey for the Israeli planes. The Israeli pilots put the quietus on Egyptian counterattacks before they could be launched and Fouga trainer aircraft attacked concentrations of Egyptian artillery. When the Egyptian retreat began, Israeli fliers started their hunt of Arab convoys. At first they strafed vehicles at the head of the convoy and then those at the rear. Those trapped in the middle caught fire and could not escape in the sand when the vehicles directly to the front and the rear exploded. The mauve and white *wadis* of Sinai were specked by burning convoys.

On the Jordanian front, Israeli aircraft delayed Jordanian armor moving up from the Jordan Valley and hit the advance force of the Iraqi Expeditionary Army. On the third day of the war, the aircraft were ordered to stop attacking concentrations of transport and armor

Top left: June 7, 1967—An Israeli tank rumbles through the Mandelbaum Gate which once separated the Jordanian and Israeli sectors of Jerusalem. [UPI]

Bottom left: Israeli paratroops gather at the Western Wall after the liberation of Jerusalem.

Top right: "We have returned to Jerusalem, never to part from her again."—Moshe Dayan [UPI]

Bottom right: Liberation forces pass the Western Wall. [Authenticated News]

Brig. Gen. Haim Herzog, commander of the Jordanian front. [Wide World]

Bottom: IDF Chief Rabbi, Maj. Gen. Shlomo Goren, sounds the *shofar* at the Western Wall after the liberation of Jerusalem.

abandoned in Sinai. Israel wanted to lay its hands on the Egyptian loot while it was still intact.

War with Jordan

Israel was reluctant to wage war on the Jordanian front. The evaluation was that war on two fronts—Egypt and Syria—was a heavy enough burden. The Jordanian border was especially dangerous because it touched on most of the concentrations of Israeli population and was accessible to essential and vulnerable targets. The border cut through Jerusalem, Israel's capital, and ran close to government ministries and the Knesset. Jordanian artillery could easily hit the suburbs of Tel Aviv and many other settlements and was within range of three Israeli airfields.

On the first morning of the war, Israel asked the UN Truce Observers Chief of Staff to approach King Hussein and convey a message

that if he would refrain from opening fire, Israel would do likewise. The message was delivered but things developed otherwise. Jordanian artillery opened fire along the whole line of the front and unleashed an especially heavy bombardment on the Jewish section of Jerusalem and the road to it. Jordanian aircraft attacked various targets in Israeli territory.

On the first day of the war, a Jordanian force seized the hill in the no-man's land where UN headquarters had been located. It gave the Royal Jordanian troops a commanding advantage over a wide area. Up to that point Israeli commanders had considered knocking out Jordanian artillery batteries only to prevent shelling of the Ramat David Airfield in the Jezreel Valley. When the abandoned UN hill was captured, Israel decided to take it and to break through to Mount Scopus adjoining the Old City of Jerusalem. Mount Scopus had been an Israeli enclave since 1948 and was the first site of the Hebrew University.

Israeli armored forces entered Jordanian territory and climbed the mountain slope toward Ramallah near Jerusalem. At first, Jordanian artillery shelled the Tel Aviv area and Egyptian commandos unsuccessfully attempted to reach Israel's Lydda Airport.

The next day, seven Jordanian infantry brigades were stationed on hilltops which provided wide firing range. In the rear, two armored brigades waited in the Jordan Valley. One brigade of the Iraqi Expeditionary Force that had moved across Jordan also reached the valley and took up a position on the east bank of the river. The Jordanians waited with their armored forces in the valley in the belief that the IDF would break through from north to south along the valley and the Jordan River with the intention of cutting off the whole of the west bank. The IDF had created that impression by deceptive activity. Eight Israeli bri-

Preceding pages: Israeli soldiers bear away a comrade wounded by snipers in Old City of Jerusalem. [Don McCullen]

A 135mm Howitzer on the northern front, June 1967. [Authenticated News]

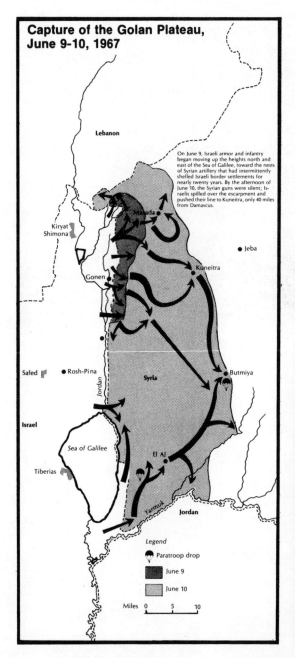

Capture of the Golan Plateau, June 9-10, 1967

On June 9, Israeli armor and infantry began moving up the heights north and east of the Sea of Galilee, toward the nests of Syrian artillery that had intermittently shelled Israeli border settlements for nearly twenty years. By the afternoon of June 10, the Syrian guns were silent; Israelis spilled over the escarpment and pushed their line to Kuneitra, only 40 miles from Damascus.

Lebanon

Kiryat Shimona

Masada

Jeba

Gonen

Kuneitra

Safed

Rosh-Pina

Syria

Butmiya

Israel

Sea of Galilee

El Al

Tiberias

Yarmuk

Jordan

Legend

Paratroop drop

June 9

June 10

Miles 0   5   10

gades, three of them armored, faced the Jordanian forces. They broke into the west bank at six locations and, although they fought courageously, the Jordanians were unable to stop the Israeli forces pouring in from all sides. Their armored units were forced to a standstill by Israeli jets before they even reached the battle zones.

Armored battles took place mostly at the northern sector of the front. The Arab inhabitants were astonished at the sight of the IDF in their towns. In Nablus, people waited in the streets for the Iraqi units and at the sight of the Israeli tanks they applauded, thinking they saw Iraqi troops passing before them. They were dumbfounded when the "Iraqis" addressed them in Hebrew.

After considerable hesitation for fear of adverse American reaction, Israel decided to take the Old City of Jerusalem. On the morning of the third day of the war, Israeli soldiers

Advancing on the Golan Heights, June 1967.
[Authenticated News]

reached the Western Wall, which Israel had lost together with the Jewish quarter of the Old City in the 1948 War of Independence. The nation trembled with emotion at the news and many regarded it as the peak of the Six-Day War. Upon the declaration of cease-fire, IDF forces controlled the whole of Judea and Samaria on the west bank. Soon afterward they captured the remainder of the Jordan River's west bank and the bridges over it.

The Syrian Campaign

Developments on the Syrian front were different. It was Damascus that had fanned the flames of war and had drawn Nasser into actions that Israel saw as clear aggression. But when fighting broke out on the Egyptian and Jordanian fronts, the Syrians did not lift a finger. Midway through the first day of the war the Syrians fell silent and thereby proved the value of military alliances in the Arab world.

Damascus had behaved similarly—though the rulers were different—in the 1956 war.

After the Egyptian defeat, however, the Syrians began a heavy bombardment of Israeli settlements in Galilee and their forces attempted to overrun two settlements in a number of assaults, but were driven off with no great difficulty.

The Syrian failure to attack at the outset of the war was a convenient development for the IDF. Full attention was devoted to Egypt and Jordan but an eye was kept on the Syrian Golan Heights where six infantry brigades were stationed, each reinforced by a battalion of tanks. Behind these were positioned another two tank brigades and two mechanized regiments.

Until the third day of the war, the Israeli Command was more concerned with blocking this force than with assaulting it, especially since most of the forces of Israel's Northern

Levi Eshkol (right) in field meeting with Moshe Dayan (center) and Maj. Gen. David Elazar (seated left).

Command were engaged in fighting on the northern sector of the Jordanian front. On the other two fronts the war was coming to an end, while on the Syrian front the sides made do with an exchange of artillery fire.

It was ironic that the extremist Syrians, who were responsible for starting the war, were to remain untouched. This was the only instance in which the Israeli civilian population actually demanded that the IDF break into enemy territory and extend the war. When the attack did not come, a delegation from the settlements of the area came to Jerusalem to bring pressure on the cabinet ministers to approve action against the Syrians. The delegation comprised representatives of many kibbutzim, including those settlements belonging to Hashomer Hatzair, the leftwing Zionist party. These settlements live under the shadow of the Syrian Heights and had suffered over the years from bombardments and attacks. They insisted that the IDF climb the Heights and end once and for all their vulnerability to Syrian attacks.

The Minister of Defense, Moshe Dayan, objected to action against Syria at that stage. He did not want to open another front before the war with Egypt and Jordan was finished. He apparently also did not want to strain the patience of the Soviet Union, which was especially sensitive to the fate of the leftist regime in Damascus. The General Staff did give an order to the Northern Command to prepare for battle, but action was postponed because of low clouds that interfered with air activity. It was not until the morning of June 9, the fifth day of the war, that Dayan suddenly changed his mind and instructed the IDF to invade the Golan Heights. Meanwhile, two armored brigades of the Northern Command completed their missions on the Jordanian sector and began to move northward toward the Syrian border.

The war on the Syrian front lasted only twenty-seven hours, but it was a hard and bloody confrontation. The terrain imposed difficult conditions. The Syrians sat on high peaks, which in a number of places rose above Israeli territory like sheer walls. The Syrian emplacement system was especially strong. Their concrete bunkers could not be breached by the many bombs dropped from Israeli aircraft. The main Israeli effort was directed at an objective that was especially difficult from the point of view of terrain on the assumption that the Syrians would station their least strength there.

The attack developed in stages because the IDF could not concentrate all its forces on the front at the beginning. The only road passing along the Syrian border was subjected to heavy Syrian fire, which interfered with Israeli preparations. Two armored brigades arrived from the Jordanian front and an additional armored brigade came up from the far south. Another paratroop unit, part of which had also fought

Israeli soldier guards Egyptian prisoners of war.

Sunken ships formed part of the Egyptian blockade of the Suez Canal. [UPI]

on the Egyptian front, reached the Northern Command. At the height of the attack, on the second day of battle, the IDF had at its disposal eight brigades, including three armored ones.

On the first day, four openings were forced into the Syrian line by Israeli forces assisted by heavy bulldozers. The advance drew to a halt at nightfall, but the escarpment was in Israeli hands in a number of places. At dawn the Israeli pressure increased and new units broke into two additional points on the Heights. On the first day the Syrian Army had fought splendidly in hand-to-hand combat, but on the second day the rout began. The first to flee were the officers. At noon on Saturday, the town of Kuneitra fell into IDF hands. The road to Damascus was open and according to the estimate of Gen. David Elazar, the commander of the Northern Command, thirty-six hours would have been sufficient to reach the Syrian capital, only thirty miles away. Suddenly the Russians issued menacing threats and Israel decided to be satisfied with the capture of the Golan Heights.

June 10, 1967: The Sixth Day

At 6 P.M. on Saturday, June 10, the sixth day of the war, the guns fell silent on all fronts.

Israel had lost more than 700 men in this short war, not a great number considering the total victory, but a hard blow in terms of the percentage of casualties to the population as a whole. It would be comparable to the United States losing some 80,000 men in a short war.

The senior command of the IDF, although confident, had estimated before the war that Israel's losses would be substantial. Chief of Staff Rabin said after the war: "I thought we would have thousands of dead and tens of thousands of wounded."[4] In Tel Aviv's parks, mass graves had been prepared in anticipation of bombing. Children were instructed at school in civil defense procedures in case of bombing and gas attacks.

Twenty-one brigades—nine armored, three infantry and armored, three paratroop (including one mechanized) and six infantry—had made up Israel's order of battle in the Six-Day War. On the Egyptian front in Sinai, ten of the brigades were organized into three corps under Generals Tal, Yoffe and Sharon. Four of the twenty-one brigades saw service on more than one front. Two armored brigades were transferred to the Syrian front after completing their attack in Sinai as well as another two armored brigades that had fought in the battle on

The aftermath: Bulldozers clear square in front of the Western Wall to make a plaza where visitors can pray. [UPI]

the Jordanian front. Vessels from the Israeli Naval Station at Eilat participated in securing the Straits of Tiran and naval frogmen infiltrated Alexandria Harbor to sabotage Egyptian vessels.

The fear of an imminent holocaust had driven IDF units to supreme effort. Self-sacrifice and acts of heroism were not uncommon and contributed to Israel's victory. With all the IDF's faith in its strength, it was the men of the Pentagon who believed more than anybody else in total Israeli victory. American generals said Israel would win, though with considerable losses, even if Egypt struck the first blow.

Causes of Arab Failure

What dictated in advance the results of the battle on the Egyptian and other fronts was the Intelligence gap between the sides. The Arab Intelligence services knew little about the IDF and what they did know was incorrectly evaluated. Their evaluations of Israeli strategy were also faulty. Moshe Dayan later commented:

The Arab opening of the war was slow, without use of the decisive potential force that could be accorded to the first blow. Another mistake was that Nasser exaggerated in his evaluation of Egyptian military force. This exaggeration primarily derived from the view of the equipment. He saw he had a lot of sophisticated equipment and became intoxicated to a certain degree, or confused the equipment with the Army and exaggerated in that he saw all this as one massivity.[5]

Israel, on the other hand, knew a lot about what was going on in the Arab armies. Israeli Intelligence knew such technical details as where the Arab planes were stationed and even where decoy dummy aircraft were positioned. After the war, General Gavish, IDF Commander of the Egyptian front, said, "It

was like a game of chess in which we knew in advance, thanks to good Intelligence, the other side's moves."[6]

Evidence of the scope of penetration by Israeli Intelligence was the taping of a conversation that took place on the first day of the war between King Hussein and Nasser in which the latter attempted to persuade Hussein, by means of false information, to throw his army into the war. Israeli Intelligence published the conversation during the war, thereby causing considerable embarrassment to the Arabs.

Israeli Shortcomings

Israel's big mistake was that the government had not formulated strategic and political objectives before going to war. All efforts were aimed at destroying the threatening concentrations of Arab armies—and no more. No contingency plan existed for establishing a Palestinian state on the west bank of the Jordan and in Gaza. Such a plan would have gone a long way toward dispelling the basic cause of conflict in the Mideast and would have served to disarm the Palestinian terrorists. After the war, Deputy Premier Yigal Allon admitted that it had been a mistake not to penetrate deeply enough into Syria to assist in setting up a sympathetic Druze state in the Druze mountain area (including the Golan Heights), which would have been a buffer between Jordan and Syria. A Palestinian state and a Druze buffer were but two of the postwar political possibilities.

The rift between the political and military leadership in the preparation of war plans was noticeable in every field. While the Army had planned its moves in terms of exact strategy years before, the politicians trailed behind developments on the battlefield.

The Aftermath

The Six-Day War changed the face of the Middle East. The shock of defeat that overcame the Arabs was greater than any setback they had experienced since the beginning of the Arab-Israeli dispute. After their defeat in 1948 the Arabs contended that they had been undone by the treachery of Arab rulers who were linked with foreign interests and were out for themselves. The Arabs believed that the Israeli victory was not definitive, and the day was not far off when Israel would be routed. The Egyptians explained the defeat in 1956 by claiming that it was not Israel that had beaten her, but France and England who made Egypt retreat from Sinai.

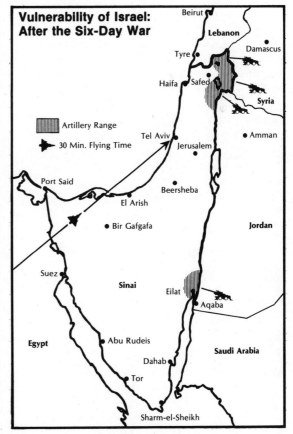

Vulnerability of Israel: Before the Six-Day War

Artillery Range
Missile Range
9 Min. Flying Time

Beirut, Lebanon, Damascus, Tyre, Kuneitra, Haifa, Syria, Tel Aviv, Amman, Port Said, El Arish, Quantara, Bir Gafgafa, Jordan, Suez, Sinai, Eilat, Aqaba, Abu Rudeis, Saudi Arabia, Egypt, Dahab, Tor, Sharm-el-Sheikh

Vulnerability of Israel: After the Six-Day War

Artillery Range
30 Min. Flying Time

Beirut, Lebanon, Damascus, Tyre, Haifa, Safed, Syria, Tel Aviv, Jerusalem, Amman, Port Said, El Arish, Beersheba, Bir Gafgafa, Jordan, Suez, Sinai, Eilat, Aqaba, Egypt, Abu Rudeis, Saudi Arabia, Dahab, Tor, Sharm-el-Sheikh

Below: [Nancy Reese]
Opposite: An Israeli New Year's postcard.

Seizure of new territories in Sinai, in Judea and Samaria on the west bank of the Jordan, and the taking of the Golan Heights totally changed the strategic situation of Israel. Most of the concentrations of population and other vital targets in Israel were now out of range of Arab artillery. In a number of places, a reverse situation had been created for the Arab states. The IDF was now closer to the Arab capitals: sixty miles from Cairo and thirty-five miles from Damascus. Israel's air warning system had changed completely. In the past Arab planes had theoretically been able to reach the heart of Israel in minutes. After the war they had no such easy access.

New geographic gains gave Israel security from attack, as was proven in the Yom Kippur War. The territories gained in the Six-Day War lessened the threat of Israel's extermination by a surprise military blow. These new territories also provided a political advantage to Israel by giving Jerusalem leverage in peace negotiations.

New options had opened up for Israel. For example, as a result of the Six-Day War, Israel had under her rule more than a million Palestinians and a considerable share of the refugees. It seemed that conditions existed for a new meeting point and for direct dialogue. But the Arab attack on October 6, 1973 brought that era to an end.

Footnotes

1 Rabin, in *Maariv*, 2 June 1972.
2 Previously unpublished interview with author, after Six-Day War.
3 Interview with author, originally published in *Ha'aretz*, 1 April 1970.
4 Rabin, *op. cit.*
5 Lecture at IDF Command School, 19 July 1967.
6 Previously unpublished interview with author, 1967.

צבא הגנה לישראל

שנה טובה

A HAPPY NEW YEAR

11. THE ISRAELI AIR FORCE

Opposite: [Marvin Newman]

Israeli Air Force roundel.

The reputation of Israeli pilots is widespread. For much of the world, the fliers symbolize the Israeli warrior more than any branch of the IDF. Thanks to the quality of the pilots, the Air Force of the IDF has been transformed into Israel's major deterrent power.

The training methods, instruction and tactics of the Israeli Air Force have aroused interest even among the world's largest and most advanced air forces. The Intelligence services of the Arab countries and the Soviet Union are particularly interested in the secret of the Israeli Air Force's success.

Ezer Weizman: Architect of the Israeli Air Force

Perhaps a key to understanding the uniqueness of the Israeli jet pilot is the personality and genius of Ezer Weizman, one of Israel's first military pilots and the man who more than any other commander shaped the Israeli Air Force. He commanded the Air Force for eight years, from 1958 to 1966. During that time Weizman taught his men to excel in aerial combat. He had unusual tenacity and succeeded in conveying to every pilot the conviction that the objective must be attained in spite of any obstacle, ground fire, enemy aircraft or bad weather.

As a former Royal Air Force pilot, the slim, tall and quick-spoken Weizman stood out among the first pilots of the Israeli Air Force. He became a model for many of Israel's fighter pilots and his influence grew when he became the commander.

Like his ex-brother-in-law, Moshe Dayan (they married two sisters, the daughters of a Jerusalem lawyer), Weizman had a reputation for pranks and flamboyant behavior. He was at first considered to be irresponsible by the young State's leaders. When Weizman's name was mentioned to Ben-Gurion by the first Commanding Officer of the Air Force as a possible future commandant of the Air Force, Ben-

Gurion retorted, "What, that goat?!" In Ben-Gurion's eyes, Ezer was certainly a fighter, but not the kind of man who could serve as a model commander. Ezer Weizman was not of the pioneering stock of the Haganah on whom Ben-Gurion relied. The son of Yehiel Weizman and nephew of Haim Weizmann, first President of the State of Israel, Ezer was considered typical of the children of the affluent known as "the golden youth" of Tel Aviv.

During the Second World War, together with several other Palestinian youths, he volunteered for the RAF. The British were at first reluctant to assign Palestinians to flying courses, so Weizman served as a driver. Later he was one of the first Israelis sent to Rhodesia for flight training. Upon completion of the course, he was assigned to a British fighter squadron at Fayid, an Egyptian airfield. More than twenty years later, in the Six-Day War, Israeli pilots struck this airfield and destroyed dozens of Egyptian MIGs.

Weizman became famous as a fighter pilot. He was one of the four pilots, two Israelis and two Jewish volunteers from the United States and South Africa, who flew the first fighter planes of Israel—Messerschmitts bought from Czechoslovakia. Their first aerial action was the May 19, 1948 attack on an Egyptian column approaching Tel Aviv from the south. This mission, in which the South African volunteer was killed, was crucial in defending the Jewish settlements in the north. The surprised Egyptians, who did not know Israel had fighter planes, stopped dead in their tracks, refusing to advance further. The bridge near Ashdod, where the battle took place, is still called by the Israelis *Ad Halom*, "Thus Far!"

About a year and a half later, on January 7, 1949, the last day of the War of Independence, Weizman took part in an aerial battle with British fighter planes. Units of the British Army were then stationed in the Suez area of Egypt.

Emblem of the Israeli Air Force.

Bottom: Ezer Weizman (center) and Mordechai Hod (right), two pilots destined to become commanders of the Israeli Air Force.

A few days earlier, Britain had delivered an ultimatum through Washington demanding withdrawal of Israeli forces from Sinai. London claimed that according to the Anglo-Egyptian agreement of 1936, she was obliged to defend Egypt. Even before that, the British had needled the Israeli forces, and occasionally sent reconnaissance planes on photographic missions over Israeli territory. In order to add muscle to her threat, she sent armed Spitfires into Israeli territory.

In aerial combat and ground fire, five British planes were shot down. This operation sealed the Israeli victory in the War of Independence and, for the first time, the Israeli Air Force became known as a force whose pilots were not afraid of confronting the glorious RAF and even capable of downing their planes. Ezer Weizman was credited with a Spitfire.

After Independence, Weizman emerged as the head and unofficial leader of the Israeli fighter pilots. He was later given a command and from the outset put his training emphasis on fighting spirit. He demanded that the Israeli pilot be in all senses an aerial warrior. For this purpose, he developed a course for battle leaders, those pilots who lead their comrades in the air and plan aerial combat.

Breast badges of pilot (top) and navigator.

Below: Ezer Weizman at the controls of a British-made Black Spitfire, used by the British during the Blitz and one of the first planes flown by the Israeli Air Force. This particular plane, the only one of its kind still in operation in Israel, is reserved for Weizman's personal use.

The Israeli Air Force had to learn everything for itself. In the 1950s, before the Sinai War of 1956, Israeli pilots were not widely accepted by other nations and Air Force requests that Israeli pilots be admitted into various courses in other air forces were usually turned down. Weizman persuaded his men that they were successfully moving toward becoming one of the best air forces in the world. He predicted that some day other great air forces would flock to learn solutions worked out by the Israelis.

The cream of Israeli youth joined the Air Force. Weizman proclaimed the slogan, "The

they feared that pilots from kibbutzim would remain in the regular army and thus become isolated from kibbutz life. In their eyes it was more natural for a kibbutz son to do his national service in the infantry and then return to work on the land. The long separation from the life of the kibbutz that the Air Force necessitated seemed dangerous and in conflict with the pioneering ideal.

Weizman went out of his way to convince the kibbutz leaders that service in the Air Force was no less important than residence in a border settlement. Many young pilots from the kibbutzim accepted his premise that there are

good ones fly," and within a few years an elite coalesced. It lived almost in isolation; it thought and spoke in its own concepts. The Air Force developed as a separate body, a kind of crack private army. Kibbutz youth and children of semi-cooperative settlements were especially noticeable among the pilots as compared to their small proportion in the general population. Being a fighter pilot was considered a glamour profession among kibbutz youth.

The kibbutzim at first took a dim view of this tendency. The heads of the kibbutz movement were not particularly worried that many of their young men were joining the Air Force, but

"pioneers at a height of 40,000 feet" and that in contemporary Israel there are other ideals than working the land. The struggle between the kibbutz movement and the IDF, especially the Air Force, gave rise to many arguments in kibbutz general meetings.

Weizman and his supporters won the arguments; many kibbutz sons remained in the Air Force.

Training

Few are accepted into the exclusive club of Israeli Air Force pilots. The club is not only a kind of national first team, but also a unique

Breast badges of bombardier (top) and paratrooper.
Bottom: Israeli youth begins flight training.

social grouping, admired and emulated by all.

Flight training attracts many, but only a small percentage is accepted. Selection takes place among eighteen year olds. The Israeli Air Force's fighter pilots are on the average seven years younger than their American counterparts and fighter pilots in other advanced air forces. The computers of the defense establishment sort the cards of candidates for the draft and select those who seem suitable for flight training. They are then invited to preliminary examinations even before they are asked whether they are willing to be pilots.

In the IDF, fliers are volunteers, similar to paratroopers, submariners or frogmen. Those who are accepted by the flying school have to serve at least five years in the Army. The number of volunteers grew after the Six-Day War. Many Israeli youngsters who were impressed by the role of the Air Force in the war sought to join. Thus the selectors have been able to choose the very best out of large groups of talented volunteers.

The volunteers come from all segments of Israeli life, from the big cities, from the agricultural cooperatives and kibbutzim, and even from development towns.

The public recognizes the exclusivity of the pilots' club. If in other countries parents take pride in a son accepted by a respected university, in Israel, in the midst of a constant state of war, many respect the son who is accepted into the pilots' course.

Parents frequently write high authorities and visit instructors to ask details about their sons in the pilots' course. Not only do members of the immediate family see the success in flight training as something special, whole settlements are proud of it. When a young man from the immigrant town of Bet-Shaan completed a pilots' course, the mayor praised him in a special session of the municipality and proudly noted that he was that town's first pilot.

Over the course of years, with the accumulation of considerable data about volunteers for flying and graduates of the course, sociologists and psychologists have attempted to create a super model of those who stand up to all the tests of pilot training. The Air Force sociologists found that those whose chances of success in flying are greatest are mostly native-born Israelis, sons of families of European origin. The number from other groups is small. As yet, the experts do not have satisfactory answers why it is these who are most successful and why the number of native Israelis of Oriental origin is so small.

Flight school instructor. [Marvin Newman]

Israeli-made Fouga trainer aircraft.

The examination and selection procedures for acceptance in the flying school of the Israeli Air Force last several weeks. After the first series of examinations, including rigorous medical checks, psychological and technical aptitude tests, successful candidates are transferred to the flying school, where they stay for two weeks.

At the end of this period only a small percentage of the candidates remain. Youngsters who are discovered, for example, to be unable to form friendships and to live in conditions demanding a communal spirit are among the first to be eliminated. The next stage of tests is intended to quickly reveal which candidates lack the aptitude for flying. A quick flying course in light planes is given. The instructors are veteran pilots and the object of the course is not to teach flying, but to find out whether a trainee is capable of mastering the plane's controls.

At the end of this screening process successful candidates are assigned to flight school, but tests continue throughout the whole course, even after the young pilot has completed his studies. For a year or two after he has received his wings, even when he is already in a fighter squadron, a flier is still subject to follow-up

testing. These subsequent checks usually show that the early evaluations were correct.

The IDF Air Force flight school is unique in that it trains not only pilots—drivers of planes—but above all superb aerial warriors. The Commandant of the Air Force school, whose name cannot be published for security reasons, says:

We are not training a pilot here but a fighter. A fighter who is also an officer and a commander. I am convinced that it is this emphasis that afterward brings the successful results in aerial encounters with the enemy. The emphasis is primarily on forging the pilot as a warrior. We pay special attention, there-

Flight school passing-out parade.

fore, to what are important character traits for a warrior: honesty, comradely relationships, mutual assistance. When a pilot leaves here, I know that he'll never abandon a wounded comrade. He'll circle above him to protect him up to the last minute and he'll come back from an attack and report truthfully. I don't know of a single case in which an Israeli pilot has abandoned a downed comrade. They leave the area only when fuel gives out or when ordered to do so.[1]

Another factor that singles out the Israeli Air Force flying school is the social responsi-bility borne by the school's cadet. This liberal approach is unusual in a military framework. A Cadet Command is set up and functions as an internal government with backing from the school commandant. It is responsible for all activities outside of training and instruction. The Cadet Command, which is changed every month, organizes social activities, lectures and entertainment as well as study circles to supplement formal instruction. The Cadet Command is also responsible for cleaning the planes used for training.

The Israeli Air Force makes an effort to

assign the best of its pilots to serve as flight school instructors. The Air Force Staff insists that educating the future generation of fighters is the domain of the best of present fighters. Outstanding fighter pilots therefore devote, by rotation, part of their service to instruction. Instructors still occasionally go out on operational sorties to relieve any feeling of frustration. There is no instructor in the IDF flight school who has not had combat experience.

The pilots' course is divided into five stages. Two-week leave is granted between each stage to lighten the physical and mental pressure. One of those weeks, however, must be devoted to attending educational lectures. The first two stages are preparatory. Stress is placed on ground training and on physical and mental conditioning. The Commandant of the school explains:

In many air forces, such as the American, less time is devoted to ground instruction. They have no preparatory stages. There is a method of instruction which could be called the black-box method. The cadet does not know what goes on inside the box. He only learns the essentials. The objective is to equip him with the barest minimum. In the Israeli Air Force the approach is different. Pilots are obliged to know exactly what goes on inside the plane. One of the results of this method of teaching is that the pilots submit proposals for technical improvements and there are those who have won governmental prizes. [2]

On the pre-preparatory level, attention is given to mathematics and physics. Cadets also learn meteorology, aeronautics, electronics, navigation and law. Those who lag behind in theoretical studies are tutored, but anyone who fails at subjects is asked to leave the course even if his overall qualifications are excellent.

Next comes the preparatory stage in which the hours of flight training are still restricted to light aircraft. The emphasis at this point is primarily on developing physical fitness and stamina. The cadets undergo officers' courses and are then sent to paratroop training. They conduct sea rescue exercises and learn topography on long marches, including night treks in which each cadet must cover twenty miles alone with a heavy pack. At the end of this period there is a further sorting of cadets. Pilots and navigators who had previously studied together are, at the beginning of the third stage, separated.

During the third training period, called the primary stage, the pilots concentrate on flying. After a few months they solo and perform aerial acrobatics to learn how to control an aircraft in emergency situations. At the end of this stage, many cadets are eliminated.

The pruning process in Israel's Air Force is stricter than that of any other air force. In Egypt and France, for example, most of the cadets who are accepted into a flight course complete it. In the United States, seventy-six percent finish, but in Israel the percentage is much less. Israeli instructors think the chief cause of failure is the inability of many cadets to think correctly while in the air. It is often shown that a cadet who possesses the required mental alertness on the ground loses this acuity the moment he goes up. Things that he learned well on the ground are forgotten when he is airborne and under pressure.

Rejection from the course is not arbitrary or sudden. Every week the cadet receives an evaluation of his progress. If he is failing, the cadet is invited to interview with psychologists and senior commanders. He is not failed before the matter has been brought before a special committee of experts who also offer opinions. In the final stages of the course the school commandant must approve every cadet rejection.

The fourth stage, known as the basic stage,

Opposite: Aerial warfare during the 1956 Sinai Campaign.

is the most difficult. Cadets learn night flying, navigation and flying in groups. Final classification comes at the end of this stage. Some of those eliminated at this point remain pilots but serve in squadrons of light aircraft as communications and backup pilots.

In the fifth stage, called the progressive, the cadets are organized into a sort of combat squadron. Here they are first introduced to the aircraft as a weapons system and they begin to operate it as such.

At the end of the course the cadets are assigned to three groups. The best are sent to combat squadrons, something which every cadet wants. The others are sent to helicopter squadrons or to transport planes. They then undergo operational courses and afterward are transferred to regular Air Force squadrons as student pilots.

Morale

Ezer Weizman developed a family feeling in the Air Force. He convinced the pilots that in the Air Force they belonged to a special family that must stay together. "If a pilot of mine divorces unnecessarily," Weizman used to say, "I must intervene, because otherwise it hits at his morale and the general morale of the Air Force."[3]

There is no doubt that one of the reasons for the high morale in the Israeli Air Force derives from this family feeling. A British pilot, a veteran of the RAF who has visited many air forces, says he has seen many air armies with fighting spirit, but the outstanding characteristic of the Israeli Air Force is the unusual self-sacrifice of its members.

Ezer Weizman has put it this way:

We here in the Air Force are one big family. A family in which everybody knows everybody, and everybody looks after everybody. And I, if this thing can be defined in nonmilitary terms,

am the father of the family. We are a closed family. We do not bother to deal in things outside our interests. Possibly this framework of the Air Force is similar to the kibbutz, and the impulses that bring us to serve in the Air Force are similar to the impulses that bring a person to live in a kibbutz—the feeling of destiny, the knowledge that where we are is the center of action. Each of us, starting with me down to the cook frying omelettes at one of our bases, has the feeling that we are doing something important. The chef can earn good money in one of the luxury hotels, but he remains because he is proud of what he is doing. This is so for the pilots, the armorers, the electronics technicians and others. What the Hasidim call "an extra spirit" can be felt and this is characteristic of the Air Force.[4]

There are those who retain their ties even years after leaving the Air Force. At Air Force parties they can be seen surveying the younger generation. They usually bring their sons and daughters to look around and soak up a bit of the special atmosphere. The fighters of MAHAL (Foreign Volunteers in the War of Independence) are also drawn to these affairs. When they come to Israel they never miss a visit to an air base. Some of these members of MAHAL come to Israel every year just for the Air Force's Independence Day party.

The families of Israeli pilots live in their own housing developments, in small houses with lawns and trees around them. Personal contacts are important for the women and children. The men go off on operations and the families live through the successes and tragedies together.

Says Amalia, the wife of a veteran pilot:

The fact that we live together makes it easier for us. The anxieties are common, and when there is fear there is somebody to talk to. It

Rena Levinson, a CHEN pilot who flew transport and reconnaissance missions in the 1950s.

Mordechai Hod as a young pilot.

makes it easier for us. But when a tragedy happens, the burden is double. It falls on all of us without exception, not only on the family of the pilot who was hit. We lose not only a colleague, but also a neighbor and a friend. The children also feel this. They know the one who fell and for them he is the father of a friend.

Sometimes we sit together, a few of the pilots' wives, and count the planes going out. We hear the planes in the air and see them take off, but we do not know which pilots are going and what their target is. We wait in tension, almost without talking. When the planes come

we count the engines again to see if all have returned. [5]

A sense of mission and strong motivation are also outstanding characteristics of the Israeli pilot. He feels he is fulfilling a role of supreme importance in defending the existence of the Jewish people. This consciousness has been instilled in all Israelis against the background of the Nazi Holocaust and the ongoing war with the Arabs.

On the eve of the Six-Day War, Ezer Weizman and Mordechai Hod, then Air Force Com-

American-made Mustang, purchased from Sweden in the fifties and used in the Sinai Campaign.

mander, visited a group of pilots. Time after time they repeated, "Remember, the fate of the nation rests on your shoulders!" One of the pilots, a farmer and an outstanding flier, broke the tense atmosphere by saying innocently: "I do not mind carrying out any mission, but to place on my shoulders the fate of the whole nation—that's not fair. Really not fair!"

The following morning, when the Air Force planes took off on their missions, General Hod published his battle orders. He purposely created an historic perspective for the war:

Again enemies have joined together against us on every side. The spirit of the heroes of Is-

Theory of Defense

Ezer Weizman is not university educated, but his contribution to the theoretical-strategic aspect of the Israeli Air Force has been considerable. He says Israel's best defense is in the skies of Cairo and this view has largely determined the methods and strategies of the Air Force, and indirectly the strategic plans of the entire IDF.

Weizman made as his ultimate aim the destruction of enemy air forces at their own airfields. Every effort was directed toward this end—training, maneuvers, attack techniques and mental attitudes. This approach neces-

rael through all the generations will accompany you into battle. The immortal heroism of the warriors of Joshua Ben-Nun, the heroes of King David, the Maccabees and the fighters of the War of Independence and Sinai will serve you as a source from which to take strength and willpower to strike the Egyptian enemy that threatens our security, independence and future. By his overwhelming defeat, we will guarantee peace and security for ourselves, our children and the generations to come. [6]

A similar spirit was instilled in the pilots during the Yom Kippur War.

sitated developing combat leaders of a special type. Weizman selected promising candidates from the ranks of pilots for advanced training while eliminating those who seemed to lack combat initiative. This process determined the character of the Israeli Air Force by making it clear that the commander and his top deputies would come from the ranks of the fighter pilots rather than from administrative or support officers.

Weizman's confidence in the ability of the Air Force occasionally seemed exaggerated. His remarks often sounded like bragging intended to raise morale. They sounded this way not only to cabinet ministers but also to the commanders of other branches of the IDF. Weizman was not able to prove his claims because the Air Force was not really put to the test in the 1956 Sinai Campaign . Ben-Gurion and Dayan, who was Chief of Staff, would not permit a major assault on Egypt and relied on French planes for air defense. Weizman's assertion in 1966, in a forum of senior commanders at the Command and Staff College, that in the event of war the Israeli Air Force would destroy all the Arab air forces within six hours, appeared to many unrealistic. He was, of course, vindicated in the Six-Day War.

Weizman was once asked what it is that is unique about the Israeli Air Force:

There is no secret about it. The talent of the nation is to be found in the Israeli Air Force. We are a sensible and talented people. Jews cannot avoid this fact. The evidence: our contribution to culture, to science and the world of the spirit. Within the military these talents can be fully utilized. Within this framework there are no fakes, and orders can be given to move things.

The aircraft more than anything else is a tool of war. The use of it demands considerable intelligence. In order to activate such a complex weapons system things must be done at maximal speed. For this, the operator must have special traits and talents. Here, the Jewish people stands out more in its talent, and therefore we are more capable than the enemy.

I do not say we are the "chosen people." Other nations are also intelligent and have good air forces, but the fact is that the Israeli pilot stands out more than many others. He has a kind of control in the situations and under the various pressures to which a pilot is subjected.

On the technical side, on the ground, the intelligence of the nation also succeeded in absorbing and teaching quickly. There were always those among us who were surprised that

Israeli youth had such a quick grasp. It is because there was common sense here. The greatness of the Israeli Air Force is not only in its operational handling, but also in its maintenance. So why the surprise?

Half of the scientists in the world are Jews! In other words, our Air Force is an expression of the basic character of the Israeli Jew.[7]

Weizman admits that the Israeli Air Force has learned much from others, but he adds that this learning is of a special nature:

There is an additional factor, and this is our common sense over the years, in that we were not overdrawn into accepted principles of the wide world.

It was natural that a small nation, like any nation starting on its path anew and seeking to maintain a military force, would look at the United States or the Soviet Union, England or France, as rich in air experience, especially after the Second World War. Russia was for us a closed world even though during the War of Independence we fought with planes we received from Communist countries. Many wanted to know exactly what were the foreign tactical theories, methods of maintenance, operations, etc. in the major air forces. But some of us understood the danger in this, for not all that is good for one country must be good for another. We were able to learn from others, but not to copy them. We knew how to apply these things according to our needs, although in the beginning we had a tendency, which was quite understandable, to copy from others because of the little experience in our hands.

Among the volunteers who reached us during the War of Independence there were many who brought with them theories and experience of their own. There were those who did not understand that systems of organization and operation derive from the mentality of a nation. An American system of organization,

American-made Sikorsky CH-53, the world's most sophisticated jet helicopter.
Bottom: Paratroops training in the Negev Desert.

for example, is a logical progression of American mentality; the complicated organizational structure of the French is a logical progression of French culture and a French way of thinking. An air force is not built only on equipment, but also on contact between men; contact between the commander and his command. This also is a matter of mentality. I do not believe that a British officer, for example, could effectively command an Israeli force. Not because he does not have control over the necessary technical knowledge or because he lacks courage. Simply because he cannot penetrate the soul of the Israeli soldier. It is not puzzling that American advisers do not succeed in several countries.

We are a thinking community in ferment, and therefore we rebelled against alien things which were not suitable to us and rejected them. In 1948-49, we had no alternative because we were few. Then the volunteers came. The moment they began to try to formulate the image of the Air Force, there were conflicts with the Israelis. We knew that not everything that was good for them in technique or tactics was also good for us.

Over the years we learned to apply the maxim of quality over quantity. In the Air Force we learned not to sacrifice standards. I remember that in 1960 I had to grant a pilot's certificate to one lone pilot. He received his wings from me in my office because there was no passing-out parade. I was not prepared then to forego standards. I said I preferred that no one should complete the course—or only one man—

rather than lowering the standard only in order to take pride in a passing-out parade.

I have no doubt that on the average the Israeli Air Force is among the best in the world. I am not acquainted with the Russian Air Force, but when I see Russian equipment and examine Russian aerial tactics, doubts arise in my mind. From our meetings with the American Air Force, I learned a lot about the level of the Israeli Air Force. The U.S. Air Force is a clear criterion. It is very big, very serious and more experienced today in combat than any other air force. No other air force can serve as a yardstick. The European air forces today lag behind. When I put Israeli pilots up against American pilots, I see that in some subjects the Israeli boys are better. I want to stress that I am talking about the average. It's possible that if we had to field 4,000 pilots, then we would have to lower the level. I am convinced that on the average, the Israeli Air Force is the best in the world.

This is not because we are fighting Arabs. If we stand against the Russians, in equal numbers, we will overcome them. I am convinced that if we have to fight them—one hundred pilots against one hundred pilots—we will overcome them. If we have to stand against ten times that number, then it's clear that quantity begins to play a role. [8]

The Israeli Air Force Meets the Soviet Union

A battle between Israeli and Russian pilots actually took place on July 30, 1970, close to the

Bay of Suez over Egyptian air space. It was not an accidental confrontation. The Soviet military command in Egypt was anxious to test Israel's declaration that the IDF would not be scared off if the Russians joined Egyptian units in the War of Attrition taking place in Suez. The Russians looked for combat contact with Israeli pilots and it seemed clear that if Israel were to back off from a confrontation, Russian boldness would increase.

Although the action had a clearly defensive nature, it was difficult for Israel to decide to act. More than half of Israel's Cabinet Ministers were born in Russia or were from Eastern Europe, and their memories of pogroms and unanswerable persecution by the Russian regime and population were still vivid. It is only natural that people with this kind of background would experience a subconscious restraint against face-to-face confrontation with the traditionally feared Russian *muzhik* (peasant), especially when the *muzhik* appears in the form of a great power capable of responding ruthlessly.

Israel nevertheless accepted the Soviet challenge. Crack pilots, flying American Phantoms and French Mirages, were assigned the mission. The Phantoms went off to attack Egyptian radar stations and the Mirages gave them cover. This flight strategy was a classic trap and the Russians swallowed the bait. Israeli Intelligence reckoned that if MIGs appeared in the area over the Bay of Suez they would be flown by Russian pilots. It was known that in the division of labor between the Egyptians and the Russians, the latter were responsible for the air defense of the front's southern sector.

It was a full-scale aerial battle. Against sixteen of the MIG-21s put up by the Russians stood a squadron of Mirages and one of Phantoms. (The exact number of planes in an Israeli squadron is classified.)

The fight lasted no more than four minutes. The full details have been censored by Israel and have never been acknowledged by the Russians. But reliable sources have provided part of the story: At first the MIGs challenged the Mirages. The latter were led by a kibbutznik, one of Israel's most experienced fighter pilots. The Mirage pilots outmaneuvered the MIGs and downed one of them at close range with guns. A second MIG was hit in its tail by an American Sidewinder air-to-air missile and plunged to the earth.

Then came the turn of the Phantoms which also downed two MIGs, both with Sidewinder missiles. Only two parachutes could be seen in the skies when the MIGs were hit. Two other Russian pilots were apparently killed.

The rest of the Russian pilots seemed to panic. There was disorder in their formation and after another minute they retreated. The Israelis received an order not to follow them, but before returning to base they still had to complete their mission: the destruction of the Egyptian radar station.

An hour after the battle, the Israeli pilots related their experience at a debriefing session in which their commander also took part. They said it was a routinely easy aerial battle. Although they had made contact with many planes, they had no difficulty in bringing four down. Only recently it was revealed that a fifth MIG was hit and subsequently exploded over Egypt.

The pilots said the enemy planes came into battle "like a bull after a red flag. As though they were knocking their heads against a wall. They were like ripe fruit waiting to be picked."[9]

The Israeli pilots were not aware that their opponents had been Russians and it was only later they were told. They were unanimously astounded over how easy the engagement was.

The results of the battle produced a rather

Aircraft of the Israeli Air Force: (1) Douglas Phantom II all-weather interceptor; (2) Super Mystere training jet; (3) Vautour jet fighter-bomber; (4) Mirage IIIc jet interceptor; (5) Ouragan training jet.

Bottom: MIG-23 (fishbed) on its landing run. [Tass from Sovfoto]

1.

2.

3.

4.

5.

Top right: Marshal Kotakov, Commander of the Soviet Air Force. [Tass from Sovfoto]

Below right: Meteor, the first Jet used by the Israeli Air Force, was purchased from England and used in the Sinai War. [UPI]

Bottom: The Russian-made MIG-23, Foxbat (above) and MIG-19, Farmer.

strange reaction among Egyptian pilots. They expressed great joy at the apparent proof that they were not such bad pilots—certainly no worse than their Russian instructors. They were finally able to counter Russian contentions that Egyptian pilots were not sufficiently prepared to accept more sophisticated planes, such as the MIG-23.

But the Kremlin was shocked. For the first time since World War II, Russian pilots had gone into aerial combat, and for the first time since that war they had sustained a decisive defeat. The commanding officer of the Soviet Air Force, Marshal Pavel Kotakov, was sent to Egypt and he recommended that the most advanced aircraft the Russians had—the MIG-23 —be sent to Egypt in preparation for any future dogfights with Israeli jets.

Motivation

The sense of mission Weizman and other commanders speak of was reflected in interviews with two cadets the day before they received their wings.

The first one was twenty-year-old Amiram. Dark-haired and alert, his father Russian-born and his mother a German Jew, he was one of the outstanding cadets in the course. "It seems to me the bigger mission today is to be a pilot," he said. "To protect the skies of the State—that is modern pioneering and for this I am prepared to take risks. I'm sure we are the best, even if Russian pilots come against us," he continued rather arrogantly. "If we were in Switzerland, for example, we could not be that good. I think our character is what gives us this supremacy. It's something connected with the history of the Jewish people." [10]

His comrade, twenty-one-year-old Ram, a kibbutznik, said, "We just do not have any alternative but to be the best. To lose supremacy means for the nation to walk into the sea. I do not think it will happen." [11]

The Commandant of the pilots' school, one of the aces of the Israeli Air Force who has to his credit the downing of many Arab fighter aircraft, has a broader point of view. He tried to put his finger on the uniqueness of the Israeli pilot:

Above all is his motivation. This is the dominant factor. The central motivation of the young Israeli is a feeling of obligation, almost subconscious, to the State. The contact with the homeland, the feeling of mission. The knowledge that this is a war for existence. It's like an infusion of blood, a sense of no alternative.

Our pilot population comes from the elite of Israel. What gives us a special impetus is our war for existence. It's astonishing, but the rate of flying success of Israeli youth exceeds that of Jewish youth coming to us at a late age from the Diaspora and joining the Air Force. Israeli education makes its mark here. The impulse of the Israeli youngster to seek challenges for himself is greater than normal and above the average if you compare him to youth in an affluent society.

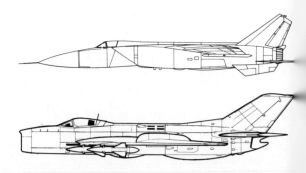

The Douglas Skyhawk A-4 fighter-bomber. [Marvin Newman]

I tried to analyze our victory in the Six-Day War from the point of view of a pilot, of a fighter sitting alone in the cockpit. I found four factors that are typical of the Israeli pilot and, in effect, determined our victory.

First, courage. Afterwards come initiative and resourcefulness and only last the level of implementation. There are many examples. A pilot arrives, for example, at an enemy airfield. He must make four bomb runs. They open fire on him and it has an influence. But men in the middle of their bombing runs ignored the fire. They aimed with single-mindedness and courage. After the war, we analyzed the level of operation. We checked, for example, the level of gunnery of the young pilots and the results were marvelous. On this, I must say that the reason for Arab failure is that the sum total of their national culture did not teach thém to deal with technological innovations. The Arabs suddenly heard of sophisticated MIG-21s, missiles and radar systems, which are a condition for the direction of aircraft of this sort, and their air force was not capable of struggling with these innovations.[12]

The Arab View

Obviously the commanders of the Arab air forces and their pilots do not accept this analysis. They have tended to blame their difficulties and failures on the weapons each side possesses. An example of this thinking was expressed in an unusual conversation that took place in the spring of 1969 between an Israeli and an Egyptian pilot. The meeting was preceded by aerial combat in the skies of Sinai.

Four MIG-21 aircraft penetrated Sinai air space and two Israeli Mirages took off to meet them. In one of the Mirages was G., a fighter pilot famous for his steady nerves. Before the first shots were fired, while the Mirages were attempting to achieve an advantage through quick maneuverings, two of the MIGs started to flee westward, beyond the Suez Canal and back toward Egypt. G. turned his plane toward one of the remaining MIGs and his partner turned on the other. The pilot of the MIG in front of G. seemed more daring than his colleagues. He did not run from the battle, and he had a certain initial advantage in height and attacking angle.

The Arab pilot opened fire and immediately G. knew he was facing a daring Egyptian but a lousy fighter pilot. He had opened fire from a bad position at which one's chances of a hit are very small. G. was sure it would only be a question of minutes until he downed the Egyptian. The first burst from G.'s cannons hit him in the tail and a flame burst from the MIG engine. It lost control and the second burst downed him. Bullets pounded on the fuselage, chunks of plane flew in all directions and finally a white parachute could be seen.

The Egyptian pilot, Lt. Muhamad Abdel-Baki, landed in Sinai on the Israeli side of the Canal and was completely stunned when Israeli soldiers reached him. At first he tried to run into the dunes with a revolver in his hand, but when a few shots were fired over him, he stopped. Dusty and grimy, with one leg dripping blood, he fell to his knees. There was fear in his eyes and apparently he was convinced that the Israeli soldiers would shoot him and that he only had a few minutes to live. He begged for his life. One of the soldiers gave him water and he was taken to a hospital.

When his wounds were healed he had an unexpected visitor—the pilot who had brought him down. This was not a routine meeting between pilots. G. introduced himself cheerfully, careful not to gloat. He said he had come to pay a sick call. Muhamad was taken aback but he realized the Israeli pilot had not come to mock his defeated opponent. The two faced each other: the twenty-six-year-old Egyptian, tall, thin and balding; the Israeli, thirty, with flecks of grey hair—the son of Cairo opposite the Israeli kibbutznik.

It was Muhamad who suggested analyzing the battle. They took a piece of paper and tried to draw the battle maneuvers. A technical conversation between pilots ensued. The Israeli tried to explain the Egyptian's mistakes and the reasons why he had lost his advantage and had been downed easily. Muhamad listened with interest. Once or twice he nodded his head, but said nothing. When the Israeli had finished, Muhamad ignored his detailed analysis, saying, "Only because of the Mirage! It's a demon, not a plane. Only because of the Mirage you succeeded in downing me!"[13]

Cutting Red Tape

The Israeli pilot is extraordinary, but what are the characteristics of the Air Force as a whole that make it unique? Military censorship, based on security considerations, prevents more than a general, theoretical discussion of this question.

In a recent interview with a veteran squadron commander this subject arose and I recall his reply:

More than once I've asked myself whether there is anything that makes us special as a force. Today I can say with certainty that we are outstanding in our operational approach and grasp. I can give examples for comparison: I visited a Phantom base of the U.S. Air Force in California. One squadron commander, a Chicano, talked to me about aerial battles. He told me that during training he would reach a decision and would want to act on it, but could not do a thing because of the bureaucracy in which he was trapped. I told him that our squadron leaders can pick up the phone to the Air Force Commanding Officer and tell him, "Sir, I have just now come back from a sortie and there's something we must do." And the Air Force C.O. says to him, "Go ahead!" It takes exactly twenty-five seconds. He looked at me enviously, this American. For us in the Israeli Air Force it's like a mechanism that maintains itself, from the operational level up to the commander who decides. You do not normally see that in other air forces. It's true that the fact that we are relatively small, compact, helps

Skyhawk in battle over Golan Heights during Yom
Kippur War.

us and gives us great flexibility. But the operational approach is important. Our squadron
leaders are permitted to take part in the pre-
planning sessions, at the time of the planning
and before orders are cut. This is exceptional.

The attack on the Arab airfields during the
Six-Day War was a good example of our
approach—straight to the point. When the
Americans attack an airfield or a battery of
anti-aircraft missiles their approach seems to
be different. They will certainly open with electronic warfare to destroy the anti-aircraft missiles, and only at the end do they reach the air-

field itself. We hit the main target first. Afterwards, if it is absolutely necessary, we hit the
periphery target.

The original operational approach can also
be seen in other things. For example, the
French Mirage aircraft. Upon receiving the
plane, we attempted to examine the French
technology developed around this weapon system. It was quite different from the way we saw
it. The French sought to produce a blind fighter
plane, capable of taking off in any weather and
firing a missile at an enemy plane. Along come
the Israelis and they give this plane guns and

Ground crew preparing the Skyhawk for its next sortie. [Marvin Newman]

bombs. *They decided that the plane must be functional for aerial combat, for air-to-ground attacks day and night. When the French heard what we were doing to the Mirage, including ground support and aerial combat at all ceilings, they could not understand it and did not believe it. This is an example of an operational approach, resourcefulness and initiative. The French learned from us about their own plane. True, our poverty imposes limitations. But it's our professional level and approach that give us the solutions.* [14]

Experience and Lessons of the Yom Kippur War

The Air Force shouldered a heavy burden in the Yom Kippur War. In addition to combat duties—interception flights, air defense and attack assignments—it was responsible for air transport of supplies to ground units at the various fronts. Israeli jets also struck deep inside enemy territory and sought to knock out as many enemy surface-to-air missile emplacements as possible. It was active on both the Egyptian and Syrian fronts.

The Air Force suffered heavy losses—102 Israeli planes were downed—largely because of

Missiles vs. Men in Cockpits

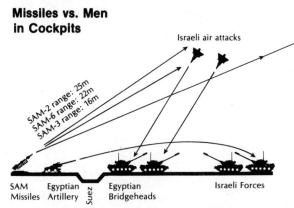

Israeli air attacks

SAM-2 range: 25m
SAM-6 range: 22m
SAM-3 range: 16m

| SAM | Egyptian | | Egyptian | Israeli Forces |
| Missiles | Artillery | Suez | Bridgeheads | |

greatly improved Arab air defense. Israeli pilots had learned during the War of Attrition how to partially neutralize the high-altitude Soviet-built SAM-2 missile and the medium-altitude SAM-3, but in October 1973 they were faced with three other highly effective anti-aircraft weapons which, particularly in the case of Egypt, bolstered Arab low-altitude air defenses. There were the SAM-6, the SAM-7 and the 23mm multi-barrel machine gun.

It was not so much the qualities of the SAM-6, about which the Air Force knew quite a lot, that caused problems. It was the sheer quantities of the weapon in the hands of the Arabs. The SAM-6 is a medium- and close-range air defense missile which made its first appearance in the Middle East. The particular SAM-6 model used in the Yom Kippur War[15] had a multiple-channel guidance system which posed electronic and countermeasure problems for Israeli forces.

The SAM-7 is a heat-seeking missile similar to the American Redeye. It can be fired by one man or mounted on vehicles and fired in clusters of four or more. The 23mm gun is a four-barreled, radar-directed weapon. The Israeli planes hit by the 23mm were, of course, flying dangerously low but that was necessitated by the danger of missiles. The range of Arab anti-aircraft capabilities was wide enough to pose a serious threat to the Israeli Air Force.

Despite these setbacks, the Air Force was in a high state of technical preparedness and had more planes at its disposal than ever before. Although heavy demands were made on stores—continually resupplied by the giant

U.S. airlift during the war—the only shortages were of certain types of ammunition.

When the war broke out, the Air Force was in a state of readiness although it, too, was hampered by faulty Intelligence evaluations. Its delay in stemming the Egyptian crossing of the Canal was because it was ready for a different type of operation—a preventative strike. Once in action, the Air Force destroyed Egyptian bridges across the Canal and inflicted damage on helicopters carrying Egyptian commandos, though it was unable to save the Canal. In the Golan Heights, however, the Air Force was instrumental in bringing about the Israeli victory.

The uniqueness and quality of Israel's Air Force derive from the special motivation prevalent among its men, the sense of mission arising from a state of war, the ability to learn special operational approaches based on rich combat experience, a tightly linked chain of command, a sense of belonging and a strong degree of camaraderie.

Footnotes

1 Previously unpublished interview with author, 1970.
2 Ibid.
3 Interview with author, originally published in Schiff, *Kanafayim meal Hanilus* [Phantoms over the Nile] (Haifa: Shikmona, 1970), pp. 9-16.
4 *Ibid.*
5 Previously unpublished interview with author, 1973.
6 *International Air Force Publication No. 1* (1967).
7 Interview with author, originally published in Schiff, *op. cit.*, pp. 146-50.
8 *Ibid.*
9 Previously unpublished interview with author, 1973.
10 Previously unpublished interview with author, 1973.
11 *Ibid.*
12 Previously unpublished interview with author, 1973.
13 Previously unpublished interview with author, 1973.
14 Previously unpublished interview with author, 1973.
15 United States Army, *Military Review* (February 1972), pp. 48-9.

12. DOCTRINE

Opposite: [Authenticated News]   B.H. Liddell-Hart.

Many military commentators consider the IDF one of the best armies in the world, with combat standards well above the average. The writings of the late British military analyst, B.H. Liddell-Hart, and American military expert, Gen. S.L.A. Marshall, are full of praise for the spirit and improvisational skill of the Israeli Army. Military men throughout the world are anxious to visit IDF installations and learn something of its theories and doctrines.

Five Basic Principles of Israeli Defense

To understand the IDF's doctrine of warfare and its strategic approach, it is necessary to examine the five basic principles that guide Israel's defense: few against many, war of survival, strategy of attrition, geographical pressures and the time factor.

Few Against Many—The knowledge that any armed conflict will pit the Israeli few against the Arab multitudes has existed since the beginning of the Arab-Israeli struggle. Israeli military people are aware that the numerical advantage will always be on the Arabs' side. Israel's War of Independence broke out when she had half a million Jews, and the Six-Day War when the population numbered somewhat more than 2.5 million. The state of Israel is today faced by some 50 million Arabs in neighboring territories (of which 32 million are in Egypt alone). To these must be added additional Arab states, such as Libya, Algeria and others who support hostile and terrorist actions against Israel. Up until the Six-Day War, Israel comprised a small area of some 12,500 square miles. After the war, her territory was 50,000 square miles (including the Sinai Peninsula), while the Arab states occupied millions of square miles that gave them a strategically important depth.

The gap can also be seen in the natural resources at the disposal of each side. Whereas

Israel's resources are meager, the Arab states possess immense quantities of petroleum. The crude oil flowing out of the Arab states brings in billions of dollars and gives them political leverage. Israel lacks these enormous resources and can rely for political support only on the United States. The Arabs, on the other hand, can count on the diplomatic and material support of Russia, China and most of Asia and Africa.

This sense of few against many takes on more intense significance because of memories of the Nazi Holocaust. The IDF and the Israeli people as a whole are therefore especially sensitive to loss of life. The heads of the IDF see extensive losses as a danger to the continuance of the Jewish nation and this is an important consideration whenever the possibility of prolonged war is discussed.

This was one of the reasons why Israel agreed to a unilateral withdrawal from the

Israel

Suez Canal after the Yom Kippur War even though her forces had captured the west bank of the Canal. A prolonged occupation of Egyptian territories on the west bank could have brought on another war and Israel, already having suffered heavy losses in the Yom Kippur War, could not allow this.[1]

A War of Survival—Unlike other nations, Israel does not face an enemy whose sole aim is to defeat her army or to conquer a specified area of land. The overall Arab plan has been and continues to be the total destruction of the Jewish State.[2] The fact is that the Mideast conflict is nothing less than a war for Israel's very existence. Many nations have lost wars yet continued to exist one way or another. Israel assumes in advance that defeat in war means an end to the Jewish nation and she wages war accordingly.

The Strategy of Attrition—There is an asymmetry in the objectives of the two sides in the dispute. Whereas the Arabs adopt a strategy of extermination, the IDF cannot, even if it so desired, operate according to such a strategy vis-à-vis the Arab world. The IDF's strategic objectives must be restrained. The Israeli General Staff cannot think in terms of a final decision over the Arabs, but only of defeat in particular battles and wars. The IDF, therefore, employs a strategy of attrition to thwart the Arab strategy of extermination. They aim to inflict heavy losses on the Arabs whenever possible to deter temporarily any renewed attacks.

Geographic Pressures—Israel is a country with its back to the sea. Prior to the Six-Day War, her geostrategic situation was grave. The ratio between the length of her borders and the depth of her territory was especially bad in terms of defense. Her only geographic advantage lay in short internal communications lines that permitted rapid movement of forces from one front to another, but even this was eclipsed

by greater geographic disadvantages.

The whole of Israel was no more than a tiny patch in the Arab world. Israel was surrounded on all sides by enemies and was the easy object of sea blockades, whether in the Mediterranean or the Red Sea. Jerusalem, her capital, was cut in half by the frontier and all her vital centers were within enemy artillery range. Egypt held military bases close to Israel in the Sinai Desert and Gaza Strip. The Syrians in the Golan Heights enjoyed virtual control over a large part of Israeli territory and a significant share of her water sources. Jordan sat facing the country's narrow waistline and could cut the country in two by one armored strike at its center. Israel was a country with no depth, all its territory a border zone, and with almost no possibility for advance warning against approaching enemy aircraft.

This situation gave rise to a deep fear against sudden Arab attack, which in turn gave birth to the acute awareness that Israel would always have to make the first strike if she were to survive. Indeed, failure to act on this conviction proved disastrous for Israel in the Yom Kippur War. And the massing of Egyptian forces in the Sinai Peninsula was a decisive factor in Israel's decision to wage the Six-Day War.

The Six-Day War brought about drastic geographic changes. Israel acquired considerable depth, and her ability to absorb offensive blows increased considerably. For the first time in her history, geographic conditions allowed Israeli strategists a degree of mental tranquility. This, unfortunately, contributed to the complacent mood of the Israeli military establishment before the Yom Kippur War.

The Time Factor—Time is the decisive factor in all Israeli operative planning. Strategists and political leaders in Israel have always feared that any outbreak of hostilities would immediately bring intervention by the Great Powers or the United Nations. The purpose of this inter-

Egypt

vention would always be to block and vitiate Israeli achievements, while it is doubtful that there would be any such intervention if the Arabs held the upper hand.[3] It is for this reason that strategy is developed to ensure that the Arabs are held back from any territorial achievement in war at the same time as Israel's objectives are obtained in the first stages of battle. The element of time takes on an additional importance because of Israel's restricted resources and her sensitivity to losses.

These calculations were upset in Egypt's War of Attrition, which followed the Six-Day War and lasted for seventeen months. Since this war did not involve any territorial achievement there was no immediate international intervention. Yet, toward the end of that war the Russians did intervene on the Egyptian side and even used their fighter aircraft.

The Qualitative Edge

In the face of the many Arab advantages, Israel has one outstanding strength: qualitative supremacy. The generally backward Arab population and society is faced by Israel's population which, though smaller, possesses a progressive social structure, a high level of physical health and a higher level of education. The war for existence has impelled Israelis to aim for excellence. While much of civilian life in Israel is plagued by bureaucratic inefficiency and indifference, the Army works. This still holds true, despite operational deficiencies during the Yom Kippur War.

The IDF exploits its qualitative edge to compensate for other disadvantages. The decisive factor is not the number of men or soldiers, but the standard of the nation; not the individual weapons, but the group weapon—the weapons systems that the nation can successfully produce and operate. In the War of Independence

Middle East Populations and Oil Reserves

(Thousands of Barrels)

Country	Population	Daily Oil Production — 1972	Estimated Daily Oil Production — 1975	Proven Oil Reserves
Algeria	12,102,000	1,150	1,200	15,000,000
Bahrein	217,000	750	1,200	12,000,000
Egypt	34,900,000			
Iran	30,500,000	5,000	7,300	55,500,000
Iraq	10,440,000	1,400	1,900	36,000,000
Israel	3,155,000			
Jordan	2,460,000			
Kuwait	900,000	3,300	3,500	66,000,000
Lebanon	2,950,000			
Libya	1,938,000	2,200	2,200	25,000,000
Morocco	15,030,000			
Oman	750,000			
Qatar	90,000	480	500	6,000,000
Saudi Arabia	8,200,000	6,000	8,500	145,000,000
Sudan	16,450,000			
Syria	6,450,000			
Tunisia	5,360,000			
Turkey	37,000,000			
United Arab Emirates	200,000	1,700	4,100	20,000,000

Sinai Peninsula   **Claimed by Egypt; presently operated by Israel. Yearly output — 6¼ million metric tons.**

weapons systems such as tanks and aircraft were only auxiliary. A transition took place during the Sinai War of 1956 when the weapons systems became the decisive factor in Israeli hands.

Israel is unique in her ability to achieve maximum mobilization of her national potential for the Army and civil defense. This extends to the mobilization of men and women for emergency economic measures. Because of her paucity of resources, Israel cannot maintain a large standing army. She has to make do with a small regular nucleus and consolidate the bulk of her power in reserve forces. It is vital that the large reserve army be properly organized, well-trained and capable of rapid mobilization to front lines.

Yigal Yadin, the eminent archeologist and second Chief of Staff of the IDF, studied the Swiss reserve organization and adopted that system for the IDF in an extended and improved form. Israel is the only country in the world which can assemble the bulk of its reserves within twenty-four hours and then transport these fully equipped units to the front within an additional forty-eight hours. Each unit summons its men by means of slogans broadcast over the radio or by unit runners. The men report to assembly points and are then taken to the unit emergency stores where they are equipped and then transported directly to the front.

By this means, and with the help of the nucleus of a relatively small regular army, Israel has succeeded in establishing the largest per capita army in the world. It is estimated that out of a population of some 3 million, the IDF can field an army of half a million men. Although caught by surprise in the Yom Kippur War, Israel was able to mobilize quickly and turn the tide against the Egyptians and the Syrians.

The organization of the regular standing army has been specifically developed to enable it to face regular armies and to maintain a high level of preparedness. Emphasis is placed on the Air Force, which is especially large and based primarily on regular units that are capable of immediate operation at full strength. Stress is also placed on a sophisticated Intelligence service that can guarantee an alert of the militia army at the right time.

The fact that the IDF is an army of the masses influences the choice of the weapons systems used by the militia army, which trains only once a year. It was decided that certain sophisticated weapons systems should only be operated by the regular army. For example, Phantom aircraft equipped with advanced computers are not usually manned by reserve pilots. To bridge the specialization gap that exists in a militia army, the IDF insists on a total population mix in all its units. By distributing Israel's technological and cultural elite throughout the whole Army, the IDF achieves a higher-than-average qualitative level within each unit and avoids social disparity between officers and enlisted ranks. A professor of science can be employed filling sandbags in Suez Canal positions; a professor of philosophy may serve as a sentry or driver with the rank of private. Israel's academic community has often attempted to abolish this custom, but the IDF has remained adamant. Though, of course, scientists with strategically valuable skills are appropriately employed. The principle of equality has thereby been maintained in the Army and has contributed to the high morale and raised the average level of equality of all the units.

The IDF General Staff is also organized in an unusual manner as compared to other armies. It is an integrated structure without separate staffs for the Air Force, the Navy and the land Army. The staff is unified and centralized. The Chief of Staff acts also as the Supreme Com-

Jordan   Lebanon

mander and, in wartime, the Air Force and Navy commanders serve as advisers to the Chief of Staff. This centralization and unification of command proved its efficacy both in the Sinai War of 1956 and in the 1967 Six-Day War.

Putting Defense Theory Into Practice

Israel's doctrine of warfare evolved out of a search for suitable answers to the problems deriving from the five basic principles introduced above. For example, an attempt has been made to compensate for the lack of strategic depth by establishing a regional defense based on border settlements, especially kibbutzim, and settlements on the second line. These settlements, organized for all-round defense, are equipped with weapons, including anti-tank guns and mortars. According to the plan, they can hold off an invader while they wear down his strength. This provides time for general mobilization of reserve forces. Regional defense saves money because it is based on existing settlements and not on the holding of a fortified line by Army units. Its operative importance lies in the fact that it releases crack units from the burdens of defense. Regional defense was crucial up until the Six-Day War, but its importance diminished following the geographical changes brought about by that war.

Israeli strategists developed the thesis of pre-emptive attack as an answer to the threat of defeat by surprise attack. In the conditions that prevailed until the Six-Day War, the opening blow was essential in Israeli planning.

Yigal Allon commented on the problem of initiative and the pre-emptive strike in 1958, in his book *Sand Screen:*

In the conditions of the country, with its long and besieged borders, little depth and flat territory, in its areas' weakness, and because of the excessive proximity of Arab air bases and enemy long-range artillery, Israel is unable to permit her enemies the taking of the first initiative. Since the enemy could well set himself the destruction of the Israeli Air Force on the ground as his first objective, Israel is obliged to exercise her moral and political right to take the operative initiative into her own hands before the enemy aircraft take off, for otherwise she may be doomed at the beginning of battle. As long as the Arab rulers continue to maintain a technical state of war the moral right of pre-emptive counterattack is the military guarantee of Israel's future existence.[4]

Another vital point of Israeli strategy centers around transferring war to enemy territory. Because Israel lacks strategic depth and because her back is to the sea, stress is placed on rapidly transferring battle away from her populated areas and into enemy territory, even if the enemy strikes first. This was amply demonstrated in the Yom Kippur War when Israeli forces crossed the Suez Canal into Egypt and advanced into Syria to within a day's march from Damascus.

IDF operational plans emphasize fast-moving, mobile attacks, the "blitzkrieg." Mobile war takes advantage of the IDF's technological superiority. In accordance with this doctrine, a precise order of preferences has been determined: The offensive arms receive top priority. First place is given to the Air Force, followed by armor. A high preference is also given to the paratroop brigades as a striking force. These units receive the best tools to guarantee rapid penetration and maneuverability in the difficult terrain of mountains and desert.

Moshe Dayan was one of the chief architects of the mobile attack and Yitzhak Rabin, who was IDF Chief of Staff during the Six-Day War, was outstanding in developing it as a doctrine.

Israel's poverty and the long periods of embargo imposed on her have compelled the IDF to learn how to improve weapons systems and

Opposite: Briefing in the field.

Below: Prime Minister Levi Eshkol delivers a speech at the grand opening of the Beit Shemesh Aircraft Engine Plant, part of Israel's burgeoning defense industry. [Authenticated News]

Bottom: American-made M-48-A-3 tank with 90mm gun.

Iraq

to exploit, perhaps more than any other army, weapons that are considered obsolete. There is no weapons system that the IDF has acquired without improving it. This includes the French Mirage, the American Phantom and Skyhawk as well as tanks acquired in Britain and the United States.

When the United States sold Israel M-48-A-3 tanks, armored workshops exchanged the gasoline engines for diesel and replaced the 90mm gun with a 105mm gun. (Israel has reached the level of a medium-sized state in her capability of manufacturing weapons systems and now belongs to the club of ten countries manufac-turing the most modern weapons.) When the IDF went to shop in the international weapons markets it searched for versatile systems. For example, the IDF was not content with a fighter aircraft that was merely a good interceptor. It wanted a plane that could attack as well.

The IDF has employed traditional combat methods, but has given them an Israeli character and set standards that are higher than usual. An example of this is the Israeli Air Force's success in attacking Arab airfields and destroying hundreds of aircraft within a few hours. Another case can be seen in the armored penetration on the Egyptian front on the first day of the Six-Day War.

Of the three traditional battle patterns—defense, retreat and attack—the IDF has been outstanding only in the last. The concept of retreat is almost nonexistent in the IDF's doctrine of warfare, and the defensive method is relegated to second place. During the War of

Independence, the IDF made use of defensive tactics but since then this doctrine has remained on paper. The military schools have generally ignored it, and the first time the IDF was compelled to think about defensive warfare was after the Six-Day War, during the War of Attrition.

The name of the game is offensive action. The IDF found many advocates of this approach in its early stages; Yitzhak Sadeh and Orde Wingate were most notable. Within the IDF itself, Moshe Dayan is noteworthy for his aggressive spirit, Ariel (Arik) Sharon for the development of small-scale combat and highly mobile tactics, Israel Tal for tank warfare and Ezer Weizman for the development of aerial combat. These commanders have been the embodiment of Orde Wingate's maxim, "The best defense is attack."

The IDF excels in offensive planning, especially when the strategy of the indirect or improvisational approach is involved. But long-term planning has suffered from many defects because the General Staff has always been caught up with current problems.

Much attention is given to the question of how to overcome Arab superiority in fire power and combat weapons. Operative and tactical planning is based on the fastest possible route to face-to-face combat in which the superiority of the individual fighter can be decisive. The IDF does not waste much time on the preparation of the classic opening moves. Commanders have learned not to make assault conditional on x number of hours of artillery softening up or the destruction of ground-to-air missile systems before the planes attack objectives defended by the missiles. In the Six-Day War, for example, Israeli Air Force planes did not strike first at Egyptian missiles, but went directly to the airfields. They found time for the missiles only on the third day of the war, and only when the missiles had begun to

interfere with the aerial cover given by the Air Force to armored columns advancing through Sinai.

One of the classic ways of shortening the early stages of battle is the use of darkness. The IDF has achieved impressive results in this field. Technical means of exploiting the night as an assault opportunity were developed both on land and in the air. Beginning in the 1950s, when commando units were used for nighttime reprisal actions, and culminating in the Six-Day War with the great night offensive at Abu Ageila in Sinai, the cover of darkness has been well used by the IDF. Night does not restrict the IDF in its use of large-scale forces and in carrying out the most complicated offensive.

Another characteristic trait of the IDF is that it is the only army that has developed on both the theoretical and operational levels a doctrine of warfare to counter the Soviet strategy employed by Egypt and Syria. IDF experts have thoroughly studied Soviet theories and know their weak points. Training installations in Israel have been built according to the Russian doctrine and armored and infantry units are familiar with Soviet tactics.

Full utilization of armored strength has also been developed as an essential doctrine in the IDF. The prime mover of this concept is Maj. Gen. Israel Tal. His central idea is that tanks must be considered as a group and not as separate and independent weapons systems. Tal uses tanks not for armor-against-armor battle, but to break through enemy lines. He has devised a special organization of armored units to implement this aim.

The IDF doctrine of warfare as described above relates to battle with conventional weapons. The entry of nuclear weapons into the Middle East will change the entire picture and new strategies will have to be devised.

The principles mentioned in this chapter were in effect without change until the Six-Day

Arik Sharon with staff officers in the field during the
Yom Kippur War. [Shabtai Tal]

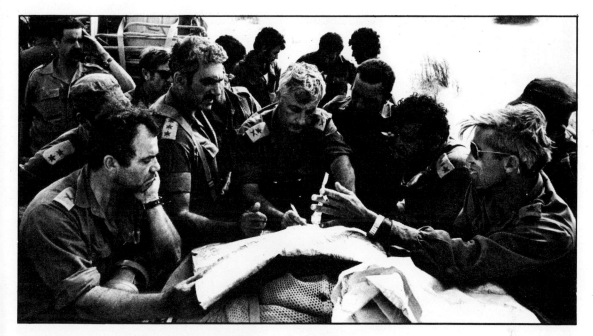

War. The geostrategic changes which took
place following that war have occasioned some
modifications, but the basic tenets remain.

The improved level of Arab military performance evidenced in the Yom Kippur War
must now be taken into account. The need for
pre-emptive attack on threatening enemy concentrations still appears to be essential and
the IDF has not forsaken the principle of transferring the war into enemy territory. However,
changing political and territorial realities require constant revision of tactical planning.
Israeli strategists still live with the fear that
a foreign power could intervene on the Arab
behalf as Russia threatened to do during the
Yom Kippur War. Above all, Israel continues
to wage war for her very existence, a war of
few against many.

Footnotes

1 Former Prime Minister Golda Meir voiced this opinion
   in her speech to the Knesset, 22 January 1974.
2 For post-Yom Kippur War writing supporting this view,
   see Gil Carl AlRoy, "Do the Arabs Want Peace?"
   Commentary (February 1974), pp. 56-61; and Amos
   Perlmutter, "The Covenant of War," *Harper's* Mag-
   azine (February 1974), pp. 51-61.
3 This was demonstrated at the United Nations during
   the Yom Kippur War when the Soviet Union moved in
   the Security Council for a cease-fire only when it was
   clear that Egypt was losing.
   Allon, *Masach shel Hol*, p. 68.

بسم الله الرحمن الرحيم

الجبهة الشعبية لتحرير فلسطين

THE POPULAR FRONT FOR THE
LIBERATION OF PALESTINE
(P.F.L.P.)

PALESTINE

وراء العدو في كل مكان
WE SHALL FIGHT THE
ENEMY EVERY WHERE

For three days in November 1973, Arab terrorists held a Tokyo-bound Dutch jumbo jet with 288 people aboard as it hopscotched around the Middle East. The action, carried out by the little-known Arab Nationalist Youth for the Liberation of Palestine, was front-page news for nearly a week. It was directed not against Israel but, in effect, against her friends. The KLM plane was the target of the hijacking reportedly because of Dutch support of Israeli interests. The Arab nations had already imposed an oil embargo on the Netherlands for her part in the Yom Kippur War — it was suspected in Arab circles that Dutch airfields and airliners were used to transport Israeli reservists home from Europe to fight in the war. One of the hijackers' stops during the air marathon was Cyprus, where they demanded the release of seven Arabs being held there for the April 1973 bombing attack on the home of Israel's Ambassador to Cyprus and on an El Al airliner at Nicosia Airport.

Sixty-eight hours after taking possession of the plane, the hijackers surrendered to authorities in the sheikdom of Dubai. No one had been injured and no prisoners had been released, but once again the war of terrorism against Israel had spilled beyond the narrow confines of the Middle East.

The increasing incidents of terrorism and air piracy marked a new stage in an old war. In recent years, Arab terrorists have extended their activities outside the boundaries of the Middle East, bringing their struggle to the attention of the world but at the same time threatening the rest of the world with the consequences of their terror. There is a chilling nihilism about fedayeen activities that has put air travel and even such mundane acts as opening a letter into the realm of peril. The word *fedayeen*, from the Arabic "to sacrifice," implies the suicidal recklessness that characterizes many terrorist actions in Israel and abroad.

The Hundred Years' War against Israel

Arab terrorists have been waging a fierce but undeclared war against Israel since the days of the first settlements in Palestine. The conflict has waxed and waned, subject to political conditions in neighboring Arab countries and circumstances within Israel and the leadership of the guerrilla bands, but the threat has always been there. Escalation of terrorist activities has been intimately tied up with the declared wars Israel has waged with its neighbors, and most often the terrorism has acted as a catalyst in these wars. The fedayeen, unrestrained by Big Power diplomacy, treaties, cease-fire agreements and national boundaries, are relentlessly dedicated to driving the Jews from what they consider to be the Palestinian homeland.

Defending Israel's borders against terrorist activities has presented the IDF with a specific set of problems. It is forced to wage guerrilla warfare against a hidden but ubiquitous enemy and, in large measure, has been limited to retaliatory action. Unlike the fedayeen, the IDF must guard against international sanctions and must always be wary of accusation that Israel is the aggressor. But guerrilla warfare is not completely alien to the IDF. The spiritual heritage of the Palmach, ETZEL and LEHI, clearly guerrilla units, carries on into the IDF. The techniques of those organizations serve as models for the regular army.

Arab leaders speak of waging a hundred years' war against Israel. In fact, the war has already passed its ninetieth year. The Arab guerrilla war began many years before Israel achieved independence and long before the Jews of Palestine learned to organize themselves for defense. Nor are the activities of Fatah and other fedayeen groups an invention of the 1960s and 70s. These terrorist organizations are treading a well-paved path whose beginnings go back to the days of renewal of

Opposite: The Givati Brigade patrolled border
settlements to deter Arab marauders.

Jewish settlement in Palestine in the 1880s.

The tactics have changed with the circumstances. At first, assaults on settlements and
destruction of orchards and crops were the
major perils to be feared. This has mush-
roomed into the hijacking of aircraft over
international airspace and the posting of
explosive letters in Europe and the United
States.

The first wave of this war began when Jews
moved out of the mixed towns and started to
erect independent agricultural settlements.
Thus began the struggle over the soil of Palestine. In those early years, there was no veteran
moshava that had not been attacked by its
Arab neighbors. Among these, Petach Tikvah
was brutally assaulted by terrorist bands in
1886 but the settlers managed to drive back
the attackers. Other settlements did not succeed, there being no organized group or plan
for self-defense — robbery, murder, rape and
destruction of crops were common experiences for these early settlers. The Jews
appealed to Ottoman authorities to provide
them with protection but their appeals were
denied. Out of that necessity arose the Shomrim and Hashomer organizations previously
discussed, and finally the Haganah, the direct
forebear of the Israel Defense Forces.

Pre-Statehood Waves of Terror

Between these early beginnings and the
establishment of the State of Israel, there were
three more waves of terror and guerrilla warfare. They took the form of flare-ups; the
battles were indecisive and hostilities subsided with no real solution. The first wave, the
Arab Riots of 1920-21, was religio-political in
nature. Action was concentrated against the
urban settlements in Jerusalem, Jaffa and Tel
Aviv but soon spread to the agricultural settlements. By that time the Haganah had been
established and was able to provide some

measure of defense.

Eight years later, a second wave of terror
engulfed Palestine, and the Jews, amid great
suffering, were compelled to abandon a considerable number of settlements. The primary
motivation for the 1929 disturbances was
again religious. In 1929, the outbreak began
when Arabs in Jerusalem tried to prevent Jews
from praying at the Western Wall, a fragment
of Solomon's Temple which stands on ground
that is also sacred to Islam. The fighting spread
to Hebron, Nablus, Gaza, Tulkarem, Jenin and
Bet-Shaan. Many Jews fled these mixed towns
and again the fighting died down as quickly
as it had begun.

It was seven years before hostilities again
erupted. The Arab Revolt, considered the most
serious of pre-Statehood waves of terror,
began in April 1936 and lasted until the beginning of World War II. Arab guerrilla attacks
were more forceful in this round but the Jewish forces also succeeded in considerably
improving their countermeasures. In addition,
the British Army stood behind the *yishuv* since
the Arab Revolt was also directed against the
British mandatory authority.

The Early Fifties: Border Raids and
Robbery

After the War of Independence, guerrilla
warfare once again emerged but it was of a
different character. Although religious differences still existed and were again a point of
irritation, the real issue was political and territorial, as homeless Arabs attacked occupants of the new Jewish homeland. The guerrillas were no longer waging war from a position of strength, as they had in the past, and
the war entailed crossing borders from the
neighboring Arab countries.

Hundreds of thousands of Arab refugees
had abandoned their homes and villages after
the State of Israel was established and settled

in temporary camps near the armistice lines. Egypt and Israel maintained a joint camp in the demilitarized zone of Nitzana and had established joint patrols which, in cooperation with the UN, traversed the length of the armistice lines. Egypt was in charge of the administration of the Gaza Strip, another refugee area. The refugees lived in squalor, were under martial rule and were not granted rights of citizenship by Egypt, who considered the area to be an economic and political burden.

It was against this background that the seething resentment of Palestinian Arabs grew. The stagnation of the refugee camps and the frustration and hatred toward Israel, which had taken what they considered to be their homeland, provoked many into crossing the border and raiding the farms and orchards of Israel. At first, thieving bands raided agricultural settlements near the border; later activity penetrated the cities. One infiltrator from Jordan was arrested in Tel Aviv after having committed five robberies. In Jerusalem, houses were plundered and tires stolen from cars. Saboteurs began to specialize in the murder of Israeli watchmen from whom they

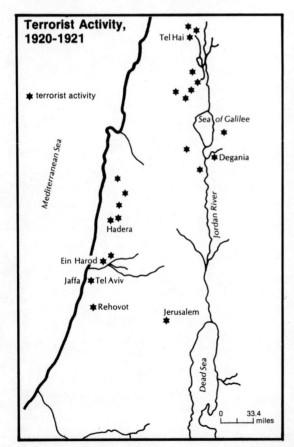

Terrorist Activity, 1920-1921

★ terrorist activity

Tel Hai

Mediterranean Sea

Sea of Galilee

Degania

Jordan River

Hadera

Ein Harod
Jaffa Tel Aviv

Rehovot

Jerusalem

Dead Sea

0   33.4
└──┴──┘ miles

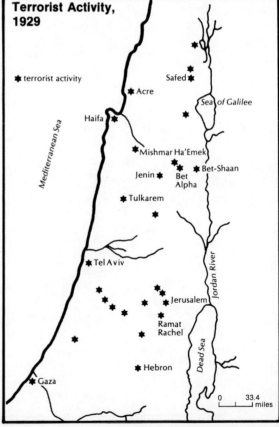

Terrorist Activity, 1929

★ terrorist activity

Safed

Acre

Sea of Galilee

Haifa

Mishmar Ha'Emek

Bet-Shaan

Jenin   Bet
Alpha

Tulkarem

Mediterranean Sea

Jordan River

Tel Aviv

Jerusalem

Ramat
Rachel

Dead Sea

Hebron

Gaza

0   33.4
└──┴──┘ miles

stole weapons. Numerous raids on IDF camps netted guns and ammunition for the guerrillas. In 1952, a band of robbers stole three tons of military rations from an army camp in Eilat. In many cases, gangs were organized by rich Arabs in Jordan as a business venture. These groups would penetrate Israeli territory by night and steal any property of value, taking livestock, engines, irrigation pipes, building materials and crops. During the citrus season, Arab trucks would cross the border and return loaded with oranges. The thefts were often accompanied by brutal acts of murder.

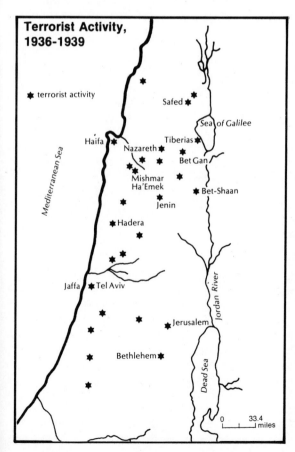

Arab activity moved beyond the bounds of ordinary infiltration when the Mufti, Haj Amin el Husseini, began to recruit among the refugees those who were willing to conduct sabotage raids inside Israel. He still hoped to establish an Islamic Palestinian state and was attempting to awaken a militant nationalism among the refugees. Sabotage activities unconnected with looting and theft of property began to be felt in Israel in 1950. Fields were set afire, water pumping stations were blown up, trees were uprooted, roads were planted with mines, railroad tracks torn up and miles of telephone wire cut and confiscated.

The Arab Legion and the Egyptian Army objected to the Mufti's independent activities but the Intelligence services of both armies began to make their own use of infiltrators. They were prepared to ignore the border crossings of the looters if they brought back military information about Israel along with their plunder.

1951: Israel Begins to Fight Back

In mid-1951, Israeli Intelligence began to receive information that the Mufti was behind the sabotage activities. The danger had increased to such a point that it was time to take positive action. This was Israel's first military challenge since the War of Independence and the qualitative decline of the IDF in the early 1950s had left its impact on the operational competence of the Army. Defensive measures had not succeeded; the time for retaliation had come. Initially it was decided to act upon the refugee camps and Jordanian villages from which the infiltrators came, in the hope of forcing the inhabitants of those areas to pressure the infiltrators into ceasing their activities against Israel.

Eighteen missions were carried out in 1951 but they were small operations and were hardly methodical. It was largely a matter of tit for tat. Mines were laid in enemy territory

Opposite: The cave office of "Abu Sallem," *nom de guerre* of a PFLP leader. [*Ha'aretz*]

in response to the laying of mines in Israel; thefts of irrigation pipes and telephone lines were undertaken by IDF soldiers beyond the frontier; herds of cattle were stolen, abandoned villages demolished, and crops sown by Jordanian villagers were reaped by the IDF. None of this prevented the flow of infiltrators.

Of eighty-five retaliatory actions carried out by the IDF by the end of 1953, only thirty-eight were listed as successful. It was a signal to IDF leaders that the Army was sorely in need of reform and rededication. In explaining the background of these failures, Moshe Dayan said, "We came out of the War of Independence with high standards of defense. I do not think that this war gave us high standards of offense. The main reason for this lies not only in lack of combat experience, but also in moral aspects. Defense flows in our blood; retreat as a concept has never existed. On the other hand, why fight to the last man for a hill with nothing on it, even if it is militarily important? This is not the same thing as standing to the last man in a settlement for which we fought. There was a moral defense."[1]

In the summer of 1953, a turning point came in the IDF response to the problem of guerrilla raids. Ariel Sharon, a twenty-five-year-old university student who had served in the IDF as an Intelligence officer during the Independence War, was called back to form a special raiding unit. It was designated Unit 101 and, in practice, it existed as an independent force for only six months. No more than forty men, hand-picked by Sharon for their commitment, high morale and tactical abilities, undertook the task of retaliation.

Unit 101 was an effective force and its leader an important figure in the reform of the IDF. It was through his activities with Unit 101 that Sharon became commander of the paratroops and under his command that the combat standards of that branch of the Army were raised

to a very high level.

A joint action under Sharon's direction upon the Arab village of Kibya in October 1953 had a profound and shocking effect on the history of terror and counterterror. A woman and her two children had been killed by a terrorist grenade in an immigrant settlement near Lydda and the Jordanian village of Kibya was earmarked for a retaliatory raid. After a short battle, the village was seized and the IDF demolished forty-six of its 250 houses. It was believed that most of the inhabitants of the village had escaped in the early stages of battle but, when the smoke had cleared, sixty-nine men, women and children were found dead in the wreckage of Kibya.

The public outcry was great, both in Israel and in the UN. Ben-Gurion's government gave an evasive answer to accusations about the attacking—he claimed it had not been a military action, but rather that the families of victims of Arab terrorism had undertaken their own revenge. Nonetheless, it became policy thereafter that any future retaliatory actions be reserved to military targets.

It had become clear through Israeli Intelligence that there were, in fact, military targets close at hand. Sponsorship of terrorist activities had moved beyond the Mufti; it was no longer sufficient to aim at the small villages and refugee camps which nurtured fedayeen sentiments.

1954: Egyptian Sponsorship of Fedayeen Activities

In 1954, the guerrilla war had already ceased to be spontaneous and had been transformed into terror organized by Egypt. Following the British evacuation of Egypt, the Egyptian General Staff unleashed fedayeen units for war on Israel. Nasser's plan was to harass Israel without exposing his own country to all-out war. Hundreds of Palestinians in the Gaza Strip were recruited into fedayeen units

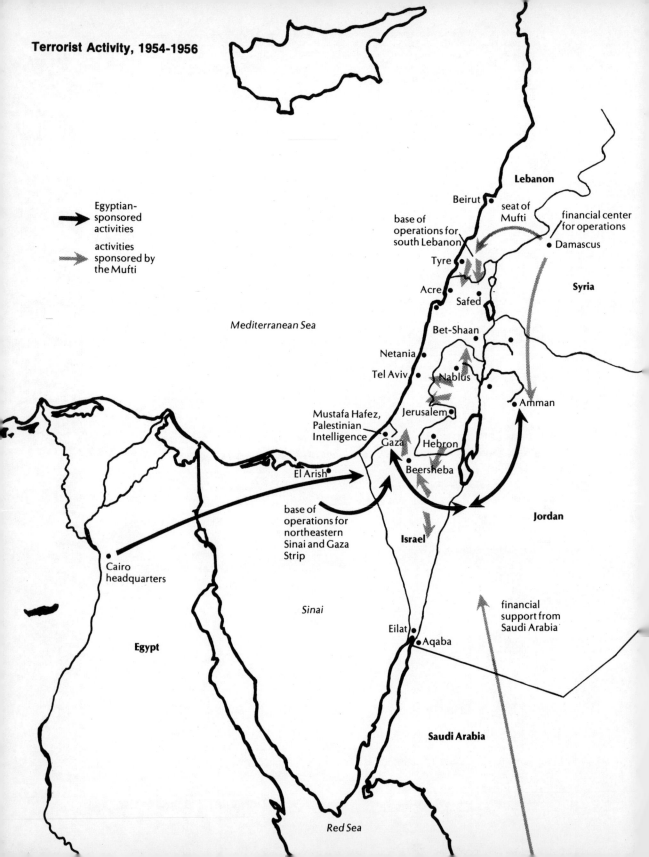

Terrorist Activity, 1954-1956

Egyptian-
sponsored
activities

activities
sponsored by
the Mufti

Lebanon

Beirut

seat of
Mufti

financial center
for operations

base of
operations for
south Lebanon

Damascus

Tyre

Syria

Acre

Safed

Bet-Shaan

Mediterranean Sea

Netania

Tel Aviv

Nablus

Amman

Mustafa Hafez,
Palestinian
Intelligence

Jerusalem

Gaza

Hebron

El Arish

Beersheba

Jordan

base of
operations for
northeastern
Sinai and Gaza
Strip

Israel

Cairo
headquarters

financial
support from
Saudi Arabia

Sinai

Eilat

Aqaba

Egypt

Saudi Arabia

Red Sea

Above: Fedayeen dead after clash with Israeli patrol.

Below: Thirteen were killed in the ambush of this bus by fedayeen, 1954. [Israeli Army]

Above: A fedayeen land mine knocked over this produce truck in southern Israel, 1955. [Israeli Army]

Below: UN observers examine damage in an Israeli settlement attacked by fedayeen, 1956. [Israeli Army]

and scores of convicted criminals were released from prison on the condition that they operate in Israeli territory. The Egyptian military attachés in Jordan and Lebanon organized Palestinians in these countries for sabotage operations in Israel. In 1955, after a number of extensive Israeli reprisals against Egypt, the fedayeen activity became more serious. It was mostly directed against civilian targets and manifested itself in ambushes of vehicles and the demolition of houses in border settlements.

Nasser may have hoped to avoid direct military confrontation with Israel but his part in the terrorist waves was known and can be seen as part of Israel's justification for launching the Sinai Campaign. The heavy toll in lives and property had rendered the situation intolerable. Defense of the borders and sporadic retaliation had not succeeded. Israel was ready to teach Nasser a larger lesson and found an ally in France, whose own struggle in Algeria was made the more difficult, it was believed, by Egyptian support of the FLN.

Thanks to the Sinai War, Israel's borders gained a measure of security. Egypt's fedayeen

Below: Israeli commanders plan retaliatory action
against fedyaeen, 1955. [Israeli Army]

Bottom: Yasir Arafat. [Wide World]

units were disbanded and infiltration had
dropped to minute proportions. In 1965, however, this tranquility was upset by the emergence of Fatah.

The Late Sixties: The Rise of Fatah

Founded in 1959 by Yasir Arafat, Fatah
eventually became an important force in the
Middle East. Its name is an acronym for Movement for the Liberation of Palestine— *Haara-
kat Tahrir Falastin*—which has been reversed,
since *hataf* means sudden death in Arabic.
Fatah is the Arabic word for conquest.

Because the atmosphere in Egypt was no
longer cordial to fedayeen activities after the
Sinai War, Arafat based himself in Lebanon.
Fatah found allies in Algeria, whose FLN had
successfully ousted the French colonial rule,
and later in Syria. By 1963 the leftwing Baath
Socialist Party had taken over in Syria and was
interested in wresting from Nasser some of the
power he wielded in the Arab world. Its support
of Fatah was a tool in that struggle.

The first Fatah operation in January 1965 was
directed against Israel's National Water Carrier. Frustration had again given birth to a new
wave of guerrilla warfare but this time it was
also aimed at the Arab states, however indirectly. The Arab leadership refused to go to
war against Israel and it became Fatah's objective to aggravate matters and turn the uneasy peace into war. Their plan involved
carrying out sabotage operations in Israel in
order to provoke reprisals against the Arab
states, thereby setting the two sides off down
the slope to war. Their program proceeded
well, at least in terms of this objective—Fatah
became one of the major factors leading to the
outbreak of the Six-Day War.

Fatah operations up to the Six-Day War were
not militarily significant, though they took on
greater weight after the Damascus government
began to support Fatah in an attempt to em-
barrass Nasser. Israel viewed the small-scale

Young *ashbal*—lion cubs—trained in terrorism by Fatah. [Israeli Army]

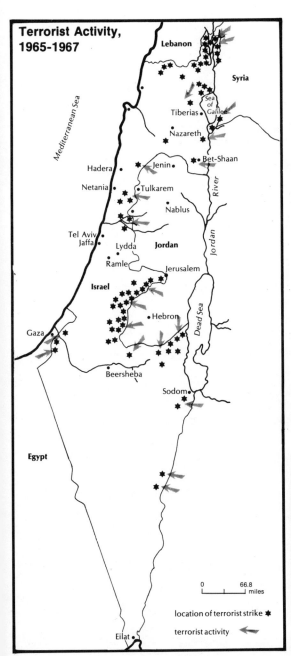

**Terrorist Activity,
1965-1967**

Lebanon

Syria

Mediterranean Sea

Tiberias • *Sea of Galilee*

Nazareth

Hadera • • Jenin • *Bet-Shaan*

Netania •

• Tulkarem

Jordan River

Nablus •

Tel Aviv •
Jaffa • Lydda • **Jordan**

Ramle •

Jerusalem •

Israel

• Hebron

Dead Sea

Gaza •

Beersheba •

Sodom •

Egypt

0   66.8
⊢————⊣ miles

location of terrorist strike ✸

terrorist activity ⬅

Eilat •

operations of Fatah with a severity far greater than their military significance. After eight relatively quiet years, Israel feared a return of the terror of the early 1950s. But the severe reprisals taken against Syria helped exacerbate the deterioration in relations that led to the Six-Day War. In practice, Israel played the role that Fatah had intended for her.

Fatah achieved its objective in June 1967 but the results of the Six-Day War were hardly what Arafat had hoped for. The Arabs were defeated and their armies routed. Yet, the geographic changes effected by Israel's control over new territories gave birth to new and much more convenient conditions for guerrilla warfare against her. The occupied territories could provide more convenient hiding places (though not comparable with the jungles of Vietnam or the Philippines) for the guerrilla fighters. A population of a million Palestinians was added to the 300,000 Israeli Arabs.

The Israeli government was viewed as an occupying regime by this population. This was the first time that the right conditions existed for the establishment of guerrilla bases within territories ruled by Israel; for the first time Fatah could find cover in the human forest of

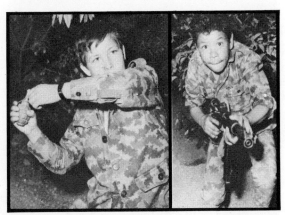

PFLP leader "Abu Sallem" and fellow fedayeen planning a raid on Bet-Shaan Valley near the Sea of Galilee. [*Ha'aretz.*]

Opposite: Israeli Druze anti-fedayeen border patrol in northern Israel. [Israeli Army]

the local population, especially in the Gaza Strip, which was overflowing with masses of refugees.

In fact, the saboteurs were aided considerably by Israel's liberal approach to the Arab population. The Israeli government decided to open the bridges over the Jordan and permit the Israeli Arab population to continue its commercial, cultural and personal contacts with the Arab countries. Despite the state of war, thousands of Arabs from the neighboring countries poured into Israel on family visits and a lively commercial traffic crossed the bridges. This was a calculated risk on the part of Israel. The saboteurs did indeed exploit the open bridges for smuggling of equipment and arms, infiltration of trained men and the maintenance of constant communications with their personnel in Israel.

The Fedayeen after the Six-Day War

One of the fedayeen organizations' achievements after the Six-Day War was their success in inciting the Palestinian masses. After the defeat of the regular armies, the fedayeen were considered the only warriors still dedicated to the redemption of Arab honor. Fatah grew from a small band to a mass movement. Other fedayeen organizations arose, at one point numbering sixty. Among them were five larger and more prominent organizations—Fatah, the Popular Front for the Liberation of Palestine, the Popular Democratic Front for the Liberation of Palestine, *SAIQAH*—and the Popular Front General Command. They claimed a membership in the thousands, all armed and dedicated to the extermination of Israel. They hoped to achieve by guerrilla warfare and terrorism what the regular armies had not done on the battlefield.

The fedayeen organizations also became a part of the inter-Arab battle. There was almost no Arab state that did not adopt its own fedayeen organization. Weapons were drawn from

Top: Fedayeen commandos during penetration raid. [UPI]

Middle: Two members of PFLP practice planting land mines. [*Ha'aretz*]

Bottom left: Dr. George Habash, leader of the Popular Front for the Liberation of Palestine (PFLP).

Bottom middle: Naif Hawatmeh, leader of the Popular Democratic Front for the Liberation of Palestine (PDFLP).

Bottom right: Cartoon by "zeev" which appeared in *Ha'aretz*, an Israeli newspaper. Yasir Arafat is the travel agent.

Middle Eastern Airlines plane, one of thirteen blown up in December 1968 at Beirut airfield in retaliation for fedayeen attacks on El Al planes.

Middle: Israeli reconnaissance patrol. [Israeli Army]

Bottom: A terrorist is flushed from his cave refuge. [Israeli Army]

the arsenals of the regular armies, and funds flowed in from the rich petroleum emirates and countries like Saudi Arabia and Libya.

As time passed, the fedayeen organizations tended more to the Left. Their connections with the Soviet Union and the People's Republic of China strengthened, and weapons flowed to them from these two countries. Their rhetoric was designed to portray them as a liberation movement; they likened themselves to the Viet-Cong and the IDF to the United States Army in Vietnam. The analogy, however, is not so neat. Unlike the United States, Israel is fighting in her own home for her very existence. Further-more, as time passed, the majority of Arab states refused to play the role of Hanoi for the fedayeen.

The fedayeen organizations found connections with leftwing extremist underground movements, such as the Red Army in Japan and the Turkish Liberation Army. They recruited mercenaries from among them and elsewhere. As their operational failures multiplied, they began to make use of foreigners, whether for hijacking of aircraft or for murder operations. The massacre at Lydda Airport in May 1972, in which twenty-eight tourists were killed, was carried out by three Japanese. And there have been numerous cases of foreign tourists who have been apprehended carrying bombs, some-times planted without their knowledge, in-tended to blow up aircraft for the fedayeen.

Israeli Action against the Fedayeen after the Six-Day War

In the period after the Six-Day War, the IDF joined forces with the various Intelligence branches in Israel to eliminate the fedayeen menace. Direct military action was combined with infiltration by security agents as more in-formation was gathered on the location and identity of guerrilla strongholds. Although she had a freer hand within her own territories,

Below: Katyusha 130mm rocket and launcher of Chinese manufacture destroyed by an IDF retaliatory strike in the Mt. Hermon area. [Zeev Schiff]

Weapons of the fedayeen—anti-personnel bomb and mine of Chinese manufacture. [Israeli Army]

Israel was treading dangerous ground elsewhere. A truce had been declared and a state of peace existed between Israel and her Arab neighbors. Nonetheless, military action had to be taken against the fedayeen who sought refuge in those countries. Israel was, therefore, highly vulnerable to criticism from the world at large and to retaliation from those Arab states that continued to support the fedayeen.

The fedayeen failed to establish guerrilla bases in Israeli-occupied territories. Although the Arab population hardly welcomed the Israeli conquest, it was not prepared to take the risk of active assistance to the fedayeen.

Israeli Intelligence services succeeded in penetrating the organizations and, through the exploitation of internal disputes, they slowly but systematically eradicated the fedayeen organizations in the territories in Israeli hands.

The government of Israel, feeling that she had the upper hand, decided not to impose the death penalty against those among them—including Arab citizens of Israel—who were caught in attempts to murder civilians and lay explosives in public places like supermarkets, cinemas and bus stations. Even Kozo Okamoto, who participated in the massacre at Lydda Airport, was not sentenced to death. The prisons

filled up with thousands of saboteurs. Two years after the Six-Day War, there were 3,000 fedayeen in Israeli prisons, but as the guerrilla activities died down Israel began to release those convicts who had been sentenced to short terms.

The policy banning capital punishment for terrorists was seriously reconsidered after the massacres at Kiryat Shimona and Maalot in the spring of 1974. The imprisoned fedayeen, many Israelis felt, represented a tempting motive for seizing Jewish hostages.

Having routed the fedayeen camps in Israeli-occupied territories, the IDF turned to guerrilla bases beyond the borders. First priority was accorded Jordan, followed by Lebanon. Thousands of saboteurs were concentrated in bases close to the borders of these two countries, within artillery range. From there they attempted to cross the border into Israel, in order to reach areas populated by Arabs. To cope with these bases, Israel made use of frequent aerial attacks, airborne commando raids and penetration by armored columns, which reached as far as the Litani River in Lebanon. In her war on the fedayeen, Israel did not recoil from massive bombing of military and strategic objectives in Syria in order to bring pressure on Damascus and force the Syrians to forbid fedayeen expeditions into Israel from Syrian territory.

In September 1970, the Popular Front for the Liberation of Palestine hijacked four international jetliners to Jordan, where they destroyed the planes after holding the passengers captive in the desert. The event spurred an international outcry and precipitated a civil war in which King Hussein moved to crush the fedayeen presence, which had become a state within his own state. Many hundreds of fedayeen were killed, often by Palestinians serving in Hussein's Army. The Syrian Army invaded Jordan to give assistance to the fedayeen, but

Bottom left: Maj. Gen. Aharon Yariv, former Chief of IDF Intelligence, anticipated the rise of Black September. Yariv is currently the director of Israel's clandestine anti-terror war.

Bottom right: Black September hijackers Therese Halaah (right) and Rimma Tannous stand trial in Israel.

was driven back by the Jordanians and the threat implied by the concentration of Israeli forces on the Syrian border. By spring of 1971, the fedayeen in Jordan had been defeated.

1970: Black September Escalates the Terror

The fedayeen Black September movement was born against the background of the September 1970 disturbances in Jordan. This organization, an ultra-extremist arm of Fatah, started out with political assassinations in Jordan and then moved to personal terror against Israelis outside the borders of Israel. The hijacking of aircraft, including non-Israeli planes, to gain release of those imprisoned for sabotage activities in various European countries, became frequent. Activities spread to the Netherlands, Belgium, Germany, Italy, Switzerland, Austria, Greece, Great Britain, Denmark and the United States. Planes were hijacked

and blown up, assassination attempts were made, bombs were planted in factories, schools and apartment houses. Letter bombs were sent to Israeli diplomats, terrorizing postal workers and natives of the countries in which they were stationed. These operations reached their peak with the murder in September 1972 of eleven Israeli athletes at the Munich Olympics.

The fedayeen felt themselves more secure in war outside of Israel, in places where there was no fear of direct confrontation with the IDF. They relied on the fact that the countries in which they were operating were reluctant to jeopardize their relationships with the Arab states, and in the final event would release the culprits. Their hunch was indeed proven correct. Most of the Arab fedayeen arrested in Europe on various charges, including murder, were released without trial. Among these were three of the terrorists who participated in the Munich Olympics murders.

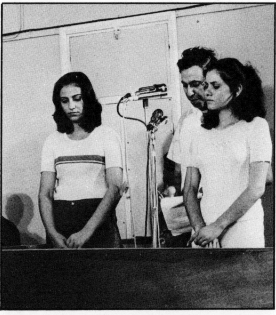

Left: Captured fedayeen blindfolded by his IDF captors.

Right: Moshe Dayan tours Gaza with Gen. Haim Bar-Lev at the height of fedayeen action in that area, 1971. [Israeli Army]

Bottom: An Israeli unit moving through "Fatahland" in southern Lebanon during May 1970 retaliatory raid. [Zeev Schiff]

Ghasan Khanafani, spokesman for the PFLP, was killed by a boobytrap in his car shortly after he claimed credit for PFLP in the 1972 Lydda Airport massacre.

Bottom: Fedayeen captured by an Israeli patrol.

Israel Answers Terror with Terror

In the early seventies, retaliatory action was stepped up by the military and Intelligence agencies in Israel. Terrorist leaders also began to receive explosive letters. In Beirut and Libya, a number of them were killed or wounded by parcels or booby-trapped cars. Ghasan Khanafani, spokesman for the PFLP, was killed when his car exploded shortly after he had boasted that his group had engineered the Lydda massacre.

Israel is careful not to take credit officially for these actions. It has become cloak-and-dagger warfare—the identity of agents and the details of operations are secret. However, after the Munich murders, Israel announced that the game would be played by new rules. The representatives of fedayeen organizations in Paris, Rome and Cyprus were assassinated and others were injured.

Nor did Israel ease her blows against terrorist bases in the Arab countries. She mounted long-range commando actions deep inside Arab territory. Hand-picked commando units landed from helicopters and came by sea to hit at bases hundreds of miles from the Israeli border. These operations reached their peak with a bold penetration into the heart of Beirut

Suspected collaborator in village of Habirah is questioned by Israeli soldiers. [Zeev Schiff]

Middle: Collaborator is held in an army vehicle while his house is blown up as punishment for his cooperation with terrorists. [Zeev Schiff]

Bottom: Fedayeen in Israeli prison prepare camouflage netting for Israeli Air Force. [Zeev Schiff]

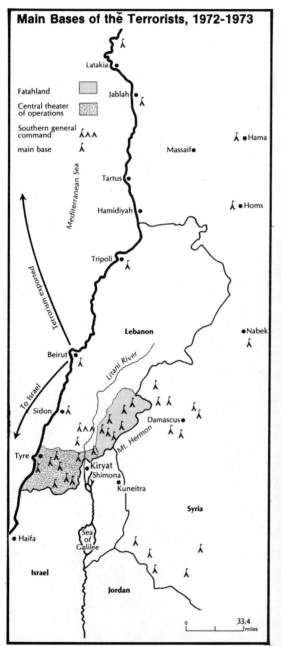

Main Bases of the Terrorists, 1972-1973

Latakia

Fatahland

Central theater of operations

Southern general command

main base

Jablah

Mediterranean Sea

Hama

Massaif

Tartus

Hamidiyah

Homs

Terrorism exported

Tripoli

Lebanon

Nabek

Beirut

Litani River

To Israel

Sidon

Damascus

Tyre

Mt. Hermon

Kiryat Shimona

Kuneitra

Syria

Haifa

Sea of Galilee

Israel

Jordan

0   33.4
|———| miles

Czechoslovakian anti-vehicle mine used by fedayeen.
[Israeli Army]

in April 1973. There the commandos located
the apartments of three Palestinian fedayeen
leaders, two of whom were connected with
Black September, and killed them together
with their bodyguards.

In August 1973, Yosef Tekoah, Israel's Ambassador to the United Nations, explained that,
in the absence of effective international sanctions against terrorist activities, Israel had decided to act dramatically in her own defense
against the "orgy of bloodshed by Arab terror."
Such action, he said, was represented by the
diversion of a Lebanese jetliner to an Israeli
airfield the previous August. Israel had been
severely censured for that action and the UN
Security Council had even gone so far as to
pass a vote of official condemnation. Particularly frustrating was the American willingness
to later approve a Security Council resolution
condemning Israel's retaliation for the Kiryat
Shimona massacre in April 1974 without condemning the terrorist action itself. The failure
of the UN to act against terrorism aroused
the anger of many Jews who feel it represents
the world's indifference to Jewish suffering.
Again the dilemma has to be faced: How can
Israel protect herself from the actions of terrorists in a manner that is effective and at the
same time escape criticism from the United
States and Israel's enemies who watch the
uneasy peace in the Middle East with ner-
vous eyes?

Israel has not won her war against terrorism.
Fedayeen activities continue to flare up and die
down in parallel to political developments between Israel and her Arab neighbors. During
the peace negotiations between Israel and
Egypt following the Yom Kippur War, a new
wave of terrorist activities in the Middle East
and abroad could be seen as a fedayeen attempt to sabotage any peace agreement.

The extremism of the terrorists increases in
proportion to the chances of peace in the Mid-

east. They have succeeded in the past in drawing the Arab states into war against Israel and
they take seriously their role as the relentless
antagonists in these struggles. What their role
will be in the future remains to be seen, but
there is no doubt that the fedayeen present a
special challenge to the Intelligence forces
and the IDF.

Footnotes
1 Israel Defense Forces, *Tenth Anniversary Publication*
(Tel Aviv: 1968).

14. THE WAR OF ATTRITION

Chief of Staff Haim Bar-Lev, 1968-1972

Despite the crushing defeat of the Arab armies in the Six-Day War, it was not long before fighting against Israel was renewed. This extension of the Six-Day War into a prolonged conflict with Egypt was an arduous experience for Israel.

After the June 1967 war there was talk of reducing the IDF to a minimal force. Those who argued for troop reduction contended that it would take years for the Arab armies to regain the strength necessary for a new confrontation. But even as the debate over the size of the postwar Army continued, a new war was begun.

This fourth war was known as "the war after the war" or "the War of Attrition," the latter being a reference to Egypt's stated aim of wearing Israel down by hammering away at her defenses and by inflicting consistently heavy losses. Israel officially dates the War of Attrition from March 1969—when the sporadic clashes along the Suez Canal developed into daily occurrences—until August 1970 when an American-sponsored cease-fire went into effect. In fact, the war started much earlier.

September 1967: The Khartoum Decision

The Arab states convened in Khartoum, Sudan in September 1967 and made a decision based on three no's: no peace with Israel, no negotiation with her and no recognition of her territorial claims. The outcome of the meeting was a shocking disappointment to the Israeli public who had hoped that the great victory of the previous June would naturally and necessarily be followed by a peace agreement with the Arab states.

The implications of the Khartoum decision became evident on October 21, 1967. During a routine patrol of the Sinai coast, the destroyer *Eilat*, flagship of the Israeli fleet, approached too close to the Egyptian-held Port Said at the entrance to the Suez Canal. As the destroyer passed in front of Port Said, a Russian-made Ussa missile boat stationed in the port sud-

denly launched three missiles which sank the *Eilat*. Of the 200 crew members, 47 were killed and 91 wounded. Israel was suddenly made to face the reality that despite her great victory in 1967 there was, in fact, no end to the war. The Arabs had been defeated, but not finished.

Israel retaliated four days later when her artillery struck oil refineries in the Egyptian town of Suez, setting them ablaze.

September 1968: The War Spreads

The new small war soon spread to the Jordanian and Syrian frontiers, where the Palestinian terrorist organizations launched an effort

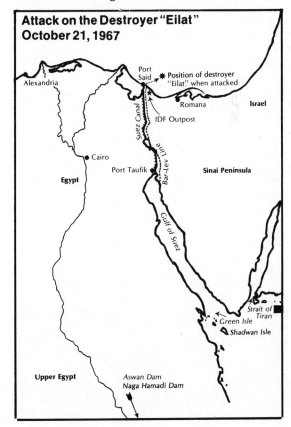

**Attack on the Destroyer "Eilat"
October 21, 1967**

Gen. Haim Bar-Lev with Moshe Dayan, July 1970.
[Authenticated News]

to establish bases in Israeli-occupied territories or close to her borders. The IDF replied with punitive expeditions and aerial attacks. Though aimed at the fedayeen, there was no way of avoiding clashes with the Jordanian and Syrian armies. In September 1968, IDF forces on the Suez Canal were bombarded by Egyptian artillery. Within a few hours, hundreds of Egyptian guns rained down more than 10,000 shells on the Israeli lines along the whole front. They inflicted many casualties on Israeli soldiers who sought shelter in emplacements and bunkers which failed to provide cover against heavy shells and direct hits. The Egyptians demonstrated their advantage: fire power produced by an overwhelming number of guns, used in a static battle in which they had no fear of advancing Israeli columns. Seven weeks later, they repeated the exercise and again caused serious casualties in heavy bombardment.

The IDF was presented with a new military challenge. The commanding officer at the Egyptian front, Maj. Gen. Yishayahu Gavish, said: "The first barrages shook us. The Egyptians then had 150 batteries of artillery. They fired delayed action fuses in order to penetrate the bunkers."[1]

Again, as they did after the sinking of the

Eilat, the IDF sought retaliatory strategy. They chose an indirect approach, far away from the front: an airborne invasion deep into Egypt. An electric transmission station on the high tension line between the Aswan Dam and Cairo was blown up. The Air Force also damaged a Nile bridge and the Naga Hamadi Dam in upper Egypt. These incursions convinced Nasser that his hinterland was not yet prepared for war. The strategy was successful inasmuch as the massive Egyptian activities of the War of Attrition were again postponed for a few months.

The IDF Adopts a Defensive Strategy

The War of Attrition confronted the IDF with military problems it had never before known, or had ignored since the War of Independence. Since the 1948 war, the IDF General Staff had emphasized offensive planning. Plans, operations and energy had always been directed toward attack patterns. The military thinkers devoted little time to defensive maneuvers. The rule was that war would have to be resolved by rapid offensive and forward movement. A complete generation of commanders and soldiers had based themselves on this, so much so that the study of defensive strategy and "digging in" had been deliberately neglected. However, as the situation emerged after the Six-Day War, the IDF was compelled to concentrate on defensive planning. It was feared that since the IDF had for years been geared to advance, break through and rapidly resolve a battle, the new routine of defense would change the character of the Israeli soldier. Previously known for his initiative and aggressiveness, would he now be stymied by defensive thinking?

For the first time in its history, the IDF was compelled to wage war from static lines along the borders. The IDF General Staff had always avoided such confrontations and, since the mid-1950s, had held almost no troops in border

"The war of attrition should be outmoded by now . . . too often it is not."—Napoleon Bonaparte [Culver Pictures]

Bottom: Gen. David Elazar on maneuvers in Sinai.

strongpoints. Defense of the border had been based on small mobile units which patroled the area, while the bulk of the IDF force was in training in rear camps and other nonstrategic points. But in 1968 a large proportion of the regular army and many reserve units were compelled to take up positions along the borders in emplacements and fortresses on permanent defense lines. This kind of fighting necessitated division into small units, a radical change from the normal procedure of operations in large formations to achieve rapid decisions in battle.

"Digging in" became, of necessity, the central task of the Israeli Army. The Army had never used as much barbed wire, mines, shelters and strongpoints as it did in the War of Attrition. It signaled a change in attitude since the 1950s when it was believed that fences and mines would not stop infiltrators from crossing borders. They were stopped by the deterrent power of the IDF and the Arabs' knowledge of what to expect if their people did cross. The change stimulated development of various electronic tools and the installation of electronic fences. The heavy Egyptian bombardments taught that sandbags did not provide adequate shelter to soldiers. Israeli Army engineers began constructing bunkers and trenches, pulling up railroad tracks that crossed the length of Sinai to strengthen these new emplacements. Ironically, Soviet field manuals provided the best instructions on proper construction and reinforcement of bunkers.

1969: The Bar-Lev Line

The search for new strategies also found expression in the essential question of how to defend the most important border of all—the Suez Canal. The choice was between a defense based on a fortified line along the banks of the Canal, or defense by mobile forces stationed in the rear, out of range of light weapons and

Bottom: Israeli position on the Bar-Lev Line.   Gen. Arik Sharon at the Bar-Lev Line.

mortars, but ready to push back anybody who crossed the Canal. The supporters of mobile defense, among them Maj. Gen. Ariel Sharon, contended that the strongpoints along the waterline would not serve as a delaying factor or as firing positions in the event of a general attack, but only as convenient targets for the Egyptian artillery. They said this would unavoidably increase Israeli casualties. Those who thought differently contended that if the IDF did *not* sit on the waterline, small Egyptian units could cross the Canal and dig in on the Israeli side. This would result in a chain of battles that could be prevented in advance.

In 1969, a decision was made to construct a fortified line along the Canal. It became known as the Bar-Lev Line, after Lt. Gen. Haim Bar-Lev, IDF Chief of Staff at the time. Unlike the Maginot and Mannerheim Lines, which were continuous defensive chains, the Bar-Lev Line consisted of many fortified positions linked by a road. Armored reconnaissance units roamed between the positions and armored striking forces were distributed behind them so that within minutes they could reach any point along the Canal. The uniqueness of the line was in the mobile armored and artillery forces.

Israeli armored unit in Sinai with self-propelled
155mm artillery piece. [Israeli Army]

One of the IDF commanders in Sinai commented that while the fighting that took place along the Canal was *not* best suited to the character of the IDF, "We tried to wage this static war in the most mobile way possible. And we depended greatly on the initiative and independence of commanders in the lower echelons. In this way we adapted to the new situation."[2]

Egyptian Army Advantages

The Egyptians enjoyed a number of advantages in the War of Attrition. Because it was a static war, they were less vulnerable to the command weaknesses that had been exposed in the highly mobile war of 1967. Furthermore, the Egyptian Army's land forces had superior fire power. This was especially clear in terms of artillery: The Egyptians had nearly twenty times as many guns as the Israelis, thanks to continued Soviet arms shipments. Their Russian guns fired ten times as many shells as did Israeli artillery.

Up until the Six-Day War, the Israeli artillery had been of secondary importance in General Staff plans. At the end of the War of Independence, the standard artillery piece in the

IDF was a 75mm gun, a 1906 Krupp model. In the 1956 Sinai War, Israeli artillery consisted mainly of British 25-pounders and a few French 155mm guns. The Six-Day War found Israeli gunners with very few self-propelled 155mm artillery pieces. The War of Attrition was the turning point for Israeli artillery, which has since become almost entirely self-propelled. The artillery succeeded in concentrating its forces although the number of guns at its disposal was small. The Israeli gunners excelled in rapid action and good communications while moving from position to position under fire.

Another Egyptian advantage lay in their ability to sustain casualties with a certain resignation inherent in Islam. The Egyptians, both as soldiers and civilians, tend to accept tragedy fatalistically. The size of the nation (33 million), the high percentage of illiterates, faulty communications between the different strata of the nation and a controlled press all help obscure the scope of loss and defeat and prevent the nation from rebelling against its rulers.

This is not so in Israel. It seems that there is no nation more sensitive to sacrifices than the Jews of Israel, who are still burdened by memories of the Nazi Holocaust. The Egyptians, with Nasser at their head, were well aware of this Israeli sensitivity. In speaking of the War of Attrition, the Egyptian President once said: "I cannot conquer Sinai, but I can grind Israel down and break her spirit."[3] Egyptian commentators explained that cutting down seven Israeli soldiers every day on the Suez Canal would be enough to force Israel to the breaking point and to bring her to her knees.

The Egyptian General Staff believed it could achieve local aerial supremacy in the Canal zone. They thought that the arms embargo imposed against Israel by France after the Six-Day War and the fact that U.S. Phantom aircraft had not yet reached the IDF would make it easier for the Egyptians to achieve that aerial supremacy. Then, after systematic artillery pounding and inflicting many losses on the IDF, the Egyptian Army could cross the Canal and seize control of all or at least part of the waterway.

Nasser's assessment of Israeli sensibilities was accurate. There was nothing more painful or demoralizing than the photos which were published daily in the newspapers of Israeli soldiers who fell in the War of Attrition. Nothing influenced the morale of the Israeli public more in those days than the sight of those young faces. No less painful was the feeling that the war was purposeless since it did not seek to defeat the enemy army. The feeling of frustration grew when the Russians deepened their military involvement on the side of the Egyptians. Among the civilian population and within the Army, the question—where will it end?—was asked with greater frequency. Defense Minister Moshe Dayan attempted an answer in a speech delivered in August 1969:

This question was born with the first Hebrew—with Abraham our father. Jewish anxiety throughout the ages has been a double anxiety: fear for the individual—the Jew—and for the entirety—the nation. Anxiety for the physical fate of the Jew and the spiritual continuity of the Jewish people. For these, we have been condemned to struggle through all the generations. When the Creator said to the Jewish nation: "Fear not, O Jacob, my servant!" he did not intend to give us an insurance policy. The meaning is that we are condemned to constant struggle and we must not fail because of cowardice.[4]

The Body Count

During the War of Attrition, the IDF set up the most intensive military medical system of any army in the world, and one that was without precedent in its proximity to the front lines.

The achievements of this system were reflected in the lowered death rate among casualties.

But Israel still paid a heavy price. The total dead in the War of Attrition was no less than in the Six-Day War. From the end of the 1967 war until the cease-fire on August 7, 1970, 721 Israelis were killed in battle and terrorist attacks. Of these, 594 were soldiers. The number of wounded reached 2,659. The highest casualty rate was at the Egyptian front where 367 Israelis were killed and 999 wounded.

The Arabs also paid a heavy price—their dead numbered many more. Among the Palestinian terrorist organizations alone, the dead totaled, according to IDF computation, 1,828. The heads of these organizations contended that their losses were even greater. To these must be added 2,500 of their personnel caught and put behind bars in Israel. The Egyptians did not publish casualty figures, but Nasser admitted in a letter to the President of Iraq that close to 100 Egyptian soldiers fell weekly. At the peak of the War of Attrition, when Egyptian missile units were being bombed, the Egyptian Chief of Staff admitted their death rate was at least 300 a day. Aerial photographs of Egyptian cemeteries in the Canal Zone alone showed 1,801 graves in this period. Abdul Moneim Riad, the Egyptian Chief of Staff, was among the dead. He died from wounds received in shelling on the Canal.

Egyptian towns along the Canal were almost totally destroyed and some 750,000 residents were evacuated. Important industrial plants were wrecked and with them the refineries and oil port of Suez. Inhabitants of Jordanian border villages in the Jordan Valley where the Palestinian fedayeen organizations had their bases also suffered from Israeli retaliation.

IDF losses on the Canal led to the decision to put the Israeli Air Force into action, and the War of Attrition escalated. A raid by Egyptian commandos on an Israeli tank unit at the Port

Chief of Staff Bar-Lev announces that Russian advisors have fired SAM-3 missiles at Israeli planes over the Suez Canal, July 1970. [UPI]

Bottom: "I cannot conquer Sinai, but I can grind Israel down and break her spirit."—Gamel Abdel Nasser [Nancy Reese]

Taufik jetty on July 12, 1969 was the turning point. The unit suffered heavy losses and the government finally agreed to proposals to make use of the Air Force against the Egyptians. At first, the air strikes were sporadic actions, but as the war spread, so the activities of the Israeli Air Force intensified.

Israel's flying artillery cut down considerably Egypt's advantage in fire power and changed the situation on the front line. Israeli casualties dropped from month to month. At the same time, the IDF increased its incursions into Egypt, beginning with commando raids deep into Egypt, and moving to shorter penetrations near the front line.

One of the most impressive raids was the armored "excursion" of September 1969. Israeli landing craft dropped a column of tanks and half-tracks on the Egyptian coastline in the Gulf of Suez. The column consisted of Soviet armored vehicles captured by the IDF in the Six-Day War, and reconditioned for battle. The column moved up to the main road and started southward. For nine hours it moved forty miles from one Egyptian objective to another, destroying everything in its path—guard posts and camps, coastal positions and radar stations. The Egyptians could not understand what was happening, and it was only a news agency report from Tel Aviv about penetration of Egyptian territory that awakened Nasser and his General Staff. Egyptian cars moved past the armored column, which seemed Egyptian in every detail, and were destroyed by machine-gun fire and artillery. The Egyptian Commander of the Suez Gulf area was killed in one of these cars. A senior Russian military adviser was also killed during the incursion. Some 150 Egyptian soldiers lost their lives and much equipment was destroyed.

The Egyptians were stunned. Nasser removed his Chief of Staff and the Commander of the Egyptian Navy. Earlier, after two Israeli

Mirage aircraft had flown low over his own home outside Cairo, Nasser had fired his Air Force Commander and Aerial Defense Commander. A few days after the Israeli raid in September 1969, Nasser suffered his first heart attack, but it was kept secret. He died of a second heart attack a year later.

The Israeli Phantom F-4E jet.

Bottom: A Soviet missile cruiser in the Mediterranean, March 1969. [Wide World]

Three months after the armored raid, IDF planners of special operations again demonstrated considerable boldness. An Israeli force, landed inside Egypt by helicopter, dismantled and flew away with an entire radar installation. The captured Russian P12 radar, which was effective in all weather against low-flying aircraft, provided the IDF with valuable new technological information.

The Egyptian operators and technicians were also captured and brought to Israel. Like other prisoners, they were questioned by Israeli sociologists and psychologists who wanted to compile a complete profile of the Egyptian soldier. In addition to tours of Israel, including visits in Israeli homes, these prisoners were given various aptitude tests. It was found that sixty-four percent of the Egyptian officers in Israeli captivity could not have passed the entrance examination to the IDF Officers' School.

January 1970: A Turning Point

In January 1970, the War of Attrition reached a significant turning point, which indirectly stimulated Russian military involvement. Israel began deep bombing in Egypt, mostly around Cairo and in the Nile Delta. As the War of Attrition had stretched on, some Israeli strategists wanted to exert heavier pressure on Nasser's regime in an effort to bring the war to an end. The first signs of this kind of thinking could be detected in Moshe Dayan's remarks in the summer of 1968: "If we want to and have to, we can undermine them through the civilian population. Our presence in Sinai permits us to strike terror in Arab cities if we really need to. This means that we could break the Arab willingness to fight."[5]

It was the arrival of Phantom aircraft in Israel that undoubtedly impelled the decision to bomb deep inside Egypt. On September 6, 1969, Israel announced that the first Phantom aircraft had arrived from the United States. From that point on the Israeli Air Force would have a tool of technological ability far greater than it had ever had before: The plane's unusual carrying capacity, its abilities in aerial combat and its long-range, electronic instruments permit the rapid identification of targets and accurate hits. To these advantages is added immense take-off power and high speed that permits the planes to break off contact and get away safely.

In December 1969, a convenient diplomatic climate existed for Israel's decision to undertake penetration bombing. The United States' anxiety over the Middle East and Nasser's extremism was growing. American spies had reported that Nasser was recovered from his heart attack. A shift to radicalism was felt throughout the Arab world. In Libya, King Idris had been

Libyan President Muammar Qaddafi. [UPI]

Bottom: Presidents Nasser and Qaddafi with
Egyptian Minister of Defense Fawzi observing
maneuvers of the Egyptian Army.

deposed by Colonel Muammar Qaddafi. In
Saudi Arabia, a plot against King Faisal had
been uncovered, and Lebanon was in the
throes of conflict with Palestinian terrorists,
stirred up by the Russians and the Syrians. The
Israeli-Arab dispute served as a lever for the
Russians and Nasser held one of the handles.
It was clear to Israel that the Nixon Administration would prefer to see Nasser struck down
again.

The hints given to Israel were less than subtle.
At a cocktail party in Washington, one of the
heads of the State Department, as though in
passing, remarked to an Israeli diplomat that

the United States objected to Israeli activities
against Jordan and Lebanon, but had never said
anything about bombing Egypt. In the same
month, Yitzhak Rabin, Israel's Ambassador in
Washington, returned home and reported that
Israel was not making use of the options the
new circumstances afforded her.

While the American position was more or
less defined, how the Russians would react to
bombing deep in the heart of Egypt was in
question. Israel became increasingly willing to
test the Soviets and to assume the risks involved. Israel concluded that the Russians were
more tolerant of Israel's forcefulness than had
previously been thought and that the Russian
bear was, in fact, very limited in his reactions.
The question was just how far this game could
go. Israeli strategists set themselves two limits:
Israel would have to avoid hitting the Arabs
so hard that the Russians would have no alternative but to save them, and Israel would
have to act in such a way that the Soviet Union
would think it not worthwhile to react against
Israel and risk American involvement.

Thus, on January 7, Israel opened a new stage
in the War of Attrition. Israeli aircraft were
sent to two new targets, both in the area of
the Egyptian capital: an army camp where
Egyptian commando headquarters was located,
next to Inshas, and an army camp near Hilwan.
These were impressive targets: The center of
Egypt's scientific research is in Inshas and it
is there that Egypt's atomic reactor is being
planned; Egypt's military factories are in Hilwan. Israeli Phantom aircraft hit daily at these
and other targets not far from the suburbs of
Cairo and inflicted heavy damage, both psychological and physical. Egypt's planes were
incapable of shooting the Phantoms down and
the Egyptian pilots could not counter the
Phantoms.

Egypt was highly vulnerable and each week
brought her nasty surprises. The damage was

Green Isle, captured by an Israeli commando force during the War of Attrition and later recaptured by Egypt. [Israeli Army]

great because every Phantom carried from four and one-half to six tons of bombs on each sortie. The targets chosen were all military, but on February 12, an accident occurred. A Phantom, intending to hit a military camp, hit by mistake a pipe factory next to the camp. Hundreds of workers were employed there and seventy of them were killed. Among the four and one-half tons of bombs dropped on the plant was one with a delayed action fuse that was due to explode a day later. When the pilot's mistake became known, Israel informed Egypt through the Red Cross that in the ruins of the plant there was a delayed-action bomb, and it would be wise to prevent access to the place. As a result, many civilian lives were saved that would otherwise have been lost.

The increased penetration bombing and Israel's taking and holding for a few days the island of Shadwan at the southern opening of the Gulf of Suez were the straws that broke the

camel's back. Nasser left secretly for Moscow in January 1970 and informed the Kremlin that he was incapable of thwarting the Israeli aircraft, and had no idea how far Israel would go. He was, in effect, admitting the failure of his War of Attrition. He demanded direct Soviet assistance and the Kremlin agreed to block the penetration raids.

A Russian airlift to Egypt was arranged. It transported sophisticated SAM-3 missiles, anti-aircraft guns with their crews, and new radar and technicians. These were the vanguard of a complete system. They were followed by modern fighter planes and Russian pilots. This was the first time that complete Russian military units reached Egypt. Until then, Russians has come as experts, advisers and instructors. The latter had worked as individuals in the Egyptian General Staff, in training bases or in the various units of the Egyptian Army. Now, they were bringing in whole units. The Russians quick-

Soviet J-Class missile submarine in the Mediterranean. [U.S. Navy]

Bottom: Mahmoud Fawzi meets with American Secretary of State Rogers. [UPI]

ly built missile bases around the port of Alexandria, Cairo and the Aswan Dam. Egypt was soon covered by eighty batteries of missiles. The number of Russians in Egypt grew monthly and reached 15,000 by mid-1970. Israeli bombing in the heart of Egypt slowly dropped off until it completely stopped in mid-April 1970.

April 1970: Soviet Involvement Is Increased

But this was only the first stage of Soviet involvement. The IDF began to detect their presence in the Canal zone. Russian advisers no longer made do with giving advice; they began to take part in the management of war and encouraged the Egyptians to intensify their attacks. This evidenced both a desire to convince the Egyptians that Soviet doctrines of war were valid in confrontation with the Israelis, and a personal interest in proving that their presence improved the performance of Egyptian units. Egyptian planning was routine in character and always lagged behind developments in the field. It did not find answers to the tactical challenges presented to it by the IDF. Because of the Russians, who began to intervene in every plan, operation and shooting schedule, reactions from the Egyptian side of the front were faster. The Israeli Army could tell that somebody endowed with better reflexes was holding the steering wheel. But overall implementation remained in Egyptian hands.

On Saturday, April 18, 1970, it became clear that the Russians had made a step forward and taken on themselves the defense of Egyptian skies—at least in the central and inland regions. Israeli aircraft flying near Cairo on reconnaissance and photography missions were met by MIG-21 fighters. The MIGs bore Egyptian markings, but the pilots conversed among themselves and with the control towers in Russian. The first confrontation with the Russian

pilots was kept secret by Israel but the United States was informed.

To Israel's surprise, American officials suggested that Israel publicize the presence of Soviet figher pilots. The Nixon Administration was having information problems over its military expedition in Cambodia. Publication of the affair of the Russian fighter pilots in Egypt was likely to help the Administration convince the American public that the Soviet Union was organizing a general offensive and endangering essential positions of the West. Although the American proposal was in conflict with the previous Israeli decision, it was nevertheless

Below: [Israeli Army]

decided to leak the information and it was planted in the New York *Times.*

Israel made it clear that she would not flinch from a fight with Russian pilots if the latter attacked or attempted to prevent Israeli aircraft from operating in the Canal region, but Israeli planes stopped their penetration raids. This tactic had failed to create the conditions for Nasser's overthrow.

The Russians defied Israel's cautious warning. They brought their fighter planes forward over the front line of the Suez Canal. On July 25, 1970, MIGs flown by Russians attempted to shoot down Israeli aircraft flying over the Canal. They fired on the Israeli planes and

followed them beyond Suez. The Russians were probing to see just how far they could extend their military intervention without getting involved in a Vietnam of their own.

Russia's aerial battle with Israel on July 30 (described in an earlier chapter) showed the Russians that in a confrontation their pilots were inferior to the experienced Israelis who were fighting near home. The Russians realized that if they really wanted to beat Israel they would have to bring hundreds of thousands of soldiers into the area. The aerial battle led Moscow to increase pressure on Egypt to accept a cease-fire, and later, to warn Cairo not to break the cease-fire.

With Russian help, the Egyptians moved missile batteries close to the Canal and some Israeli aircraft jets were downed by the SAMs. Electronic warfare was playing a far greater role than ever before.

August 1970: Stop Shooting, Start Talking

In August, the United States got Israel and Egypt to agree to a cease-fire as part of an

Defense Minister Dayan visiting graveyard of
soldiers killed during the War of Attrition.

overall plan for Israeli withdrawal from part
of Sinai in return for Egypt's participation in
negotiations on a final peace settlement. There
were no talks, but the cease-fire remained in
effect from August 7, 1970 until October 6, 1973.

Egypt violated the stand-still provisions of
the cease-fire agreement later in August 1970
by moving SAM missiles forward to close gaps
in her air defense system near the Canal. Israel complained to the United States, which
was slow to accept the validity of her claims.
Nevertheless the cease-fire held and arguments
over Egyptian violations were obscured in 1970
by other events: The wholesale hijacking and
destruction of European and American jetliners
by Palestinian terrorists, the civil war in Jordan between Hussein's Army and the fedayeen, and Nasser's death at the end of September all served to further change the complexion of the Middle East.

Israel welcomed the cease-fire. It came at the
right time. Although the Egyptians had been
hard hit, the IDF had been in danger of conflict
with Russia. The cease-fire prevented that and
two years later the Egyptians would ask the
Russians to remove their units and advisers.

The War of Attrition exacted a heavy price
from Israel and necessitated a constant state
of military preparedness. Compulsory service
for men was extended after the war from the
previous two-and-a-half years to three years.
And reservists, almost all of whom had been
called up during the War of Attrition, had to
serve as much as two months a year after the
war. Israel's defense budget also grew. In 1966-
67 the defense budget had reached 10.7 percent
of the gross national product, but in 1968-69
it rose to 18 percent, and in 1971-72 it climbed
even further to 24.7 percent.

Israel's losses in the War of Attrition were
heavy, but at least she preserved her military
achievements from the Six-Day War. Although
the Arabs had been able to inflict death and
injury, and despite increased Soviet military involvement, Israel had stood the test in another
episode of the unending Mideast War.

Footnotes

1 Previously unpublished interview with author, 1970.
2 Previously unpublished interview with author, 1970.
3 From *Al Ahram*, quoted in Schiff, *op. cit.*, p. 22.
4 Lecture at IDF Command School, August 1969.
5 Lecture in Tel Aviv, July 1968.

15. THE QUEST FOR ARMS

Opposite top: Hawk missile. [Wide World]

Opposite bottom: Patton M-48 tanks. [Israeli Army]

The massive American airlift of arms and matériel to Israel during the Yom Kippur War marked the culmination of Israel's long struggle to obtain a steady and reliable source of military equipment. Although her arms industry has developed significantly in the years since Independence, Israel is by no means self-sufficient in this area. The quest for a strongly committed supplier of arms and armaments has been a central factor in Israel's foreign policy and the results of this quest have been closely tied to worldwide balance-of-power politics.

Knocking on America's Door

In the 1950s and early 1960s, Israel's arms industry was in an embryonic state: Manufacture of ammunition and small arms was developing; technicians studied foreign armaments and were developing designs for Israeli-made weapons; weapons obtained from other sources were adapted for use by the IDF. On the whole, Israel was dependent on other nations for heavy equipment, bombs and missiles.

At that time, the United States was reluctant to make a military commitment to the young state. Despite pressure from American Jews, a policy of nonalignment was maintained. This policy was a continuation of the American stance during Israel's War of Independence.

In 1947, after the UN Partition Plan was announced and hostilities broke out between the Arabs and Jews of Palestine, the United States declared an arms embargo on all countries party to the dispute. Appeals by Israeli leaders and American Jews that the embargo be imposed only on those Arab countries that intended to violate the UN decision by invading Palestine were to no avail. In fact, the United States did more than forbid the shipment of arms to the struggling state. Travel restrictions were placed on those Americans suspected of supporting Israel. Many who wished to join the Israeli Army were required to travel via

Europe after assuring American immigration authorities that business matters were taking them abroad. In September 1948, Washington strongly censured the Czech government for its support of the Israeli war effort insofar as Czech landing facilities were being made available to American citizens en route to Israel.

After the armistice agreements were signed in 1948, restrictions on shipments of arms to the Middle East were cancelled and the embargo imposed by the Security Council during the summer truces was lifted. Still the United States continued its embargo. The United States gave Israel its economic support but took care that no weapons would be supplied. This policy was strictly enforced and until 1961 the defense relationships between Israel and the United States were, at best, marginal.

Every year, Israel would submit a list of weapons which she sought to purchase in America, but every year, the reply was negative. There were minor deviations from this automatic no. For example, Israel was permitted to buy a small number of Browning machine guns. In the late fifties, another breakthrough occurred when Washington agreed to sell Israel radar and six recoilless 106mm guns.

This sale, however, set a precedent for the limitations placed on any arms deal with the United States. Arms might be supplied on some occasions but only if they were clearly used as defensive weapons and only if the transaction were kept secret. This latter limitation was particularly irksome to Israel since it was not only American arms that were needed; American support, openly declared, was at least as important. The light guns were defined as defensive antitank weapons and Washington insisted that the transaction should not be publicized.

These sales proved to be exceptions only. Other Israeli attempts to purchase weapons were always turned away. Washington pledged

Two early tanks from Britain: (left) the Cromwell MK-IV and (right) the Comet A-34.

Bottom: The British-made Centurion MK-V tank to which Israel added a 105mm gun. [Marvin Newman]

President John Kennedy meets with Israeli Premier David Ben-Gurion at the Waldorf Astoria, May 1961. [Wide World]

economic support but advised Israel to seek other markets for armaments. Israeli representatives were directed to Canada to buy war planes and to England for missiles, tanks and other equipment.

Israel nonetheless maintained a special purchasing mission of the Ministry of Defense in New York. Because of the practical embargo, the mission concentrated on procuring trucks, other vehicles, spare parts, radio sets, various electronic equipment and medical equipment. The Americans watched the purchasing mission to ensure that Israel honored the provisions of the embargo. They methodically collected information on Israeli procurement, including civilian equipment, and frequently let Israeli representatives know that Washington was aware of the details of all procurement activities and even knew where the goods were stored.

In the 1950s, the appointment of military attaché in Washington was considered in Israel to be an exile post, the end of a military career rather than a stepping stone. The life of an Israeli military attaché in Washington was difficult in a period when Washington was courting the Arab countries.

At the beginning of the 1960s, the Kennedy Administration was convinced that an occasional gesture to Nasser would underscore the policy of neutrality in the Israeli-Arab conflict. During this period, the Egyptians were developing ground-to-ground missiles. They approached a number of countries, including the United States, for assistance in that area. The Egyptian military attaché tried to buy two or three missile propellant systems in the United States. The State Department favored approval of the transaction as a token gesture but it became known to the Israelis, and when they objected the transaction was cancelled.

The first real Israeli penetration of American arsenals occurred at the end of 1962 when

Washington agreed to sell Israel Hawk ground-to-air missiles. Although it was again emphasized that the sale was of a clearly defensive armament, it marked a major victory for Israel.

In 1960, David Ben-Gurion had personally submitted a request for ground-to-air missiles. Israel got the same negative answer that she had received on all requests to date. In May 1961, Ben-Gurion returned for a private visit with President Kennedy. The meeting took place not at the White House but in the Waldorf-Astoria Hotel in New York. Israel's shopping list for weapons was again officially submitted. Planes, tanks and also anti-aircraft missiles were requested.

In his conversation with the young American President, Ben-Gurion said: "In the event of war between Israel and the Arab countries, what worries me is not what will happen on the battlefield. There I am sure of the ability of

A plane is downed by an Israeli Hawk missile. This remarkable weapon—the Homing All the Way Killer—can change directions to pursue its target. [Authenticated News]

Hawks on launcher. [Wide World]

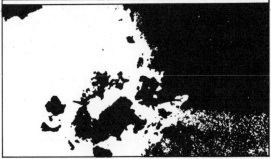

our Army. The civilian population worries me. It is vulnerable to the bombers that the Egyptians received from the Russians."[1] Ben-Gurion continued to define Israel's needs as defensive. Kennedy mulled over his remarks and promised sympathetic examination of the request. He recognized that he owed much to Jewish votes and campaign money. He knew that Israel had cause to be worried. The Egyptian Air Force had received Ilyushin-28 bombers from Russia and was at that time negotiating for more sophisticated and faster bombers.

At first, Washington tried to direct Israel to England for the purchase of anti-aircraft mis-

siles. England was the only other western country producing ground-to-air missiles at that time. But the Israelis contended that the English Bloodhound missile was not suited to Israel's needs. What the IDF was seeking was a missile capable of hitting planes flying as low as tree-top height. The only operational missile suitable for this was the American Hawk, and Washington agreed to sell.

On the eve of the Jewish New Year 1962, the IDF attaché was summoned to the Pentagon and given an official notification of the sale. The Israeli Deputy Minister of Defense, Shimon Peres, and the Commander of the Air Force, Ezer Weizman, came to negotiate and sign the transaction. The Americans imposed certain restrictions on the sale of the Hawk missiles, refusing to sell Israel the most sophisticated Hawk system. Further, the United States insisted that overhaul of the missile battery system be done in the United States, thereby ensuring that Israel remain technologically naive as regarded the Hawk.

Shortly before the Six-Day War, when Israel was in an economic recession, she requested that the U.S. provide information that would allow her to repair these systems at home. The request was primarily motivated by economics —to keep money in the country and bolster Israel's own arms industry. Washington re-

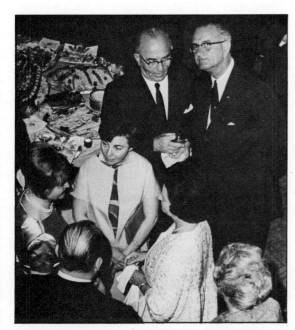

Levi Eshkol with Lyndon Johnson during visit to U.S. when sale of Phantoms was arranged. [Israel Information Service]

fused and held to that decision until after the Six-Day War, when defense relationships between Israel and the United States underwent a drastic revision.

The Shift Is Made from Defense to Offense

Another breakthrough occurred during the Johnson Administration when Washington was compelled to approve the sale of arms considered to be aggressive weapons. The web of special relationships between Israel and West Germany played a part in the change of policy. For a number of years, Israel had developed well-concealed security connections with the West German government. The contacts were established between the Ministries of Defense of the two states. According to a special arrangement, military equipment such as heavy trucks, light planes and a number of helicopters were given to Israel. The details of these transactions were known to the United States.

In 1964, Israel requested heavy weapons from the United States. This time, Israel insisted that the balance of power in the Middle East was being upset to her disadvantage. Pentagon experts confirmed this, but Washington was not yet ready to sell weapons considered to be aggressive directly to Israel. The solution was a triangular arrangement which utilized the arrangements between Israel and West Germany. Washington agreed that American tanks used by U.S. Army units in Germany could be turned over to the German government, which would then transfer them to Israel. Three hundred Patton M-48s which were due for overhaul were involved in the transaction. Israel accepted the triangular arrangement willingly and the first tanks were delivered to her workshops. However, a CBS television report of the deal provoked a storm. Nasser and the Arab countries started to scream; Bonn found itself in the cauldron of the Middle East dispute. The Germans stopped the flow of weapons in an attempt to appease Nasser, but at the same time decided to open full diplomatic relations with Israel. The cancellation of the tank transaction did not raise the prestige of West Germany in Arab eyes. In response to the opening of diplomatic relations with Israel, a number of Arab states decided to open diplomatic relations with East Germany, an act that necessarily meant breaking off relations with Bonn.

Israel came out of the affair damaged militarily but she finally had some leverage on the United States. The CBS leak had sabotaged the deal and Israel brought pressure on Washington for direct and fair compensation. It was this pressure that finally forced the United States to openly supply offensive weapons to Israel. As a face-saving measure, Washington nonetheless insisted that the Patton tanks she would sell directly to Israel were in fact defensive armaments. Israel accepted them, as

American-made Skyhawks. [Israeli Army]

defined by the United States, since the real victory was the end of clandestine dealings with the Pentagon.

Israel paid the full price for the Patton tanks. She requested rapid delivery of the tanks and U.S. Army commanders came to her assistance. The IDF attaché in Washington, Col. Ram Ron, met with American generals who agreed to forego their requests for additional tanks for American forces in Korea. These tanks, including some in which the standard 90mm artillery piece was replaced by a more modern 105mm gun, participated in the Six-Day War on the Egyptian front.

"The Nebbish Samson"

Israel's next objective was fighter planes. Success in procurement would mark a turning point in U.S. policy but many of Israel's leaders doubted that the United States could be cajoled. It was 1965 and intimations of war had begun to pervade the Middle East. The Arab states had established a Joint Arab Command and had decided to divert the Jordan River sources. At the same time, saboteurs of Fatah had resumed their activities.

In October 1965, Israel was invited to send experts to Washington for open discussion on her defense needs. The first subject for discussion was aircraft. Ezer Weizman, Commander of the Air Force, outlined Israel's requests in a document he referred to as "Samuel I," named after the book of the Bible and for Uncle Sam. Weizman's shopping list was ambitious but it proved to be realistic. Israel requested sixty-five Skyhawks and forty-five Phantoms.

As on many other occasions, Israel had to assume a posture that was strong and weak at the same time—strong enough to restrain the Arabs and raise the morale of the people of Israel, but not so strong that the Americans would doubt her need for modern weapons; weak enough to warrant American assistance,

but not so weak as to encourage Arab aggression and lower the morale of the Israelis. When Weizman consulted the Prime Minister on the problem of Israel's image, Eshkol quoted the famous Yiddish proverb: "You must represent Israel as though you are the poor unfortunate strongman, the nebbish Samson." Weizman's main contention in his appearances before the representatives of the Pentagon and the State Department was that the weaker Israel is, the more it is prone to pre-emptive attack at a moment of danger.

One Saturday toward the end of 1965, the Israeli Ambassador to the United States, Avra-

ham Harman, Foreign Minister Abba Eban and Col. Ram Ron were informed that President Johnson had approved the sale of fifty Skyhawks. Contrary to his usual custom, the Israeli Foreign Minister said little but his great pleasure was apparent. After the meeting, Eban said to Colonel Ron: "You can't understand how excited I am. I was Israeli Ambassador in the United States for ten years. I submitted many requests for procurement of weapons. The last time, I asked for approval of sale of mortars to Israel, but was turned down, and now they are ready to sell us fighter planes."[2]

There were, of course, some strings attached

to the sale. Israel was asked to guarantee that the planes would be used for defensive purposes only. Furthermore, Eban was told that the United States planned to supply tanks to Jordan and that Israel was not to protest that transaction.

In fact, Eban was asked to lobby among Israel's sympathizers who were expected to protest sales of arms to Arab states. This was not the first nor the last time Washington asked Israel to legitimize a sale of weapons to Jordan. The American administration considered Jordan to be a friend among the Arab countries and wanted to strengthen Hussein's position vis-à-vis the rest of the Arab world. Israeli collusion was required as part of the price of American arms.

Publication of the agreement to sell Skyhawks to Israel was delayed for some months. A date had been set by both countries, but was delayed because of the visit of Soviet Prime Minister Kosygin in Egypt. It was believed that such an announcement would annoy the Arabs and push them closer toward the Soviet Union. It was not until May 1966 that official notice was issued that the United States would supply tactical aircraft to Israel for defense purposes. The Israeli Air Force did not receive the planes before the Six-Day War. "If we had received the Skyhawks during the Six-Day War," an Israeli pilot said, "the Air Force would have been able to carry out the same missions with half the planes."[3]

Despite the improvement in defense relationships between the two countries, Israel did not support the American war in Vietnam. Washington had expected moral support but Israel, headed by Eshkol, not only refused to establish diplomatic relations with Saigon, but avoided the sale of supplies and food to the American armies in Vietnam.

A somewhat overly harsh application of Israel's counter-embargo concerned a military doctor, Lt. Col. Ami Giladi, who had been sent to the United States to study the treatment of burns. In those days, many burn casualties from Vietnam reached the hospital where he was working. The hospital authorities approached the Israeli military attaché, Gen. Yosef Geva, with a request to permit Dr. Giladi to treat, among others, Americans wounded in the Vietnam war. General Geva agreed and remarked that Israel considered it a humanitarian duty to treat even the wounded of Israel's enemies. She would certainly help in medical treatment of American soldiers. But when the story reached the ears of ministers in the Israeli government and upper echelons of the IDF, they responded with severe opposition to Dr. Giladi's work.

The Role of Balance-of-Power Politics

For years, Israel had hoped to have her opinions and evaluations of Middle East matters heard in Washington and eventually to establish a free exchange of views and information between the two countries. Such a relationship existed between Israel and France and it is believed that Washington's disinclination to open such a two-way street herself was influenced by France's role. And so it seems to have been true—a basic change in Washington's position took place when relationships between France and Israel went completely sour.

At the beginning of the 1950s, an idyll prevailed in Franco-Israeli relationships. The French had responded to all of Israel's applications for weapons. Fostering procurement in France seemed more realistic than the poor chances in the United States. There were those who believed in continuing the orientation toward France and even dreamt of joint development of armaments systems. Others, headed by Prime Minister and Defense Minister Levi Eshkol, demanded that Israel harness up for an ef-

Top: American made 105mm self-propelled gun.

Bottom: June 3, 1967—An Israeli freighter is loaded with armored half-tracks. Also among the cargo are 105mm shells and other ammunition as well as Sherman tanks. [UPI]

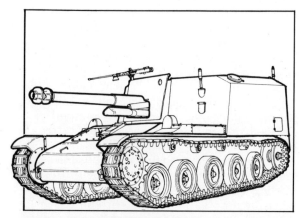

fort in the United States, even if the chances seemed slimmer. "We must not put all our eggs in one basket," Eshkol said.[4]

It was during the Six-Day War that Israel lost France as an ally. President de Gaulle saw his country at last freed of the Algerian problem and began to think of establishing a French sphere of influence in the Middle East. The Arab countries were a much richer market for French arms and they, in turn, had the oil that France required. The apparent cause of the breakdown in relations between France and Israel was Israel's snubbing of de Gaulle's advice on the eve of the Six-Day War. He had

tried to discourage Israel from firing first and she, of course, ignored his recommendation. France responded with an arms embargo and, having closed the book on Israel, the way was clear for her to establish relations with the Arab states.

Washington began to listen to the views of Israel military analysts but it was a one-way conversation—Israel spoke and Washington listened silently. The American experts contended that Israel was exaggerating in her assessments; that Israel often rushed to report events before they happened. When it became clear that former Nazi German scientists were in Egypt assisting in production of ground-to-ground medium-range missiles, Israeli representatives hastened to report to Washington. The Americans claimed that Israel was exaggerating the danger of these missiles. An expression of these differences of opinion could be found in the war of security leaks. While Israeli pressures on the United States for the supply of arms grew, the U.S. leaked to the American press information about Israeli transactions in Europe and production of weapons in Israel. The idea was to convince those who would take up Israel's cause that the balance of power in the Middle East was in fact weighed in favor of Israel.

After the aircraft purchase, however, the exchange of views became more frequent. Israeli generals visited Washington more often, to lecture and consult with American generals and Pentagon and State Department experts. Reservations regarding Israel's views still remained, but her opinions gradually became more influential.

And Israel began to hear the voices and views of Washington. These were not always pleasant voices. In November 1966, after Israel attacked the Jordanian village of Samua (bringing fierce demonstrations against King Hussein's moderate policies by Palestinian

The Gunboats of Cherbourg: French sympathizers sailed these boats out of port under cover of night in defiance of de Gaulle's arms embargo against Israel during the War of Attrition. [Israeli Army]

Gunboat equipped with Gabriel missile launchers. [Israeli Army]

dissidents), American representatives leveled severe accusations at Israel. They contended that Israel did not dare to strike back at Syria for fear of Russian intervention and instead attacked Jordan, a friend of the United States.

Washington foresaw the end of Israel's courtship with France long before it was sensed in Israel. While Israel still continued to make plans based on "her ally," the French, American experts were already assuming that Israel would require a replacement for this ally. This appears to have been one of the reasons that the sale of Skyhawks was approved. American experts were surprised that Israel continued to look to France and on one occasion they hinted at this clearly. When the Israeli Deputy Defense Minister, Dr. Zevi Dinstein, visited Washington, he claimed that France was willing to have the Mirage aircraft assembled in Israel. The Americans expressed surprise and said that to the best of their knowledge there was no chance that Israel would receive such a permit. In the end, Washington was right.

On the eve of the Six-Day War, after the Egyptians had closed the straits at Sharm-el-Sheikh and concentrated an immense army in the Sinai Peninsula, American sympathy for Israel was expressed in both small and large matters. The United States was reluctant to intervene directly in the war; she wanted Israel to win, but with her own forces. In these interests, the Johnson Administration was ready to contribute significantly. Countries that were considered friendly to Israel suddenly began to demonstrate a strange neutrality. While the West German government was still debating whether to give Israel gas masks that would also be used by military personnel, the Pentagon ordered a considerable quantity to be sent from the United States.

After the Six-Day War, the United States stopped supplying military equipment to Israel in the wake of strategic arms limitations talks with the Russians. But when these talks broke down, Israel decided to collect on the promise of the Skyhawk aircraft. Ezer Weizman was once again sent to Washington where he told Americans, "We didn't have enough aircraft. The Arabs knew this and therefore we lost our deterrent power. This drew Arab provocation and finally brought us to war."[5] In his remarks on the chances for peace and war in the future, he concluded by saying, "In the Six-Day War, Israel was victorious with the assistance of the French equipment that *was* at her disposal. We must prevent the next war with the help of American equipment that we *will* receive."[6]

From Skyhawk to Phantom

The Skyhawks were considered by Israel to be extremely versatile fighter planes. Although they were given to Israel, according to the American announcement, for defensive purposes, it was clear that they added an extraordinary attack power to the Israeli Air Force. Their many advantages included the ability to transport considerable munitions to the target regardless of weather, their accuracy and distance capability and their ability to refuel in fight.

The Israeli Air Force discovered American equipment through the Skyhawk aircraft. Until then it had dealt only with French equipment and thought it to be the best. The Israelis came to see American equipment as simpler but more sophisticated and much more reliable than the equipment in the French aircraft.

It was, however, the Phantom jet that became the focus of Israeli desire. The Phantom was considered to be a first-line weapon. If the IAF had this jet, it would reach the upper rung of the ladder. The Skyhawks were a significant addition to the Air Force but they did not close the dangerous gap created by the French embargo. Furthermore, the Mirages wore out and replacements could not be seen on the horizon. There was a fear that Israeli interceptor ability, which could not be based on Skyhawks, would be seriously harmed in the course of time. Thus the primary objective of Israeli Prime Minister Levi Eshkol in his visit to the United States in January 1968 was the Phantom.

The negotiation for the Phantoms was held on President Johnson's farm in Texas. All Eshkol's interest was centered on the fighter planes, while Johnson tried to bring the discussions around to programs that were likely to further peace. At one point, as Eshkol was about to reopen discussion of arms transactions, Johnson retaliated with a smile, "Maybe now we can talk a little about peace!"[7]

Israel's contention in her plea for the Phantom was that a strong Israel would be a guarantee against a new Vietnam. Israel's strength would remove the danger of American involvement in a distant war. A weak Israel, on the other hand, would inspire the Arabs into a general attack and America would be forced to intervene to preserve the balance of power. The American leaders did not see things quite that way and many were opposed to the sale of modern aircraft to Israel, among them Secretary of State Rusk and Secretary of Defense

The Phantom II attack fighter. [Israeli Army]

McNamara. General Earl Wheeler, Chairman of the Joint Chiefs, represented the supporters of military aid to Israel. After the Six-Day War, General Wheeler had observed that for the first time a democratic country had defeated countries supported by Russia without requiring even indirect action by the United States.

The decision was finally made in Israel's favor. After the Phantom transaction was signed, there were those who believed the United States was motivated for reasons other than support of the nebbish Samson. Leonard Beaton said in a London *Times* article that Israel received the Phantoms because the United States hoped by that means to delay Israel's plans to develop nuclear weapons.

(Israel's nuclear capabilities have long been grist for the international rumor mill. There are those who suggest that Israel certainly has capability; some foreign observers believe it is already on the operational scale and that Israel has nuclear warheads. However, there has been no official confirmation of these rumors and the matter cannot be stated as fact.)

President Johnson stood by his promise to conclude the sale before leaving office. On December 28, 1968, Washington officially announced the sale of the first Phantoms to Israel. Israel had traveled a long road in her fight against the American embargo. It was a great victory for Israel. After that, the other arms transactions seemed much easier. Certainly from a military viewpoint, there was room for raised spirits in Israel. Johnson's decision swept de Gaulle's embargo aside. But much more important was the fact that Israel would be equipped with a sophisticated weapon, while the Arabs lacked one of equal quality.

In March 1969, Israeli pilots, mechanics and technicians arrived in the United States to learn about the new aircraft. The Israeli pilots had considerable operational experience and within a short time they were outstanding in their course. They were especially expert in air-to-air combat and often overcame the American instructors. One of the most experienced senior American instructors never succeeded in outmaneuvering a certain Israeli pilot in aerial combat. The Israeli always succeeded in sitting on his tail; the gunnery cameras of his aircraft always proved that if he had used his cannons and machine guns he would have downed the instructor's aircraft. In one of these battles, the American instructor called out to him, "Remember this moment." After they landed, the American invited the Israeli into his office. In a burst of laughter, he locked the door behind him and said, "You are not leaving here until you tell me how you do the maneuver by which you always overcome me!"[8]

One day in early September 1969, a small group of Israeli leaders gathered at an Air Force base. Among them were Prime Minister Golda Meir, Moshe Dayan and senior commanders of the IDF. The first Phantoms were due to land in Israel at any moment. It had been anticipated that the first aircraft would arrive in 1970, but the United States agreed to speed up the deal. This was the fastest Israeli arms transaction ever made. When the first aircraft landed, the Commanding Officer of the Air Force, General Hod, said to Golda Meir, "The Air Force feels as though it has had a long pregnancy, and now has finally delivered the baby." Golda responded with a smile. "You have no idea how good you can feel at such a time!"[9]

The United States and the Soviet Union Are Committed in the Mideast

On January 7, 1970, in the middle of the War of Attrition, Israeli Phantoms began bombing deep into Egypt. This brought about the turning point in the War of Attrition but it also brought the Soviet Union into the Middle East.

Russian pilots and Russian units equipped with modern anti-aircraft missiles entered Egypt in strength. For her part, the United States strengthened the military connection with Israel. It reached a high point toward the end of the War of Attrition and there is no doubt that the major impetus was the increased participation of the Soviet Union in Arab military affairs.

Large-scale Soviet military aid to the Arab countries made Washington fearful of an Israeli defeat. This would be a serious blow to American prestige and would require a military reply from the United States. Thus, when the Russians sent pilots and missile crews to man the SAM sites against Israel, the United States stepped up its military aid. Washington was, in effect, serving notice to the Kremlin that she would not abandon Israel.

During the period preceding the Yom Kippur War, there still existed some restrictions on the sale of new equipment to Israel. The restrictive

phase ended abruptly when war again broke out in the Middle East. It was clear that Israel faced not only the Arabs, but also the logistical might of the Soviet Union.

American support of Israel at this time encompassed the massive airlift by U.S. Air Force planes. Prior to that time, Israel was respon-

UN Secretary General U Thant arrives in Moscow where he is greeted by Russian Ambassador to Egypt Vinogradov. [Tass from Sovfoto]

Bottom: The Soviet-made SAM-3. [Tass from Sovfoto]

sible for the transport of all equipment purchased in the United States. However, in October 1973, American planes flew 670 transport missions and carried more than 23,000 tons of arms and ammunition to Israel. In addition, aircraft carriers in the Atlantic and Mediterranean supplied replacements for the Phantoms lost in the war and Skyhawks were delivered from American bases in West Germany. Forty American military advisors were on hand to supervise the delivery. In all, $800 million worth of goods was delivered in the course of the war, a portion of the $2.2 billion aid package approved by Congress.

The Price of American Military Aid

American military support of Israel during the Yom Kippur War was, without doubt, a major factor in the military victory against the Arabs. Israel had a debt to pay and the currency was to be in diplomatic concessions.

After the war, Henry Kissinger told a group of Jewish Harvard professors that the Yom Kippur War had shown that in any future Mideast conflict both sides would require continuous, open lines of supply. He intimated that it would be difficult to obtain congressional approval for a massive resupply of Israel in the future and hinted that such a consideration would be a significant factor in pressuring Israel to make far-reaching concessions in the peace agreement.

Kissinger's remarks, amply reported in the Israeli press, served to underscore the uncertainty arising from Israel's heavy dependence on the United States for the crucial weapons of her defense. The events that have followed the military conclusion of the Yom Kippur War have made it clear that as long as the United States and Russia consider the Middle East an important sphere of influence, Israel will be a pawn in the international power game, and will continue to play the role of the nebbish Samson.

Footnotes

1 Previously unpublished interview between author and Yehuda Prihar, military attaché in Washington at that time, 1972.
2 Previously unpublished interview between author and Ram Ron, 1972.
3 Previously unpublished interview with author, 1970.
4 Lecture to heads of defense establishment, 1965.
5 Previously unpublished interview with author, 1969.
6 Ibid.
7 Previously unpublished interview between author and Yosef Geva, military attaché in Washington at that time, 1972.
8 Previously unpublished interview with author, 1970. Pilot was killed in Yom Kippur War.
9 Previously unpublished interview between author and Mordechai Hod, 1969.

16. POLITICS & THE ARMY

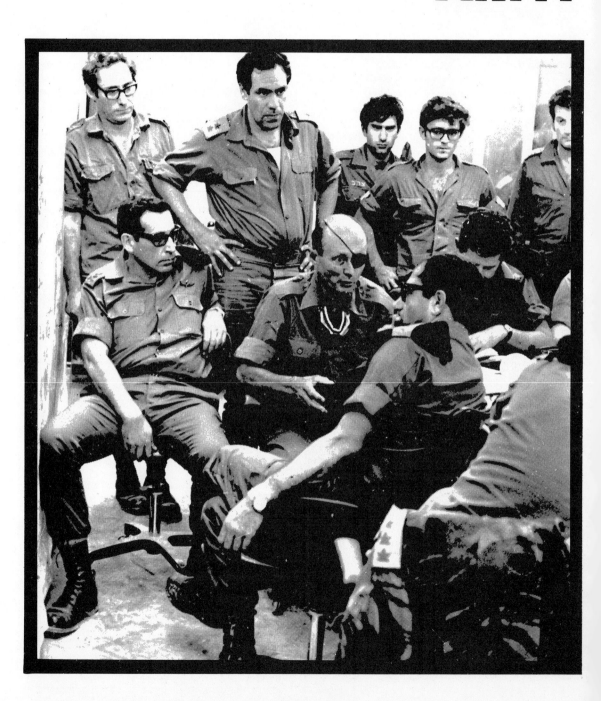

Opposite: [Israeli Army]

Egyptian strongholds on the east bank of the Suez Canal, October 6, 1973. [UPI]

Israel's embattled status creates a special tension and a dynamic that thrusts the military into practically every aspect of the nation's political, cultural and social life. The Army touches on every Israeli's existence; a consciousness of the nation's precarious position makes the fortunes of the Army a matter of vital concern to all. Most Israelis are directly involved in the IDF, either through their service in the reserves or through their families and jobs. The Arab goal of eliminating the Jewish State is firmly imprinted on every Israeli's consciousness and the garrison mentality is a necessary fact of life.

Two events of the Yom Kippur War—the Egyptian crossing of the Suez Canal and the initial success of the Syrians in the first two days of battle—were significant psychological victories for the Arab interests and served to encourage continued Arab militarism. Most Israelis live with the conviction that the Arabs are firmly determined to drive Israel from the Middle East, if not tomorrow, then twenty-five or fifty years from tomorrow. A strong IDF, prepared for any renewal of Arab hostility, is the only guarantee of Israel's continued existence and the survival of the Jewish people. No amount of reassurances from the United States can

Field Security Posters—Left: "The secret was kept, the bridge was built." Refers to the IDF bridgehead across the Suez Canal during the Yom Kippur War. Right: "Keeping a secret is a protective shield." [Israeli Government Printing Office]

change the fact that the burden of her defense rests with her own people.

These factors have permitted military interests in Israel to exercise greater influence and power over the internal life of the nation than is the case in other democratically-ruled countries. Although other mitigating factors—the absence of an established military class, as such—prevent Israel from becoming a militaristic society, the presence of the IDF in the political life of the country is a significant one.

Security and Censorship

Bitahon, military security, is a word often heard in Israel. Concern for *bitahon* is at times an obsession, at others a convenient pretext for politically expedient decisions in such areas as censorship. *Bitahon* is in some ways a sacred concept for a people whose history is one of repeated persecutions and holocausts. Security at all costs is the logical extension of the national consciousness but *bitahon* as an imperative is sometimes abused. This is one of the prices of constant vigilance, perhaps difficult for foreigners to understand unless they are familiar with the history of Arab-Israeli conflict.

Everywhere he turns, the Israeli comes across security regulations established and main-

"The government bends the news... to its administrative convenience."—Shimon Peres [UPI]

tained by the Army—whether in the form of call-up papers for reserve service, the obligation to pay a certain percentage from his monthly pay packet to the Defense Loan, a levy imposed on the population to foot Israel's enormous defense expenditure, or the necessity of obtaining a special release permit from the Army when, as a civilian of reserve status, he wishes to go abroad.

Mail is spot-checked by Army censors. The newspaper the Israeli reads is in great part passed by military censorship. Although there is no political censorship in Israel as such, anything touching on a military subject must be shown to the Army censor before it is published. If it's a question of the quantity of arms or planes or a revelation of an Army or Navy maneuver, then the issue of security is quite clear. The foreign Intelligence services of the Communist nations diligently pursue every scrap of information, so Israel's caution is warranted. Generally sensitive military information cannot appear in Israel unless it has already been published abroad. This is a frequent occurrence and a serious security problem since the Army cannot exercise censorship over foreign journalists who file their stories after they have left Israel. In this way several revelations concerning Israeli Intelligence operations, for example, have appeared in the foreign press.

Sometimes, however, the security issue is manipulated to suppress reports that the government feels will be prejudicial to internal political affairs. It is here that security censorship impinges on freedom of expression. The Israeli press continually battles this tendency. The debate is public and frequently vociferous, the press acting as protector of the public's right to know. Nevertheless when Israel politicians need to justify some action or policy, they often take the holy name of security in vain.

The IDF itself is not above using its muscle

when it feels itself under attack—a rare occurrence before the mishaps of the Yom Kippur War, when the IDF was practically above reproach. An example of the power over the press wielded by the military occurred in 1972, when Sylvie Keshet, a popular gossip columnist, wrote a scathing satirical piece suggesting that one of the IDF generals was holding lavish parties and, in violation of IDF regulations and tradition, was using enlisted men as waiters and busboys. The public was astounded that such things could take place in the IDF. Even though the column had been oblique and had avoided mentioning real names, an outraged IDF commander insisted on a front-page apology and the offending newspaper's publisher duly obeyed.

This author's own telephone was tapped by the defense establishment after a series of articles based on inside information appeared in *Ha'aretz*. The Ministry of Defense was interested in knowing the sources of this information. The phone-tapping was reported in the Israeli press.

Bitter debates have checkered Israel's history when the defense establishment has employed censorship to quash public criticism of the government. Former Deputy Defense Minister, Shimon Peres, who bore the brunt of most of this criticism during Ben-Gurion's years, conceded in 1966, after resigning his post: "The government bends the news, by means of censorship, to its administrative convenience."[1] A few years earlier, Peres himself had threatened Eliezer Livneh, an Israeli writer and past member of the Knesset, with criminal proceedings likely to end in a prison sentence. His offense? Attempting to convene a news conference to discuss the problem of nuclear armaments and the anticipated dangers to Israel if she entered the arms race. The issue was clearly a matter of dissent rather than security violation.

The Israeli-made Uzi submachine gun (top) and Galil rifle/light machine gun. The Galil outshoots the American M-16 and Soviet AK-47 and is fitted with a bottle-opener and tripod which doubles as wire-cutters.

Bottom: The Israeli-made Gabriel missile carries carries 400 pounds of high explosive in its warhead and has a range of 15-17 miles. [Israeli Army]

These practices are not the rule, but in a society in which the Army and the Ministry of Defense play such prominent roles, the exercise of political influence is at times inevitable.

The Ministry of Defense and Fiscal Matters

In addition to determining Israel's basic military strategy in its role as the parent agency of the IDF, the Ministry of Defense exercises great influence over the nation's industry and science, and so over its fiscal life. The importance of the Defense Ministry as an economic power base arises from both the preferential position of the IDF and the relationship between defense and scientific research. The Ministry's department of economics, for example, plays a strong part in planning the nation's economy and it played a key role in building Israel's two nuclear reactors.

Israel's defense budget is more than forty percent of the entire national budget of over $3 billion. Those responsible for it have considerable influence on Israel's economy. The Defense Ministry is the largest of the government ministries, in terms not only of its budget but also of its personnel. Apart from the tens of thousands of workers in the various defense industries, such as aircraft and arms manufacture, many more are employed directly by the Army and the Ministry. Some 240,000 Israelis, a fifth of the labor force, are directly or indirectly connected with defense work.

The armaments industry is an impressive example of what can be done by a small country lacking natural resources but desiring a minimum of political dependence. This was not the case prior to 1967, but following the arms embargo imposed by President de Gaulle, Israel began to develop its own defense industries. Until the Six-Day War, Israel's arms and aircraft industry was limited to the production of light, high-standard arms, light artillery,

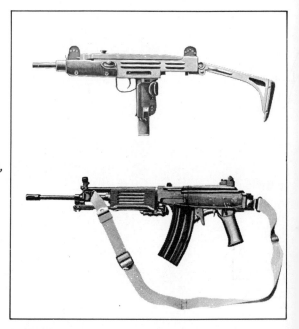

rockets, short-range missiles and missile propellants. The Israel Aircraft Industries (IAI) assembled training planes and the military industries successfully reconditioned old tanks.

The period of friendly relations with France, during which Israel acquired nearly all the arms she needed, meant that military procure-

Russian OSA missile carrier equipped with missile launchers.

Bottom left: Y. Balshnikov, inventor of the Galil gun, shown here with the Galil. [Wide World]

Bottom right: Gen. Amos Horev (Rtd.), former chief scientist for the Ministry of Defense, is now president of the Haifa Technicon. [*Times of Israel*]

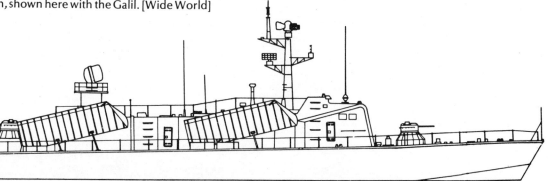

ment was a financial and economic problem, rather than a political one. This approach was found to be shortsighted. The upper echelons of the IDF in the early 1960s shared the responsibility for this view. Instead of investing funds in the development of an infrastructure for military production in Israel, those same commanders made their own short-term accounting. They demanded the required weapons at maximal speed, without considering that with a little patience they would have benefited from local development plans. Israel, as a result, cut back arms development programs and transferred investments for joint development abroad.

After the Six-Day War, Israel began to develop and manufacture modern and sophisticated weapons systems. Shocked by the French experience, Israel's major objective was to reduce her political dependence. Israel shortly became self-sufficient in the manufacture of small arms. Although precise details are classified, it is believed that she has also developed modern fighter aircraft, heavy guns and armored equipment. Foreign sources contend that Israel possesses nuclear capability but this has not been officially confirmed.

The development of Israel's defense industry has provided her with an estimated fifty percent of her armament needs. In addition, Israel has entered the arms export business and her customers number nearly fifty countries.

The Ministry of Defense and Foreign Policy

The Ministry of Defense is also deeply involved in delicate aspects of Israel's foreign policy. It has developed its own contacts and relationships with various countries and often dictates policy to the Foreign Ministry. Contacts between Israel and France in the 1950s were determined by representatives of the Ministry

Left: Soviet-made T-55 tanks captured by the IDF undergo repairs before returning to action for Israel during the Yom Kippur War. [UPI]

Right: Russian tank captured and refitted for use by IDF is displayed at 25th Anniversary Parade, 1973. [Israeli Army]

Bottom: Captured Soviet-made personnel carrier used by Egyptian Army. IDF salvage crews follow close behind the victorious Army picking up Russian equipment abandoned by the defeated Arab armies. [UPI]

of Defense rather than by the Ministry of Foreign Affairs. This was also the case when preliminary contacts were made prior to the establishment of full diplomatic representation with West Germany.

The Ministry of Defense maintains procurement and purchasing missions in various countries and it is through these agencies that the Ministry coordinates its foreign policy. Although this has certainly been the cause of friction between the Defense and Foreign Ministries, the priorities granted to defense matters have permitted the circumstance to continue. There is a large procurement mission in the United States as well as in France, England, Italy and West Germany. Other missions are maintained in Thailand, the Philippines, Japan and South America.

The Ministry of Defense has also been invited to send advisers and IDF instructors to many countries in Africa, Asia and South America. Courses have been given in Israel for army personnel and youth from these countries. The requests are mostly for consultation and guidance and the establishment of paramilitary bodies similar to the NAHAL and GADNA. Other countries have asked Israel to help them establish paratroop units and flight training and other military instruction programs. This has further intensified the military arm of government as the point of contact to the outside world.

Who Rules the Military?

The question of control over the military establishment and its accountability to the civilian government has long been a sensitive subject in Israel. The situation has evolved against the background of wars and has been colored by the various leaders who have tried to exert an influence on military power.

For the first fifteen years of its existence as an independent state, Israel's political and military leadership lay in the hands of one man. From 1948 until 1963, David Ben-Gurion exercised almost exclusive control as Prime Minister *and* Defense Minister. Most important matters were resolved behind closed doors without the advice, consent or even knowledge of the Knesset. Even the Cabinet at large was often uninformed or given only partial information on essential defense matters. The decision to embark on the Sinai War of 1956, for example, was reported to some ministers and political leaders only when it was a *fait accompli.* In response to protests of high-handedness, Ben-Gurion invoked the name of security, claiming that he could not present such secret matters to a full session of Parliament for fear of security leaks. As a compromise, he established a ministerial committee for defense affairs which, in theory, would participate in any future decisions of a political/military nature. In practice, however, the committee had to depend on the good graces of Ben-Gurion during his tenure.

For a brief period, from 1953 to 1955, Ben-Gurion was out of power. Pinhas Lavon was Minister of Defense under Prime Minister Moshe Sharett. But Lavon complained that much vital information on military affairs was kept from him by the IDF Command and upper-echelon members of the Ministry of Defense. A precedent had been set within the bureaucracy and Lavon was unable, in two years, to modify procedures.

Ben-Gurion returned to power in 1955 and again the posts of Prime Minister and Minister of Defense were unified. Representatives of the different parties, including most of those who participated in Ben Gurion's coalition government, sharply criticized the isolation of the defense establishment and Ben-Gurion's exclusive control over it.

Ben-Gurion resolutely insisted that military and defense personnel would not appear before

Prime Minister and Defense Minister Levi Eshkol greets his Army Chief of Staff, Haim Bar-Lev at Lydda Airport, 1968. [Isaac Berez]

the Defense and Foreign Affairs Committee, the most important committee of the Knesset. When the committee requested details on the selling of weapons to Portugal and the reconditioning of that country's planes, Ben-Gurion refused to give the information. In another case Ben-Gurion refused to reveal to the committee that Holland was a market for many Israeli-made Uzi submachine guns.

Perhaps the stormiest controversy caused by Ben-Gurion's autocratic ways occurred in the 1950s over the decision to build the atomic reactor in Dimona, in the Negev. This affair had far-reaching political and economic implications and to this day serves as a prime example of how decisive security decisions were made behind closed doors. The Defense and Foreign Affairs Committee had received only a general summary on the project and that only after it had been published in the newspapers. The decision to build the reactor had even been kept from members of the Knesset's Defense Budget Committee, which is usually informed of budgetary matters, be they secret or not. The outcry in Parliament was great; charges of concealment were made. But Ben-Gurion was resolute and, again, the cause of security was relied upon as justification.

Ben-Gurion's failure to develop and encourage a skilled group of civilian administrators within the Ministry of Defense meant that most of that talent resided in the officer class of the IDF and with it the real power over the Ministry's formidable economic and political resources. When Levi Eshkol became Prime Minister in 1963, Cabinet Ministers were better informed of defense matters. However, the Ben-Gurion years had established a pattern; the power of the IDF was not significantly reduced. Moshe Dayan's appointment as Minister of Defense on the eve of the Six-Day War introduced a period of greater civilian control over the defense establishment.

Who Rules Israel?

In the early 1960s, IDF generals began to make themselves felt in political spheres. The growing conflict between the civilian and political leadership reached a peak shortly before the Six-Day War. The generals openly argued with Prime Minister Eshkol, condemning his vacillation in the face of Arab threats. This dramatic confrontation in the command room of IDF headquarters underscored the division between the nation's aged, hesitant political leaders and the IDF commanders who were confident of the Army's capabilities.

Before the Six-Day War, Moshe Dayan and Yigal Allon were the only two top-ranking IDF commanders to join the civilian government, not long after departing from military service. But the political influence of the Army elite had changed with the advent of Eshkol as Prime Minister and Minister of Defense in 1963. The Chief of Staff, Yitzhak Rabin, enjoyed political status that had never been accorded a Chief of Staff in Ben-Gurion's days. Eshkol leaned on him as though he were his Minister of Defense. In the period of waiting that preceded the Six-Day Way, Rabin and his generals' evaluation of the situation and their foresight earned them an honored place in com-

The three charismatic figures of the IDF: (left) Moshe
Dayan, (center) General Ariel Sharon and (right)
former Air Force Commandant Ezer Weizman.

Bottom: Golda Meir at Ben-Gurion's funeral.

parison to the dwarfed civilian leadership.

After the Six-Day War, the willingness of
civilian politicians to hear the opinions of generals, to consult them and to exchange ideas
with them increased. A dependence on the
military leadership was evident in the decision-
making process. This dependence was even
greater during the War of Attrition when the
dangers threatening Israel were augmented by
Soviet military involvement. Chief of Staff, Lt.
Gen. Haim Bar-Lev, and Maj. Gen. Aharon
Yariv, head of Military Intelligence, were fre-

quently invited to Cabinet sessions, a rare occurrence in Ben-Gurion's time.

The military elite exploited their newly-found
influence and popularity. The political parties
began to woo them. Since retirement was close
at hand for the generals, they were attractive
prospective candidates for the election lists.
The generals, in turn, sought to influence policy
on such issues as secure borders, holding the
occupied territories, new settlements, the size
of the defense budget and even relations with
the United States and the Soviet Union. Personal rivalries in the ruling circles also accel-
erated the phenomenon. Various ministers
sought to patronize particular generals as their
private military advisers. Generals jumped
straight from military service to political life
and even to the Cabinet. Notable among these
was Lt. Gen. Haim Bar-Lev who, upon ending
his service as Chief of Staff in 1972, entered the
labor government as Minister of Commerce
and Industry. Former Chief of Staff Yitzhak
Rabin was an effective ambassador to the
United States and later an interim Prime
Minister. Maj. Gen. Ariel Sharon, who left the
Army in a protest over the government's failure to promote him to Chief of Staff, became
the rejuvenating force in the LIKUD, the center-
right opposition bloc.

Haim Bar-Lev, one of the combatants in the War of the Generals. [David Rubinger]

The War of the Generals

The Yom Kippur War elicited an angry and controversial debate over the politicization of the generals. The opening salvo in the "War of the Generals" was fired by Sharon who, in a series of foreign press interviews, said the war had been terribly mismanaged and that as a result Israel had lost her power of deterrence. For the past twenty-five years, Sharon asserted, Israel had fought to show the Arabs that she had the means to react decisively to any Arab provocation and to bring about their defeat.

"This time," Sharon says, "that did not happen. The first two days of the war were a catastrophe that could have been avoided. We had enough troops and enough contingency plans to prevent the disaster, but the forces were not deployed. The casualties we lost in the first two days were without justification.

"In the second phase of the war, Bar-Lev was brought out of retirement ostensibly to coordinate the southern front. This was a political appointment. Bar-Lev came to save his own reputation and his concept of defense."[2]

Thus against this background of differences, Sharon, who had shortly before the Yom Kippur War joined forces with LIKUD, the center-right opposition bloc composed of the Liberal Party and the Independent Liberal Party, was not only Bar-Lev's strategic opponent, but also his political rival, since the latter was an important Cabinet officer in the Meir labor government.

Bar-Lev angrily rebutted Sharon's charges in newspaper interviews, claiming that the delay in executing the Canal crossing was necessitated by real strategic considerations and the ferocity of the Egyptian onslaught. Elazar publicly chastized Sharon for undermining Army morale by his fractious attitude and forbade any further interviews. Sharon, however, was soon back in civilian clothes—he had retired shortly before the war—and continued to press his critique of the IDF command.

The War of the Generals has convinced many Israelis that the IDF has been too politicized. In a very real sense the weakness of the civilian leadership, not the political ambitions of IDF officers, is responsible for this circumstance.

Generally, the ranks of the IDF have not been hospitable to partisan activity. Young officers have backed away from aligning themselves to political parties and, with the exception of some kibbutz members affiliated with the leftist Mapam-linked movements, party membership has been uncharacteristic of the IDF. But in recent years, in the higher ranks of command, colonels and generals have been more and more outspoken as they perceive the ineptitude of the aging political leaders in evaluating Israel's strategic situation. This tendency toward public comment was evident on the eve

David Elazar on an aerial tour of Sinai defenses during the Yom Kippur War. Elazar resigned his post as IDF Chief of Staff in April 1974 in the wake of accusations by the Special Commission investigating the conduct of that war. [Israeli Army]

of the Six-Day War and has been noticeable in the aftermath of the Yom Kippur War.

The privileged position of the IDF in Israeli life allows, of course, for political influence among the Army officers but because the military is not a separate class and because retirement is early, IDF officers can find fulfillment for their political aspirations within a civilian context, not as an army elite.

Footnotes

1   Interview in *Ha'aretz*, 5 July 1966.
2   Perlmutter, *op. cit.*, p. 52.

17. THE YOM KIPPUR WAR

Opposite: [UPI]

Defense Minister Moshe Dayan at a military funeral.

The fifth war between Israel and the Arabs broke out on October 6, 1973. It was the holiest day in Judaism—the Day of Atonement. This was to be the largest war fought since the beginning of the Israeli-Arab dispute. It marked the first time that small nations activated immense quantities of weapons—more than 6,000 tanks and some 1,500 modern aircraft, hundreds of batteries of ground-to-air missiles and highly sophisticated electronics systems. Missile battles were waged at sea for the first time in history. Neither side could have used such an immensity of armaments were it not for the assistance of the great powers. Though the Soviet Union and the United States did not directly intervene in the battles, they provided massive support in arms and ammunition to the fighting parties. Both powers tried out their most modern weapons systems in this war.

On October 24, when Israeli armored columns were about to break through toward Cairo, the Kremlin threatened direct intervention and placed seven airborne divisions on alert. The United States replied by placing her forces on alert, and only by this means prevented direct intervention by Russia.

For the first time in the history of armed conflict in the Middle East, the Arab forces launched a unified and comprehensive attack against Israel. The armies of Egypt and Syria opened the offensive, but very little time elapsed before Iraqi and Jordanian expeditionary forces reached the Syrian front. They were later joined by another force from Morocco and auxiliary units from Saudi Arabia, Algeria, Libya, Tunisia and Kuwait. Pilots from Pakistan and North Korea also rallied to the Arab effort. The Arabs had for the first time in their history properly utilized their petroleum as a political weapon of war against Israel by enforcing a selective or full embargo on the states that supported Israel.

Weighing the Outcome

In eighteen days of bitter combat, the IDF lost 2,521 men—dead and missing. The impact of these losses can be compared with those suffered in the War of Independence. These two wars were very painful for Israel, but in 1948 the military achievement was clear and tangible: The State of Israel was created in the midst of battle; the Arab armies were defeated and compelled to sign armistice agreements which indirectly recognized the new frontier lines of the young state. In 1948, Israel enjoyed the extensive support of other nations. In 1973, however, Israel was isolated.

Her allies had dwindled to one: the United States. Those countries which did not directly support the Arabs adopted a stance of indifference, largely for fear of Arab oil-blackmail. Israel was compelled to pay her debts with diplomacy and in so doing lost much of the territory she had gained. But perhaps most painful was the postwar view of the future. In 1948, the joy of victory was great. People believed that by establishing the State of Israel, the Jewish people were at last secure in their homeland. By 1973, there was the overwhelming realization that Israel had been caught up in an inexorable cycle of war and that

Mother weeps over temporary grave marker.
[Shabtai Tal]

2183164

משה
רז

future generations would be doomed to un-
remitting armed struggle.

There was a decisive military victory on
the Syrian front. The Syrian Army was driven
back from the Golan Heights, and the IDF
found itself a mere twenty-two miles from
Damascus when the cease-fire took effect.
More than 1,100 Arab tanks were destroyed
on this front.

On the Egyptian front, a dramatic breakthrough was achieved. The Egyptian Army had
taken control of large areas of the Suez Canal
and many Bar-Lev Line strongholds, but the
IDF broke through the central sector of the

Canal and into Egypt. It occupied some 1,200
square kilometers, isolated the Egyptian Third
Army and held positions at a distance of sixty
miles from Cairo. But the military victory on
the Egyptian front was an incomplete one.
Israel again found that she could never achieve
a total victory over the Arabs. And in 1973, unlike 1967, the Russians stood ready to prevent
a decision against the Arab armies.

From a political viewpoint, Israel sustained
a clear defeat in the Yom Kippur War. The political and economic might of the Arabs dictated the positions of many governments in the
Middle East dispute. Members of the NATO
alliance hesitated to allow American aircraft
carrying armaments to Israel to land at their
airports. The United States supplied military
assistance of a kind that she had never before
given, but Israel's dependence increased
despite her technological progress. The IDF
was facing armies supported by the logistical
capabilities of the Soviet Union and the Warsaw Pact nations. Israel, in turn, had to rely
on the support of the United States. And in
exchange, Israel had to follow her dictates.

The Arabs did not succeed in achieving
their objectives on the battlefield, but their
political and strategic success was clear: They
changed the face of the Middle East as it had
existed since the Six-Day War, something they
had failed to do in the course of the War of
Attrition and the fedayeen and guerrilla wars.

Israeli Intelligence Falls for the Arab Bluff

The Yom Kippur War was marked by the
failure of Israeli Intelligence. The ramifications
of this failure have not yet been fully examined
but tremors have already toppled the Meir
government. Essentially, the failure was in
evaluation: Intelligence had the information
but a tradition of Arab bluffs led analysts
to put two and two together and come up
with zero.

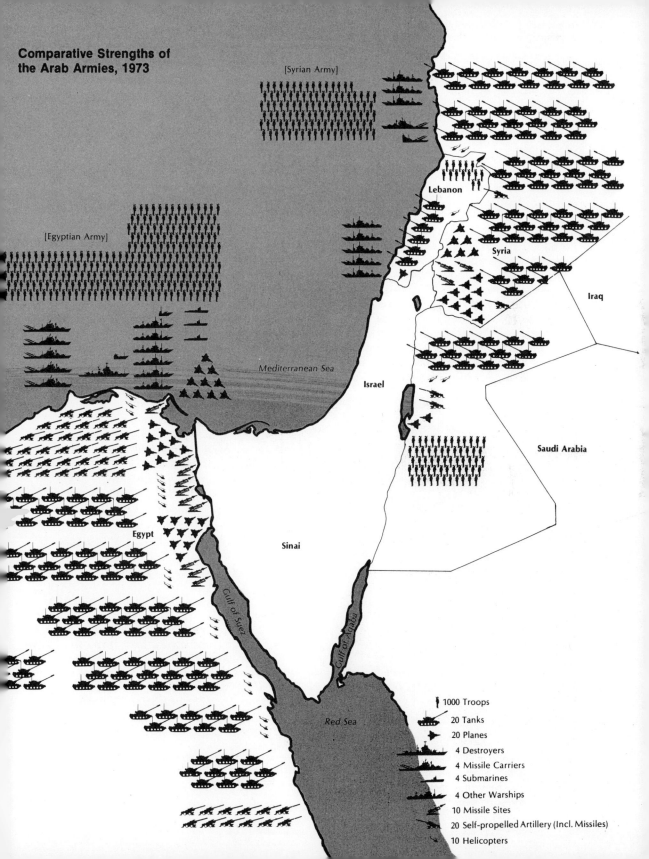

Comparative Strengths of the Arab Armies, 1973

[Syrian Army]

[Egyptian Army]

Mediterranean Sea

Lebanon

Syria

Iraq

Israel

Saudi Arabia

Egypt

Sinai

Gulf of Suez

Gulf of Aqaba

Red Sea

1000 Troops
20 Tanks
20 Planes
4 Destroyers
4 Missile Carriers
4 Submarines
4 Other Warships
10 Missile Sites
20 Self-propelled Artillery (Incl. Missiles)
10 Helicopters

Maj. Gen. David Elazar, Chief of Staff during the
Yom Kippur War.

Several times since the end of the War of
Attrition, Arab forces had concentrated armies
along Israel's borders. In December 1972,
there was a suspicion that the Arabs were
preparing for war. As a result, the decision
to shorten conscript service in the IDF was
delayed. Nothing happened. There was a similar event in May-June 1973—it was, as it has
now become clear, a kind of general rehearsal
for the Day of Atonement. The Egyptians
began massing their forces. They moved missiles from the Cairo district and fording equipment was prepared for action. At that time
Israeli Intelligence concluded that the Arabs

were not yet prepared for total war and would,
therefore, not open fire. The Chief of Staff,
David Elazar, did not accept the Intelligence
evaluation, and so extensive steps were taken
to assure alertness. New units were quickly
established, and emergency warehouses were
transferred closer to the line. Again nothing
happened. The Intelligence evaluation, coun-
termanded by the Chief of Staff, was vindicated. The confidence of Intelligence experts
in their own evaluations grew, almost to the
point of arrogance. After the Yom Kippur
War, Intelligence experts assumed that the
military concentrations in May-June 1973 were
quite possibly a part of the Arab deception
program, aimed at accustoming Israel to situations of alert along the border lines.

The Intelligence failure was all the more
serious since IDF commanders did take the
possibility of an Arab offensive into account.
Following the June alert, the Chief of Staff
spoke with me about the possibilities of war:

*The Egyptians have the motivation and
the strategic reasons for opening fire. The
Arabs have entered a stage of political stalemate, and Egypt's situation in the Arab world is
not an easy one. Among the various possibilities that the Egyptians may choose, the most
dangerous is that of total war, in partnership
with Syria and with reinforcements from other
Arab countries—especially in aircraft. This possibility is dangerous because of its massivity
and the chance of its being short. The Egyptians are likely to estimate that they will have
preliminary achievements, even if they are
restricted. They can possibly believe that the
opening blow will cause Israel heavy losses,
and then the situation will freeze on the
ground.*[1]

Asked about the Arab capability of surpris-
ing Israel with such a move, Elazar said:

It's impossible to open a general offensive

Abba Eban with Israeli commanders on tour of
occupied west bank of the Jordan River, 1973.

*in a totally tranquil situation, without us first
sensing it. The reasonable assumption is that
they will move to the alert almost publicly. In
a second stage, they will begin the offensive.
In the case of such an Arab alert before an
attack, it will be difficult to know of it in advance. Yet, I assume that the Arabs' first blow
will not be fatal. In our present situation, a
pre-emptive strike is not essential.* [2]

The Israeli Chief of Staff had set in advance
an almost complete scenario for the opening
strike of the Yom Kippur War; nonetheless
Israel was unprepared when the play opened.

In June 1973, the Intelligence assessment of
a low feasibility of war was rejected by the
Central Command. In October, however, Elazar and Defense Minister Moshe Dayan transferred the Intelligence evaluation to the Prime
Minister, without any comment. In so doing
they made themselves party to the evaluation.
It was not until Friday, October 5, that the Chief
of Staff's suspicions developed. He ordered a
high state of alert in the IDF and the Air Force
was ordered to prepare for a pre-emptive
strike. It was not until dawn of the Day of
Atonement that the Chief of Staff finally rejected the Intelligence low-feasibility evaluation—but by then it was too late.

"Israeli Intelligence knew the facts, but was
busy with conceptions," American Secretary
of State Kissinger later explained. The American Intelligence Services didn't predict the
events to follow either. The CIA had been
alerted ten days before the war broke out, but
the overly self-confident Israeli Intelligence
persuaded the Americans that war was not on
the horizon.

Israeli Intelligence did have plentiful detail;
it knew movements of almost every Arab unit.
Despite this abundance of information, it
made a crude mistake in its final evaluation.

The mistake can be partially explained in
terms of a well-established presumption: that
the Arabs would not dare to open fire for fear
of repercussions. Again, overconfidence
caused the Israeli Command to come to that
conclusion without considering the precise
details of the situation as it stood in 1973.

In a visit to Israel in 1960, the English military commentator B.H. Liddell-Hart had observed that the greatest danger threatening
the IDF, well known as a superior army, was
the tendency of victorious armies toward overconfidence. The IDF at that time had sustained
two major victories over the Arabs. Since then,
three more victories had been added to the
scorecard: the impressive campaign of 1967,
the thwarting of Arab plans in the War of Attrition and the wars against the fedayeen organizations. Liddell-Hart's warning came true to
no small extent. The general attitude in Israel,
not only that of the IDF, failed to consider the
power of frustration as a factor in determining
Arab actions. The majority of IDF commanders
saw events taking place before their eyes, but
surrounded themselves with an impenetrable
wall. Israeli Intelligence became a part of the
process. Instead of influencing, it became influenced. It served the IDF as good eyes and
ears, but was affected by the process of complacency that was overcoming the whole

Below: [Nancy Reese]

Opposite: Egyptian President Anwar Sadat. [Eastfoto]

nation. The assessments that the Egyptians would not dare to start a war were further validated each time Sadat promised war but did not begin it. The Arabs were crying wolf and Israel fell into the trap.

The Handwriting on the Wall

Three weeks before the war, Israel first noticed that Syria had begun to concentrate her military forces and was erecting an extremely dense system of anti-aircraft missiles along the border. Israeli Intelligence regarded this troop movement as a response to an aerial battle on September 13, in which the Syrians lost thirteen MIGs. When information was received that Egypt was also beginning to move units, Israeli Intelligence assumed that Egyptian forces were merely conducting their annual fall exercises. The fall exercises were a part of the Arab deception plan. The Egyptian General Staff played out its role as though it were holding an extensive exercise but, according to the plan, war was to begin when the exercises reached their peak. The Arab maintenance of the secret was excellent. Few were made a party to it, and even the senior commanders received their orders for war only a day before the beginning of battle.

Israel's suspicions grew two days before the war began, when it was reported that the Soviet advisers and their families were beginning to depart from Syria and Egypt. At dawn on the Day of Atonement, Intelligence received a report that the Arabs were intending to open fire that day. According to this particular piece of information, the battle was to begin at six in the evening. Nevertheless, Intelligence did not give it credence and stuck to its overall evaluation that the feasibility of war was low. The Chief of Staff did demand total mobilization of reserves and permission to use the Air Force to strike a pre-emptive blow, but his requests were rejected. The pre-emptive strike was turned down by the Prime Minister and

the Minister of Defense. They believed that, because of the territories added to Israel in the Six-Day War, she could risk holding fire until she was attacked. As for the mobilization of reserves, Moshe Dayan opposed full mobilization in an attempt to ensure that Israel would not later be accused of provocation. However, Prime Minister Golda Meir intervened on Elazar's behalf and partial mobilization was ordered. Again, it was too late. Under the best possible circumstances, Israel needs prior warning of twenty-four hours to move part of the reserve units to the front areas. The decision to mobilize reservists was made after eight in the morning. By two in the afternoon war had broke out.

Even after it was reported that war could be expected that very day, Israel behaved unlike a country vulnerable to attack. Golda Meir asked the United States Ambassador in Israel to inform his government and request them to

tell Egypt that Israel was aware of the war to come. The hope was that such a message would deter the Arabs. It did not. In fact, according to one Monday morning quarter-back, the announcement was instrumental in the Arab decision to attack four hours earlier than had been planned.

In the face of all this, an order was issued by the Israeli Command that armored forces in Sinai were not to move toward the Canal. It was feared that a change in disposition of armor would incite the Arabs to act. As a result, the Israeli tanks were not in position at the Canal when the battle began, and the main armored units were to the rear—in central Sinai.

The Arabs Take the Initiative

The Yom Kippur War was the first armed conflict that the Arabs planned thoroughly. They had the advantage of initiative and surprise on their side. In 1948, the Arabs initiated the invasion of Palestine but their strategy was faulty and their military preparedness poor. Coordination between the various Arab armies was nonexistent. In 1956 and 1967, it was Israel who opened fire. Though the Arabs had created a *casus belli* for the Six-Day War by imposing a sea blockade on the Straits of Tiran and concentrating considerable forces in Sinai, Israel still held the offensive initiative. In the War of Attrition, the Egyptians were the initiators, but the objectives of that primarily static semi-war were limited.

Matters were different in 1973. The Arabs set the date of war. They enjoyed the advantage of surprise and initiative, in addition to greater quantities of armaments and superior fire power. The Arab operational plan was based on two principles: The war would begin on Arab initiative and be waged on two fronts simultaneously. Because they understood that the IDF was highly mobile and capable of rapid reaction, the Arab leadership, adopting one of the essentials of IDF doctrine, determined that most of the achievements be made in the first stage of the war. Later, they would move to a prolonged war of attrition bolstered by the immense quantities of armaments and manpower which were expected to flow in from the other Arab countries. They counted on Arab quantity to defeat Israeli quality.

At ten minutes before two, the assault began on two fronts. The Syrians opened with three divisions and a number of independent brigades. In all, some 800 tanks took part in the first assault waves. Their function was to reach a depth of six miles and open a way for two armored divisions, which would come in the second stage and break through as far as the Jordan River. This was a deluge of armor operating in a relatively small area.

Though Israel had reinforced the Golan Heights with an additional armored brigade on the eve of war, the Israeli defense numbered no more than 180 tanks. The numerical gap between the attacking and defending forces was felt immediately. The speed of attack was so great that the Air Force found it difficult to supply support. Syrian tanks approached very close to Israeli tanks, and the Israeli pilots could not distinguish between the two. As darkness fell, the Syrians carried on their attack. Their tanks plunged forward with the assistance of infra-red equipment and SLS, starlight systems that intensify available light for night fighting. The IDF armored forces, which were spread over an extensive area, were slowly worn down, tank by tank. After midnight, the Syrian tanks surrounded Israeli headquarters on the Golan Heights. Maj. Gen. Raphael (Raful) Eitan, who was responsible for the blocking stage of the Golan Heights battles, was compelled to leave his command post as Syrian tanks approached the entrance to the bunker from which he was controlling the battle. The Syrian tanks then crossed the

The Suez front: Egyptian MIGs (top) take off for battle [UPI] as Egyptian soldiers (bottom) cross the Canal [Wide World].

main road and approached the Bnot Yaakov Bridge over the Jordan.

The first Israeli reserve unit—a reinforced armor company—reached the Golan Heights at three in the morning, and immediately went into battle. As day dawned, another Syrian tank unit approached the bridge close to the Jordan estuary at the Sea of Galilee. The IDF forces were thinner on the southern edge of the Heights, so the work of blocking until the reserves arrived fell on the shoulders of the Air Force. The situation was so difficult that Moshe Dayan suggested to the Prime Minister that the IDF retreat to the slopes of Golan. The proposal was rejected as more and more reserve units reached the front and joined in the blocking action.

The blocking of the Syrian front lasted until Tuesday noon. On Monday, October 8, the Syrians had begun a renewed offensive. They threw a division of heavy armor into the battle in the northern sector near Kuneitra. It was faced by a regular armor brigade of eighteen and nineteen year olds. The attack lasted eight hours and at times it appeared that the Syrian tanks would succeed in breaking through the front line.

The Syrians Take Mt. Hermon; The Egyptians Cross the Canal

The Syrians' most outstanding achievement in the first stage of war was the conquest of the IDF position on Mt. Hermon. Syrian commandos surprised the position which housed a radar installation. Some of the men surrendered after a battle, while others continued to fight from within the bunkers until they were overrun. A few soldiers succeeded in escaping. Other IDF positions along the line withstood attacks. The Syrian tanks passed between them, and only in the second stage assaulted these strongpoints. Apart from one position that was abandoned by its men, all the others stood until IDF forces linked up with them.

An Egyptian soldier jumps out of a disabled Israeli tank in Sinai. [Wide World]

Following pages: Mirage IIIc's. [Marvin Newman]

The assault on the Egyptian front was of a different nature. After a heavy but brief bombardment and an attack by 150 Egyptian planes on various objectives in Sinai, the land assault began on the Suez Canal. The first waves of assault troops were infantrymen. Ten thousand men crossed the Canal in hundreds of small boats, and established a bridgehead for the men and armor that were to follow. They occupied the embankment erected along the Canal by the IDF and from there attacked the IDF strongholds.

By nightfall, the Egyptians succeeded in transferring some 40,000 soldiers across the Suez Canal. In all, five Egyptian divisions took part in the attack wave which was a complete success. A mere 1,000 IDF men faced them on the front line. Several hundred manned the strongholds while others operated alongside the few artillery batteries. About ninety IDF tanks were on the front line during the opening assault wave.

The Air Force could do little to help. It struck at the bridges but again had difficulty distinguishing between the attacking Egyptians and the Israeli tanks.

The Air Force's primary achievement in this stage was the downing of Egyptian MIG air-

Israeli soldiers captured on the Egyptian front.
[Israeli Army]

Bottom: Soviet-made RPG7 rocket-assisted grenade.

craft, and of some twenty helicopters that carried Egyptian commandos seeking to seize the Mitla and Jiddi Passes deep inside Sinai, in order to delay the flow of IDF reserve units to the front. Facing the Tel Aviv coastline, an Israeli Mirage shot down a ground-to-air Kelt missile which had been fired at the city from a distance.

The roads to Sinai are very long. An order was given to send tanks on their own tracks, rather than on transporters, to hasten arrival at the front line. Speed was given priority but many tanks were dispatched with incomplete stocks of ammunition and even incomplete

crews. Artillery received a very low priority for transporters moving into Sinai, one of the grave errors of the Israeli Command.

In the first stage of combat Israeli armor was faced by an enormously effective Egyptian infantry equipped with antitank weapons. The Israeli units were not sufficiently equipped with artillery and mortars and they were not prepared for that sort of confrontation. The IDF rushed to the front, expecting a mobile war based primarily on tanks and artillery like that of 1967. The Egyptian Army forced Israel into a static war, based on massive fire power.

The Egyptian strength lay in her possession of two antitank weapons, mobile Sagger missiles and RPG7 bazookas. The Sagger (its Russian name is Malyotka, meaning small) has a range of about two miles. Two men are needed to operate the missile which can be carried in small suitcases, and aimed with the help of a telescope. The RPG7 bazooka is very light, easy to carry and can penetrate any armor. With the help of the Sagger, the Egyptian infantry had a longer arm than the Israeli tank guns. As the first night of battle passed, a considerable share of the Israeli armored force was worn down—of the 265 tanks that were in Sinai at the beginning of battle, only 100 remained.

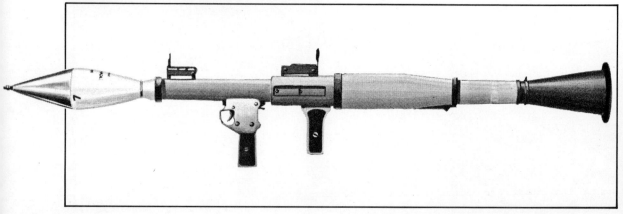

October 11, 1973: A surrounded stronghold of the
Bar-Lev Line is finally occupied by Egyptian
Forces. [UPI]

Weakness in the Israeli Infantry

Another defect in the structure of the Israeli units also derived from the special priorities that carried over from the Six-Day War. That primarily mobile war relied upon the tank as the center of land activity. In order to facilitate tank mobility, the IDF neglected other elements that are traditionally considered a part of the armored force team. The fact that budgets at the IDF's disposal were limited only served to intensify this neglect. Artillery, as previously mentioned, was slighted. Also given low development priority was the infantry which operated out of armored personnel carriers. When the Israeli tanks were unsuccessful in opposing the Egyptian infantry, the Israeli infantry was called in. But in the first stage of war, there were few elite infantrymen in Sinai. Luckily for the IDF, the capacity for improvisation among its junior officers is excellent, and in the midst of battle the unit commanders were able to find tactical answers in the field to the problems presented by the Egyptian infantry.

Within less than twenty-four hours, it became clear that the Bar-Lev Line strongholds were hopelessly surrounded and cut off. One of the strongholds fell in the first Egyptian assault,

An Israeli infantryman prays before going into battle. [Israeli Army]

Bottom: IAF pilot in Skyhawk. [Marvin Newman]

six others were abandoned and the men extricated, though losses were heavy. Nine more strongholds fell before the war was over. Only one, on the coast in the northern sector of the Suez Canal, held fast until IDF forces succeeded in linking up with it.

The reserve forces that raced to the front did not at first succeed in moving to the counterattack. The fact that the regular army had been worn down in blocking engagements on the Canal compelled the reserve units to bolster the blocking force. These units arrived in haphazard fashion; the battle resembled a street fight.

Minister of Defense Dayan suggested establishing a second line of defense, in Sinai, close to the Mitla and Jiddi Passes, but his proposal was rejected. The Military Command, led by the Chief of Staff, insisted that the blocking actions take place no further than six miles from the Canal.

Achievements of the Air Force

The Air Force encountered serious problems in the Yom Kippur War. Though the IAF was not surprised as was the armored force, it had to pay a heavy price for its achievements. It succeeded in hermetically sealing the populated area of Israel against enemy aircraft; it more or less maintained clear skies over the front. In ninety percent of the aerial battles, Israeli pilots were victorious and they succeeded in reaching every target selected within the Arab countries. Nonetheless they had great difficulty providing support to ground forces on the front line because of the Arabs' anti-aircraft missile systems.

With the assistance of the Soviet Union, the Egyptians and Syrians had built missile systems even denser than those at the disposal of North Vietnam. These systems were composed of many missile batteries of different types, and thousands of radar-operated guns. Among the missile batteries was the brand-new SAM-6,

Egyptian missile apparatus captured by the IDF.

Bottom: May Day Celebrations in Moscow, 1968, showing the SAM-1 anti-aircraft missile. [Tass from Sovfoto]

which is very difficult to spot in flight, and which possesses electronics as yet unknown in the West. The missile systems were responsible for the heavy losses of the Israeli Air Force and its restricted freedom of action.

In eighteen days of combat, the IAF lost more than a quarter of its combat aircraft (104 planes of different types). In aerial combat, the IAF downed 450 Arab aircraft.

The Navy Prevails

The only good news of the first days of war came from the sea. Equipped with advanced weapons systems and strengthened by the addition of twelve French-built missile boats and two larger missile boats that were constructed in Israel, this force was concentrated in the Mediterranean area. (Israel had not succeeded in mounting a naval-air system in the Red Sea. The force of small craft, without a single missile boat, could not, therefore, react to the

Bottom: Soviet-made Styx ground-to-ground missile has an estimated range of 15-20 miles. [Novosti from Sovfoto]

Israeli missile ship patroling the Mediterranean. [Israeli Army]

closing of the Bab-el-Mandeb Straits, 1,250 miles from Sharm-el-Sheikh. The small Red Sea navy made do with actions in the Bay of Suez and the Gulf of Aqaba—and most of these involved the naval commandos.)

The Navy adopted an offensive approach in the Mediterranean. It was able to limit its coastal protection missions, which freed it to go out and seek the enemy. Within a few days, it created a situation in which the movement of Egyptian and Syrian fleets was completely circumscribed. The supply of weapons to the ports of Latakiye and Tartus in Syria was carried out in Russian ships, under Red Fleet escort. Nevertheless, Israel succeeded in maintaining free navigation in the Mediterranean.

The hardest blow was sustained by the Syrian Navy. Eight of its missile ships were sunk, as were a minesweeper and a torpedo boat. The Egyptians lost between five and six missile boats, a patrol ship and many other

Israeli naval gunner lunches at his post. [UPI]

October 8, 1973: Israeli soldiers advance to Syrian front. The body of a Syrian soldier lies on the side of the road. [UPI]

vessels, including eighteen fishing boats that were armed for action in the Red Sea. In the missile battles, the Israeli boats were successful, though the range of their Gabriel missile is some ten miles less than that of the Russian Styx with which the Syrian and Egyptian boats were equipped. The Israeli Navy was the undisputed victor; it lost not a single vessel of any kind in the naval battles of the Yom Kippur War.

Ironically, the Navy was the only unit that did not record a victory in the Six-Day War. A few months after that war, at the end of 1967, the Navy sustained a heavy blow when its flagship—the destroyer *Eilat*—was sunk by missiles off Port Said. It was these defeats that impelled the Navy to more intense activity in drawing the lessons of battle, without overconfidence clouding its vision.

The IDF Command Regroups Its Forces

During the first four days of war, command decisions were influenced by the shortage of tactical reserve forces. The High Command had to face the critical question of how to best utilize its reserve while there was still a danger that the Jordanian Army would open a third front to the east. The question was whether to mobilize the reserves, or to wait for unexpected

developments. And if to throw it into battle, on which front—on the Suez line, where the enemy was strongest, and where a territorial achievement of any kind would radically change the political and territorial status quo; or on the Syrian front, closer to populated areas in Israel, where there was also a greater chance of beating the enemy because of the preliminary balance of forces? A decision was made to move forces to the Syrian front where they assisted in repelling the Syrians from the Golan Heights. Thus, on the fourth day of war, the center of gravity was transferred to the Syrian front.

At the Golan Heights: (left) An Israeli 175mm self-propelled artillery piece fires on Syrian positions [UPI]; (right) a tank reconnaissance unit [Treen Art]; and (bottom) an Israeli 175mm self-propelled artillery piece in action.

Opposite: 122mm Soviet-made artillery piece captured by the IDF in the Six-Day War, used during Yom Kippur War at Syrian front.

Syrian tanks in flames near the Golan Heights.
[Israeli Army]

Bottom: Helicopter photo of Syrian tanks caught in
an Israeli antitank ditch. Two Syrian-built bridges
are visible in the background. [Israeli Army]

Giant American C5 Galaxy cargo jet, used in the American airlift of arms and ammunition to Israel. [UPI]

The previous day an Israeli counterattack near the Canal failed after Major General Adan's division was thrown against the bridgehead of the Egyptian Second Army. This local failure made the decision in favor of an offensive on the Syrian front, leaving for the time being a relative stalemate on the Egyptian front.

After one day of regrouping, IDF forces opened a general offensive against Syria. Two divisions broke through toward Damascus. Major General Eitan's units broke through on the northern road, from Kuneitra to the length of the Mt. Hermon foothills. To the south, on the Kuneitra-Damascus road, Gen. Dan Lanner's forces broke the Syrian defense network. The Syrians had been hard hit the two previous days by the IAF which had begun heavy strategic bombing deep within Syria. In addition to military command posts and the Defense Ministry, the Air Force hit power stations and fuel reservoirs.

The Arabs Are Bolstered by Russian Supplies

On the third day of war, the Soviet Union's involvement underwent a significant change. Giant Russian transport planes began to land in Syria, and later in Egypt. The speed with which the airlift was effected indicated that the Kremlin had prepared considerable equipment in advance and was a party to the Arab decision to go to war. At first these planes brought thousands of anti-aircraft missiles. Later, they began to transport other equipment—ammunition and weapons. Freighters were also hastily loaded in Black Sea ports.

Within the Soviet Union, the largest transport operation of the last twenty years took place, as all trains moved to the Black Sea ports and airfields in Hungary and Yugoslavia. The quantities needed by the Arabs were so great that it was necessary to take equipment out of the

stores of regular Red Army units. Later, Warsaw Pact armies were requested to transfer weapons and equipment from their stores. At the peak of the airlift, Russian planes were landing in Egypt every ten minutes. Scores of freighters, loaded with tanks and other weapons, reached Syrian, Egyptian and Algerian ports throughout the war. Dismantled planes were transported by their big sisters to Syria, where they were reassembled by Russian technicians, and then flown to forward airfields.

Israel had attempted to destroy the Syrian landing strips on which the Russian transport planes were to land, but this was a useless race. The Syrians hastened to fill in the holes on the strips, and there was a risk of confrontation with the Soviet Union.

America Drags Its Heels

American aid to Israel was not quite so quick. On the second day of war, Jerusalem approached Washington with a request for rapid aid, especially in aircraft, bombs and sophisticated ammunition. Two days passed before the Nixon Administration decided to supply Israel with equipment and to replace those arms destroyed in battle. At first, Washington anticipated that her action would not be publicized, and that Israel would herself transport

The IDF advances on Syrian positions in the Golan Heights. [Treen Art]

the considerable equipment. Chartered aircraft began to shift equipment to Israel, but it quickly became clear that Israel alone could not take care of the quantities to be hauled. A decision was made to activate an American airlift to Israel, but by that time the Russian airlift was at its peak. It was October 14 before the first American Galaxy C5 aircraft landed at Lydda International Airport.

Though the IDF destroyed considerable quantities of arms and equipment belonging to the Arab armies, it became clear that even in victory the wear and tear on equipment in modern war is immense. The quantities re-

quired were so great that they even strained the reserves of a power like the United States.

The Russian and American airlifts did not take place under equal conditions. The Russian airfields were a mere two hours flying time from Syrian airports. Even at sea, their ships needed no more than three days to come from the Black Sea ports to Latakiye in Syria. In addition to the relatively shorter distances, the Soviet Union was assisted by the airfields of Hungary and Yugoslavia, and was able to transfer military equipment by train through the Eastern bloc. Squadrons of Russian planes even passed over Turkey, without receiving

October 11, 1973: Israeli troops dance a hora to
celebrate crossing the Syrian border on the road to
Damascus. [UPI]

prior permission.

The United States, on the other hand, found
herself almost isolated in her attempts to help
Israel face the heavy Arab attack. Her colleagues in the NATO alliance refused to play a
part in the operation. Fearing an Arab oil embargo, various European countries told Washington that they could not permit American
planes carrying arms to Israel to land at their
airfields. The only exception was Portugal.
West Germany even protested that the United
States was removing military equipment from
her bases in Germany and transferring it to
Israel. England announced that she was im-

posing an embargo on weapons for the Middle
East. Clearly, the worst hit by such an embargo
was Israel, since the Arab countries received as
many arms as they could possibly want from
the Soviet Union. In London Airport, medical
equipment destined for Israel was held up for
a few days while bureaucrats debated whether
this supply might not be considered military.

The Soviet Union Unites the Arabs

Russian intervention in the war extended
even as far as the persuasion of other Arab
states to send expeditionary forces to the front.
Its attempts were fruitful. The first to intervene

Defense Minister Moshe Dayan at an observation post in the Golan Heights. [UPI]

The Israeli flag rises over Syrian territory. [UPI]

directly in the battles was Iraq. An Iraqi division of 16,000 men with 200 tanks first clashed with IDF units on Friday, October 12. The Israeli Air Force did not succeed, as it had during the Six-Day War, in locating the Iraqi force on its way to the Syrian front. The Iraqis had moved under cover of darkness. It was known that they were en route to Syria, but the IDF forces were surprised by the sudden appearance on the front line of British-made Centurion tanks, with which some of the Israeli armored units were also equipped. Iraq had purchased the Centurions in the early sixties.

The Syrian front had been broken the previ-

cient to cause the Soviet Union to make threats of her own. On Saturday, October 13, the Soviet Union announced to Washington that she was placing two paratroop divisions on alert. The staff of one of the Russian advisory divisions departed for Syria. It was clear that the Soviet Union had resolved this time, as she had not in the Six-Day War, to prevent a decisive defeat of the Arab armies. At the moment that the tide began to turn against the Arabs, the Russians began more active involvement.

The Soviet Union had learned about the fallibility of Arab Intelligence during the Six-Day War and resolved not to rely solely on Arab

ous day and the Syrian forces were already retreating toward Damascus. The Syrians hoped that while the Iraqis took on blocking tasks, they could succeed in erecting a new defense line on the way to the capital. But the Iraqi division came into battle unprepared and was not a serious obstacle for the IDF. That day, and the following, it was hard hit in armored battles.

On October 12, IDF units came within artillery range of Damascus. An airfield to the south of the city was shelled, but Israel decided not to strike at Damascus itself for the time being.

The very fact that the IDF was sitting within artillery range of the Syrian capital was suffi-

Mobile field showers in Sinai.

Bottom: Entertainment for soldiers in Sinai.
[Israeli Army]

Israeli soldier prays while on duty at the front.
[Israeli Army]

sources. Rather they launched six espionage spacecraft which provided them with a constant source of reliable information about troop movements. In addition, Soviet espionage ships in the Mediterranean maintained perpetual surveillance. On October 16, Soviet Prime Minister Kosygin arrived in Cairo to take a close look at events on the battlefield.

The Egyptian Front

On Thursday, October 11, the IDF Southern Command again recommended a break through the Egyptian lines to the west side of the Suez Canal and on into Egypt. For the pre-vious two days, a balance had been achieved as far as the Israeli armor was concerned. The IDF had by then several hundred tanks in the field, and the Egyptians had lost more than had Israel in local armored battles. The Southern Command had three divisions at its disposal —in the south, that of Maj. Gen. Albert Mendler, who had been commander of IDF forces in Sinai when battle commenced; in the center, Maj. Gen. Arik Sharon's division; and to its north, the division of Maj. Gen. Avraham Adan. Another force, under the command of Maj. Gen. Kalman Magen, was operating on the northern sector of the Suez Canal.

Moshe Dayan (center) with Maj. Gen. Avraham Adan (left) and Dayan's aide-de-camp Lt. Col. Arye (use of his last name is prohibited for security reasons) observes the field situation along the Egyptian front. [UPI]

Bottom: The first moments of the crossing to the west bank of the Suez Canal by Sharon's forces. [Shabtai Tal]

The plans for fording the Canal were presented to the General Staff and the government by Haim Bar-Lev, IDF Chief of Staff during the War of Attrition and Minister of Commerce and Industry in the Meir Government. At the outbreak of fighting, Bar-Lev had been mobilized and sent to the Egyptian front. Though

he received no appointment as front commander, it was clear that he was to control the battles as an officer senior to the Commanding Officer of the Southern Command, Maj. Gen. Shmuel Gonen, who had received his appointment only three months before the war.

Though it was clear that the battles on the Syrian front were about to stabilize, the war cabinet found it very difficult to decide on the proposal to cross the Canal. Apart from determining the location of the breakthrough point and the direction of operations after the establishment of a bridgehead, there was another highly critical question: when to break through? On the one hand, time was pressing. As long as the war was prolonged, the wear and tear on the IDF increased, and there was a danger that the Egyptians would establish positions in Sinai. On the other hand, the Egyptian heavy armor divisions were still on the west side of the Canal and so presented a defensive threat. While the debate in the war cabinet

Gen. Elazar looks over the battlefield in Sinai.
[Zeev Schiff]

Israeli armor crosses the Suez Canal. [UPI]

was at its peak, information arrived that the Egyptians were making comprehensive preparations to transfer a few hundred of their tanks into Sinai, with the intention of opening a new offensive to break through the Mitla and Jiddi Passes. The Syrians had demanded that Cairo launch this offensive to ease the pressure on them. The Egyptians believed that their chances for crossing the Canal were better while most of the Israeli Air Force was occupied on the Syrian front. This information caused the Meir Cabinet to delay the fording operation until after the anticipated Egyptian offensive.

The Egyptians activated 1,300 artillery pieces

Ariel Sharon's sketch of the breakthrough plan
for the crossing the the Suez Canal. The advance
was to begin at 5:00 PM October 15 and be
completed by 1:00 AM, October 16. The
breakthrough forces are referred to by the first
name of the officer in charge, a security precaution.

in the heavy bombardment that preceded the
offensive. Maj. Gen. Albert Mendler was killed
when his command half-track took a direct hit.
Mendler reached Israel as a sixteen-year-old
boy. Together with his mother and brother,
he had escaped from Austria after the Nazis
took control. He was the only general in the
Yom Kippur War who had been through the
Nazi terror. He had fought in all of Israel's wars
and, on the eve of the Yom Kippur War, was
about to be appointed Commanding Officer of
the Armored Corps. His place as division commander was taken by Maj. Gen. Kalman Magen.

The Egyptian offensive began in the early
hours of October 14. The previous day, hundreds of tanks of their heavy armor divisions
were moved to Sinai. Eight hundred Egyptian
tanks participated in battles the length of
the front, while the IDF activated 700. This was
the first time that such extensive mobile battles
took place on this front. This battle marked the
first turning point to the benefit of the IDF. At
the end of a day of combat, it was clear that the
Egyptians had lost more than 250 tanks, while
the IDF had lost only 10. The time was ripe to
break through the Egyptian front and cross
the Canal.

The fording operation has been presented by

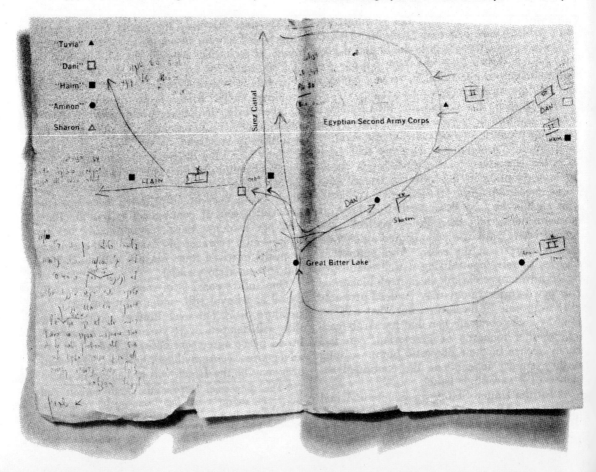

Above: Stretcher bearers in Sinai. [Shabtai Tal]

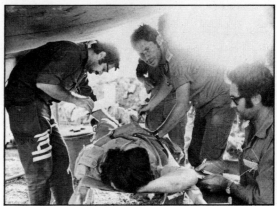

Below: Doctors treat wounded at IDF field hospital. [Israeli Army]

military commentators as a bold and cheeky action. If the truth be told, the IDF only returned to its own self on the Egyptian front when this operation began. The place chosen was in the center of the front, and not on the flank. This "seam" between the two Egyptian armies, to the north of the Great Bitter Lake, was a soft spot that had been noted about a week earlier by scouts from Sharon's division.

The first penetration took place before the Egyptians could discover it was happening. Without waiting for big bridges, which were held up at the rear in a traffic jam of vehicles moving toward the Canal, Sharon transferred the first force onto rafts which crossed the Canal without any opposition. This force included paratroops and thirty tanks. Once on the other side, they began to hit at rear echelons, command posts and missile batteries.

On the first day, they penetrated as deep as twenty miles west of the Canal, but toward the evening received an order to concentrate closer to the Canal banks. From that moment, the original Egyptian plans were upset and their reactions became slower. The commanders of the Egyptian Army did not correctly evaluate the objectives of the IDF. They thought that this was a small task force that would limit itself to raids in the rear and then return to Sinai. The Egyptian Command was convinced that their armies would be able to easily overcome the Israeli "task force," if it remained to the west of the Canal.

According to plan, Sharon was to erect the bridgehead, expand and enlarge it, and then consolidate his forces while Adan's armored units were to pass through. After the first breakthrough, a stormy debate developed over the continuation of the operation. This debate would never have occurred were it not for the fact that the IDF bridges had been held up at the rear, either because of Egyptian artillery fire, or because of traffic jams on the roads

leading to the bridgehead.

Sharon demanded that he be allowed to continue the breakthrough without waiting for the arrival of the bridges. His intention was to break through with his forces, and meanwhile transfer the armor in rafts. The enlargement of the bridgehead would be begun at the same time and then be completed by Adan's forces which, in theory, had been intended to make the first breakthrough. The Command was convinced that this was too dangerous an approach. It was impossible to consolidate the breakthrough of a large army to the west of the Canal based on pontoon bridges and a very

Israeli paratroops advance in the northern sector of the Suez Canal. [Israeli Army]

Bottom: An Israeli tank in Sinai seen through the shattered windscreen of another vehicle. [UPI]

An Israeli soldier in an Egyptian fez sips his morning coffee in Israeli-occupied Suez City. [Wide World]

Below: A group of Egyptian peasants salutes two Israeli soldiers who stopped them outside a village on the west bank of the Suez Canal. [Wide World]

Bottom: Egyptian officers return home as part of the prisoner exchange. On their backs the letter *sin*, first letter of *sa'vooi*, the Hebrew word for prisoner. [Frederic Lewis]

narrow bridgehead, which could easily be closed. The bridgehead had first to be enlarged, roads opened to it, and real bridges laid across the Canal. As for Sharon's contention that this delay might cause a significant slowdown in the political timetable, Bar-Lev replied that in any case the timetable was not determined by hours and days, but first of all by events in the field. The Soviet Union would intervene to impose a cease-fire earlier if it noticed that the Egyptian Army was crumbling.

The decision was in favor of Bar-Lev's approach. On the evening of Wednesday, October 17, after bitter battles waged by the paratroops and armored men to evacuate the roads, the first bridge was erected across the Canal. A short while later, Adan's tanks began to cross. The Egyptian Command finally understood that this was not a small task force, but a movement that threatened to choke off the Egyptian Army from the rear. They began to concentrate scores of gun batteries against the IDF bridgehead, and to send in wave after wave of aircraft on suicide attacks. Despite the heavy fire, the army engineers erected another two bridges to the north of the Great Bitter Lake by the morning of Friday, October 19. A part of Magen's division also crossed the Suez. While Sharon continued to hold the bridgehead and mop up to the north on both sides of the Canal, Adan and Magen began a race over open, flat land. Magen at first moved west toward Cairo, while Adan's armored vehicles began an encirclement action, in a southwesterly direction— to cut off the Egyptian Third Army. By the time the Egyptians saw what was about to happen to their army, it was too late. Within two days, Adan's forces took up position on the main roads between Suez and Cairo.

The Soviet Union understood very clearly what was going on. On October 19, Kosygin left Cairo convinced that the Egyptian Army's defeat was imminent. The Egyptian forces were indeed sitting in a part of Sinai, alongside the

October 17, 1973: Israeli troops in armored personnel
carriers advance on Damascus. [UPI]

Canal, but there were only 150 Egyptian tanks
between the IDF columns and Cairo. On the
Syrian front, the IDF was threatening Damascus. The Golani Brigade had meanwhile, despite heavy losses, retaken the Mt. Hermon position from the Syrians, while a paratroop reserve unit had occupied the Syrian side of
Mt. Hermon.

A Cease-fire Is Declared on the Eve
of Israel's Victory

On October 19, the Kremlin announced to
Washington that it was resolute in its decision
to stop the battles immediately, and therefore

suggested a meeting with the American Secretary of State. When America tried to delay the
meeting, the Kremlin retorted that this was a
critical matter. Henry Kissinger decided to hold
the meeting with the Russians in Moscow.
Thus, he thought, he would be able to give
Israel another day to exploit its success to the
west of the Canal.

Signs of a collapse of the Egyptian Army
were apparent on the west bank of the Canal.
While Sharon's forces were finding it difficult
to advance through the heavy foliage toward
Ismailia, the rear echelons of the Third Army
crumbled in the face of Adan and Magen's

Top: American Secretary of State Kissinger arrives in Israel to negotiate the cease-fire. [Frederic Lewis]

Middle: October 20, 1973—Kissinger meets with Soviet leaders in Moscow. Leonid Brezhnev faces him across the table, Foreign Minister Andrei Gromyko listens at left. [Wide World wirephoto from Tass]

Bottom left: Members of the Jewish Defense League stage a protest outside the American Embassy in Tel Aviv. [Wide World]

Bottom right: Israeli and Egyptian officers talk after the war. [Shabtai Tal]

forces. Israeli tanks overran missile batteries, and Air Force planes could now give close and more massive ground support. Close to 8,000 Egyptian soldiers surrendered.

On October 22, the UN Security Council declared that a cease-fire was to take effect that evening. Council members had previously refrained from making this decision, since the majority of the members of the Council, being pro-Arab, were interested in permitting the Arabs to act against Israel until the moment that it was clear the IDF would overcome them. The cease-fire was due to take effect at nightfall, but the battles continued. The IDF utilized

Opposite: Cattle herders evacuate Ismailia after the water supply to the city has been cut off. [Wide World]

Bottom: November 2, 1973—Egyptian soldiers prepare to ship water to the encircled Third Army in Suez City. [Wide World]

the time to complete the encirclement of the Egyptian Third Army, while Magen's tanks reached the Bay of Suez at the port of Adabiya. On October 23, the battles stopped on the Egyptian front. One day later, the Syrians also announced agreement to cease-fire.

The completion of encirclement of the Egyptian Third Army, after the time set for cease-fire, caused an angry reaction from the Soviet Union. The Kremlin announced an alert in all its paratroop and marine divisions, and told Washington that it intended to send forces to the Middle East. As a reaction, the United States declared an alert of its forces. The tension

lasted a few days, until it became clear that Moscow had given up the idea of direct intervention. On the other hand, Washington demanded that Israel permit the transfer of supplies and water to the isolated Egyptian Third Army.

The Aftermath

Foreign military analysts have concluded that Israel's performance in the Yom Kippur War was essentially similar in style to the Six-Day War—speed, firepower and tactical air support were their great strengths. The IDF used battle-tested equipment and Israeli battle per-

UN observer at headquarters in Kuneitra, the abandoned capital of the Golan Heights. [Wide World]

An armored scout car at the cease-fire line on the Syrian Front. [Wide World]

Bottom: A Syrian soldier in Damascus, Oct. 2, 1973. Earlier that day, the Syrian government announced it would accept the U.N.-sponsored cease-fire.

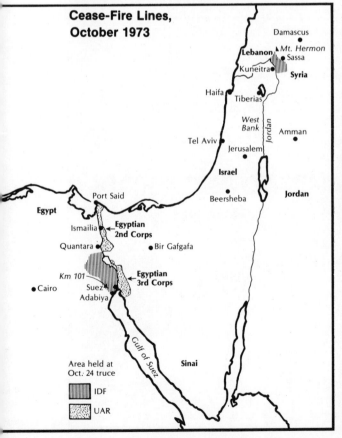

Cease-Fire Lines, October 1973

Damascus

Lebanon · Mt. Hermon
Kuneitra · · Sassa
Syria

Haifa
Tiberias

West Bank

Tel Aviv
Jerusalem

Israel

Beersheba

Jordan

Amman

Port Said

Egypt

Ismailia — **Egyptian 2nd Corps**
Quantara · Bir Gafgafa

Km 101 — **Egyptian 3rd Corps**
· Cairo   Suez
Adabiya

Gulf of Suez   **Sinai**

Area held at Oct. 24 truce

▦ IDF
▨ UAR

Kilometer 101: Negotiations between Egypt and Israel resulted in the November 11 cease-fire agreement. [UPI]

formance was up to standard. Improvisational skill was amply demonstrated, but no new weapons and equipment—no "smart" bombs, laser beams or new missiles—were unveiled.

The Arab forces, on the other hand, had access to much new and sophisticated weaponry and equipment which took their toll against Israel. Egypt's ability to rapidly deploy a seven-division force on the Israeli side of the Suez Canal was largely due to the new Soviet heavy pontoon bridge. The high-speed, heavy assault bridging was reportedly designed by the Russians for the Danube and Rhine rivers. The Egyptians constructed fourteen bridges across

the Suez Canal and were able to keep about seven of them operational despite heavy Israeli air strikes. The Egyptians used smoke to cover the bridges and Israeli planes had trouble pinpointing the bridges for destruction.

The Egyptian forces were also successful in night operations against Israeli armor as a result of their infra-red antitank missiles.

Military men consider the Yom Kippur War to have been a "midintensity" conflict—neither a full-scale global war nor a mere skirmish—and are studying it for lessons that can be applied to such warfare in the future.

The IDF ended the war feeling that political

November 3, 1973: Egyptian President Sadat greets Algerian President Boumedienne in Cairo as Arab leaders arrive to discuss oil diplomacy. [Wide World]

November 19, 1973: Lebanese security troops move in on guerrillas holding 40 people hostage in Beirut branch of the Bank of America. [Wide World]

Bottom: January 18, 1974—Chief of Staff Elazar and Maj. General Adan arrive at Kilometer 101 to sign disengagement agreement with Egypt.

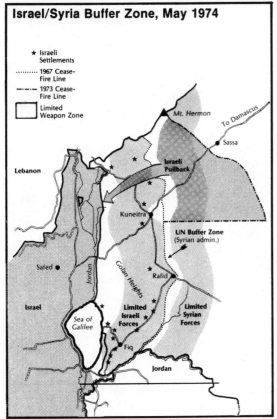

Israel/Syria Buffer Zone, May 1974

★ Israeli Settlements
······ 1967 Cease-Fire Line
—·—· 1973 Cease-Fire Line
▢ Limited Weapon Zone

Lebanon

Mt. Hermon

To Damascus

Sassa

Israeli Pullback

Kuneitra

UN Buffer Zone (Syrian admin.)

Safed

Golan Heights

Rafid

Israel

Jordan

Sea of Galilee

Limited Israeli Forces

Limited Syrian Forces

Fiq

Jordan

February 4, 1974: Israeli armored column withdraws from Egypt. [UPI]

events deprived Israel of its just reward for success in battle. The UN Security Council called for a cease-fire once it was clear that Egypt's Third Army was on the verge of destruction. After disputing the true cease-fire lines, Israel and Egypt, through the mediation of American Secretary of State Henry Kissinger, agreed on a troop disengagement.

Israel gave up the territory she had captured on the west bank of the Canal and withdrew close to the Jiddi and Mitla Passes in Sinai. Earlier a prisoner exchange was effected and Israel accepted a tacit understanding that Egypt would lift the Bab-el-Mandeb blockade at the Red Sea. Preliminary peace talks opened in Geneva and then were postponed as Kissinger tried to work out a disengagement agreement between Israel and Syria. Israel was compelled to relinquish Egyptian territory in exchange for nothing more concrete than vague assurances of guarantees by the United States.

As this book went to press, American Secretary of State Henry Kissinger was shuttling between Damascus and Jerusalem in an attempt to obtain a troop disengagement agreement between Israel and Syria. His ultimate aim is an Arab-Israeli armistice in return for Israel's withdrawal from strategically vital territories

Gen. Aharon Yariv (center), Israel's chief negotiator,
at Kilometer 101.

**Israel/Egypt Buffer Zone,
January 1974**

Mediterranean Sea

Sinai

Port Said

Khatmia Pass

Quantara

Israeli Pullback

Bir Gafgafa

Ismailia

Limited Israeli Forces

Limited Egyptian Forces

UN Buffer Zone

Jiddi Pass

Great Bitter
Lake

Suez Canal

10 miles

Mitla Pass

To Cairo

Large Egyptian
Withdrawal

Kilometer 101

Suez

Egypt

Gulf of Suez

Oil Blackmail and Shuttle Diplomacy—Top left: Egyptian President Sadat, flanked by Algerian President Boumedienne and Saudi Arabian King Faisal, arrives in Algiers for summit meeting of oil-producing nations [UPI]. Top right: Hassan el Zayyat, advisor of Anwar Sadat, leaving Paris meeting with French President Pompidou [Wide World]. Middle left: Kissinger with Sadat, December 13, 1973 [UPI]. Middle right: Kissinger with Saudi Arabian King Faisal, December 14, 1973 [UPI]. Bottom left: Kissinger with Syrian President Assad, December 15, 1973 [UPI]. Bottom right: Kissinger with Jordanian King Hussein, January 19, 1974 [UPI].

Henry Kissinger makes his magic in the Middle East
and Israel's future lies in his sleight of hand.
[Nancy Reese]

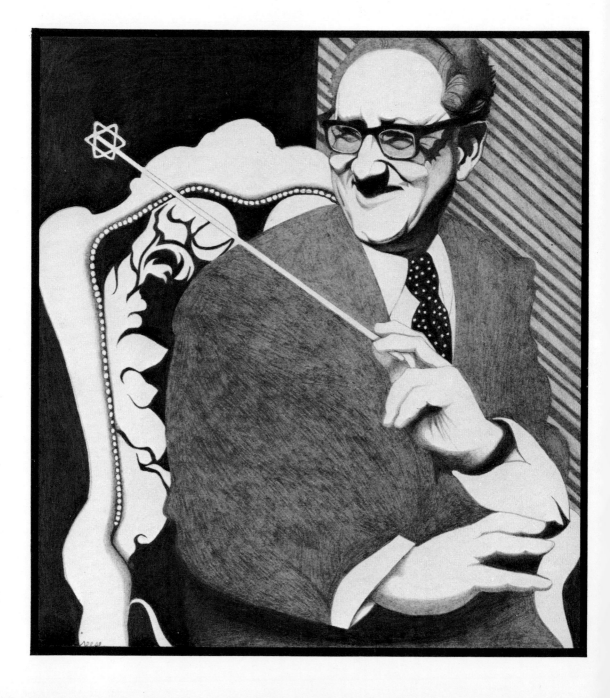

Soviet-made Scud ground-to-ground missiles, now
part of the Arab arsenals. [Tass from Sovfoto]

captured in the Six-Day War. Kissinger's plan
includes a UN buffer zone and demilitarized
areas, as well as an understanding with the
Soviet Union that she will desist from intervention on the Arab behalf; these measures, he
hopes, will guarantee Israel's security. Understandably, a substantial segment of Israel and
world Jewry are apprehensive over Kissinger's
design and its reliance on the UN as a realistic
deterrent. The continued strength and effec-
tiveness of the IDF together with America's
friendship and continued military aid never
before seemed more crucial to the survival of
the Jewish State.

The war and its diplomatic aftermath left the
Israeli government shaken. This was reflected
in the Labor alignment's poor 1973 election
showing, and the difficulty Mrs. Meir had in
forming a new government in 1974.

A sense of malaise, impotence and confusion
was further aggravated by fears over the fate of
Israeli prisoners of war in Syria's hands and the
fact that the territorial settlements resulted in
a geographical situation that was strategically
adverse to Israel. Although neither the Egyptian nor Syrian Air Force is capable of confronting the Israeli Air Force, Arab ground
forces are equipped with long-range missiles

Top: March 1974—The troubled Labor Party meets: (left to right) Golda Meir, Yitzhak Rabin and Aharon Yariv; Moshe Dayan in background. [UPI]

Bottom: Maj. Gen. Eli Zeira, head of Army Intelligence, prepares to testify before the Special Commission. [K. Weiss]

Opposite: "I have reached the end of my road. This is a burden I no longer want to bear." Thus ended Golda Meir's five-year tenure as Israel's Prime Minister. [Sherry Suris]

that can now reach almost any target in Israel.

Shortly before the war began, Egypt had received from the Soviet Union the Scud missile with a range of over 170 miles and equipped with a warhead containing over a ton of explosives. It can be assumed that Syria was also supplied with the Scud. The introduction of this weapon into the Mideast has counterbalanced Israel's deterrent strength, her superior Air Force.

An angry public outcry arose over the government's handling of the war. The role of Defense Minister Moshe Dayan was sharply criticized and what is now known as "The Gen-

erals' War" flared up in the postwar period. The conduct of the war gave rise to a bitter debate sparked by Maj. Gen. Ariel Sharon's charges that the IDF command had disastrously delayed exploitation of the bridgehead his forces had achieved on the west bank of the Canal. Both IDF Chief of Staff David Elazar and former Chief of Staff Haim Bar-Lev, who had been mobilized as an adviser during the war, refuted Sharon and defended their decisions. This Generals' War served to underscore a national sense of depression. It also provoked concern over the apparent politicization of IDF leaders since Sharon was a leader of the hardline LIKUD opposition.

After the October War, Prime Minister Golda Meir appointed a commission headed by the Chief Justice of the Israeli Supreme Court, Shimon Agranat, to investigate Israel's preparedness for the war. It was hoped that the commission would lay to rest the spirit of recrimination prevalent in postwar Israel. But the preliminary report issued in April 1974 resulted in numerous high-level resignations and a political crisis for Israel.

The report characterized Chief of Staff Elazar as overconfident, unprepared and unresponsive to the early signs of war and criticized him for his unwillingness to call up the reserves before the attack. Elazar resigned under protest on April 2.

Also named by the commission was the chief of Army Intelligence, Maj. Gen. Eli Zeira and three of his assistants. Their failure to properly assess and report signs of Egyptian and Syrian mobilization which preceded the Arab attack was noted. Zeira also resigned.

Maj. Gen. Shmuel Gonen, commander at the Egyptian front, was cited by the commission for his poor tactical control and faulty strategic decisions which, it was felt, invited defeat at the hands of the Egyptians. Gonen subsequently resigned his post.

Mordechai Gur, appointed IDF Chief of Staff after David Elazar's resignation. [Israeli Army]

Bottom left: A resident of village on west bank of Suez Canal bidding good-bye to Israeli soldiers as they withdraw. [Wide World]

Bottom right: April 23, 1974—A Syrian soldier carries an antitank weapon through the snow on Mt. Hermon as fighting continues on the Golan Heights. [UPI]

Both Mrs. Meir and Moshe Dayan were cleared by the commission. The report concluded that Dayan had been limited by the information he received from the General Staff. Mrs. Meir was criticized for not having conferred with her cabinet about Egypt's preparations for war until the eleventh hour but was commended for the emergency operations of her government.

The clearing of Dayan provoked sharp criticism in the cabinet, the Knesset and the press. The public outcry over Dayan's refusal to resign led to Mrs. Meir's own resignation and a prolonged governmental crisis.

During the Yom Kippur War, the Egyptian Army had scored a positive achievement in crossing the Canal and occupying positions in Sinai until the cease-fire. This was the first Arab military success since 1948 and it profoundly shocked Israel. As Israel saw it, this success could only embolden the Arabs and en-

courage them to attack Israel again in the future. Despite considerable rhetoric to the contrary, the Arabs have never given up their determination to see Israel's ultimate destruction. The heady experience of successes on the battlefield and the potent weapon of the Arab oil embargo gave rise to a new mood of self-esteem among the Egyptians.

Furthermore, losses in the Yom Kippur War left the command echelon of the IDF somewhat depleted. Of the 2,521 Israeli soldiers killed during the war, 606 were officers. They represented twenty-four percent of the total casualties—four percent higher than in the Six-Day War. The dead included twenty-five colonels and more than eighty majors. As a result of these losses and an increase in Egyptian and Syrian arms stocks, some observers see the possibility of a balance of power shift in favor of the Arab armies. Aware of the postwar state of the armed forces and without any realistic

Yitzhak Rabin, Israel's new Prime Minister. [UPI]

Bottom: April 17, 1974—An IDF string quartet plays Mozart during a lull in battle on the Syrian front. [UPI]

guarantees for her future safety, Israel entered a period of deep apprehension.

From the military point of view, it was clear that Israel's repeated victories over the past twenty-five years had encouraged an atmosphere of complacency. In the aftermath of the Yom Kippur War, the IDF realized that the time had come to review its operative, tactical and planning strategies and to develop methods to cope with increased Arab capacity to employ sophisticated Soviet equipment. The stagnation of complacency must end. There must be a shake-up and a revitalization of the IDF. Even if a political solution is found, the history of the Arab-Israeli conflict indicates that Israel must be prepared again and always to defend her very existence.

Footnotes

1 Previously unpublished interview with author, 14 June 1973.
2 Ibid.

FURTHER READING

Below: [Treen Art]

Allon, Yigal. *The Making of Israel's Army.* New York: Bantam, 1971.

————— *Shield of David: The Story of Israel's Defense Forces.* New York: Random House, 1970.

Bar-Zohar, Michael. *Spies in the Promised Land: Isser Harel and the Israeli Secret Service.* Boston: Houghton Mifflin, 1973.

Begin, Menahem. *The Revolt: The Story of the Irgun.* Los Angeles: Nash, 1972.

Ben-Gurion, David. *Israel: Years of Challenge.* New York: Holt, 1963.

Blankfort, Michael. *Behold the Fire.* New York: NAL, 1965.

Burns, E.L.M. *Between Arab and Israeli.* London: Harrap, 1962.

Collins, Larry and Lapierre, Dominique. *O Jerusalem!* New York: Simon and Schuster, 1972.

Dayan, Moshe. *Diary of the Sinai Campaign.* New York: Schocken, 1967.

Frank, Gerold. *The Deed.* New York: Simon and Schuster, 1963.

Glubb, Sir John Bagot. *A Soldier with the Arabs.* Mystic, CT: Verry, 1957.

Harkabi, Yehoshofat. *Arab Attitudes to Israel.* Jerusalem: Israel Universities Press, 1972.

Hertzberg, Arthur, ed. *The Zionist Idea: An Historical Analysis and Reader.* New York: Atheneum, 1969.

Hutchinson, E.H. *Violent Truce: A Military Observer Looks at the Arab-Israeli Conflict, 1951-55.* New York: Devin-Adair, 1956.

Joseph, Bernard (Dov). *The Faithful City: The Siege of Jerusalem, 1948.* New York: Simon and Schuster, 1960.

Katz, Samuel. *Battleground: Fact and Fantasy in Palestine.* New York: Bantam, 1973.

Kimche, Jon. *Seven Fallen Pillars.* New York: Praeger, 1953.

Kurzman, Dan. *Genesis 1948.* New York: NAL, 1972.

Laqueur, Walter. *The Struggle for the Middle East: The Soviet Union and the Middle East, 1958-1968.* New York: Macmillan, 1969.

Levin, Meyer. *The Settlers.* New York: Simon and Schuster, 1972.

Lorch, Netaniel. *Israel's War of Independence, 1947-1949.* Second edition. Bridgeport, CT: Hartmore, 1969.

Masters, Anthony. *The Summer that Bled.* New York: Pocket Books, 1974.

Peres, Shimon. *David's Sling: The Arming of Israel.* New York: Random House, 1971.

Postal, Bernard and Levy, Henry. *And the Hills Shouted for Joy.* New York: McKay, 1973.

Schiff, Zeev and Rothstein, Raphael. *Fedayeen.* New York: McKay, 1972.

Shapira, Avraham. *The Seventh Day.* New York: Scribners, 1972.

Sherman, Arnold. *When God Judged and Men Died.* New York: Bantam, 1973.

Slater, Leonard. *The Pledge.* New York: Pocket Books, 1971.

Tadmor, Joshua and Rothstein, Raphael. *The Silent Warriors.* New York: Macmillan, 1969.

Teveth, Shabtai. *Moshe Dayan: The Soldier, the Man, the Legend.* Boston: Houghton Mifflin, 1973.

Yaari, Ehud. *Strike Terror: The Story of Fatah.* Translated by Esther Yaari. New York: Sabra, 1970.

INDEX

List of Maps and Charts